A History of African Motherhood

This history of African motherhood over the *longue durée* demonstrates that it was, ideologically and practically, central to social, economic, cultural, and political life. The book explores how people in the North Nyanzan societies of Uganda used an ideology of motherhood to shape their communities. More than biology, motherhood created essential social and political connections that cut across patrilineal and cultural-linguistic divides. The importance of motherhood as an ideology and a social institution meant that in chiefdoms and kingdoms, queen mothers were powerful officials who legitimated the power of kings. This was the case in Buganda, the many kingdoms of Busoga, and the polities of Bugwere. By taking a long-term perspective from c. 700 to 1900 CE and using an interdisciplinary approach – drawing on historical linguistics, comparative ethnography, and oral traditions and literature, as well as archival sources – this book shows the durability, mutability, and complexity of ideologies of motherhood in this region.

Rhiannon Stephens is Assistant Professor of African History at Columbia University. Her work has been published in scholarly journals such as *Past and Present* and the *Journal of African History*. She received her PhD in history from Northwestern University.

T0381832

African Studies

The African Studies Series, founded in 1968, is a prestigious series of monographs, general surveys, and textbooks on Africa covering history, political science, anthropology, economics, and ecological and environmental issues. The series seeks to publish work by senior scholars as well as the best new research.

A list of books in this series will be found at the end of this volume.

A History of African Motherhood

The Case of Uganda, 700–1900

RHIANNON STEPHENS

Columbia University

CAMBRIDGE
UNIVERSITY PRESS

CAMBRIDGE
UNIVERSITY PRESS

32 Avenue of the Americas, New York NY 10013-2473, USA

Cambridge University Press is part of the University of Cambridge.

It furthers the University's mission by disseminating knowledge in the pursuit of
education, learning and research at the highest international levels of excellence.

www.cambridge.org
Information on this title: www.cambridge.org/9781107547193

© Rhiannon Stephens 2013

First published 2013
First paperback edition 2015

A catalogue record for this publication is available from the British Library

Library of Congress Cataloguing in Publication data
Stephens, Rhiannon, 1977–
A history of African motherhood : the case of Uganda, 700–1900 / Rhiannon Stephens.
p.   cm. – (African studies)
Includes bibliographical references and index.
ISBN 978-1-107-03080-0 (hardback)
1. Motherhood – Political aspects – Uganda – History – To 1890.   2. Motherhood –
Social aspects – Uganda – History – To 1890.   3. Mothers – Uganda – Social
conditions.   I. Title.   II. Series: African studies series.
HQ759.S6884   2013
306.874´3096761–dc23   2012049382

ISBN 978-1-107-03080-0 Hardback
ISBN 978-1-107-54719-3 Paperback

In memory of my father, Dafydd ap Glyn
Son of Doris Keturah Harry

Contents

Maps and Figure

Acknowledgements

I have had the good fortune to receive the support, generosity, and friendship of many people as this book has meandered along its way to fruition. It would never have even been started, however, were it not for the teachers who first introduced me to the vast treasury that is African history: Gunvant Govindjee at Atlantic College and David Anderson, Michael Brett, Wayne Dooling, Richard Rathbone, and Andrew Roberts at the School of Oriental and African Studies. Were it not for Richard's guidance, in particular, I doubt I would have ended up at graduate school at Northwestern University.

At Northwestern I have left a large intellectual debt, and my biggest creditor there is David Schoenbrun. He guided me through my PhD with rigour and enthusiasm in equal quantities and managed all the while to let me take my own path. I am very grateful to him too for his support in the years since I left Evanston and most especially for the conversations we continue to have about the field of early African history. A number of other mentors helped me along the way, notably Jonathon Glassman, Caroline Bledsoe, Rae Moses, and Stefan Kaufman. And I am grateful for many good conversations with and feedback from my fellow graduate students, not all of them at Northwestern: Pamela Khanakwa, Neil Kodesh, Kathryn de Luna, Karl Gunther, Carole Emberton, Emily Callaci, Jeremy Berndt, Andreana Prichard, Joe Lapsley, Jana Measells, Katy Burns-Howard, Elizabeth Prevost, Jennifer Tappan, and Marina Pyrovolaki, among others. Wasswa Ddamulira took on the task of teaching me Luganda in Chicago, for which I thank him.

Northwestern provided me with financial as well as intellectual support, which made my initial research possible: a Northwestern University

Graduate School Presidential Fellowship enabled the writing, while a Graduate Research Grant and a Research Year Fellowship made the research possible. Various awards from the Program of African Studies also facilitated my research: a Hans Panofsky Award, a Melville Herskovits Field Research Award, a Jane Guyer and Akbar Virmani Award, and a Morris Goodman Award. The Department of History generously awarded me several travel grants.

It is, of course, in Uganda that I have accumulated the largest debts. These include to the many people who patiently answered my many questions about their languages, cultures, and histories, and those who opened their homes to me as a guest and to whom I am intensely thankful: Mary Bageya, Aisha Baluka, Hamidah Ddamulira, Womali Ephraim, Isabirye Eriasa, Kalautu Gladys, Betty Okot Gonza, Tazenya Henry, Mangusho John, Helen Kagino, Ernest Kamya, Zewulesi Kantono, Veronica Kanyana, Lukoowe Kaseenene, James John Kavere, Chimendwa Kawuke, Joyce Kawuledde, Richard Kayingo, Joy Kisule, John Kunena, Margaret Kyaita, Samsom Luvunya, Steven Kaza Magaja, Henry Maganda, Tom Masaba, Denis Medeyi, Joseph Medeyi, Margaret Medeyi, Madete Mohammed, Henry Mongo, Joram Mpande, Abuna Mujwi, Peter Michael Muloit, Esther Mulowooza, Sarah Musana, Yokarasa Mutegwa, Yokulamu Mutemere, Sam Mwigo, Rehema Nakaima, Harriet Nakibanda, Mwisram Namusoso, Mary Namwano, Noor Namwebya, Maliseri Namwoyo, Manjeri Nasiyo, Kalulu Paulo, Mbasalaki Mastuula Saidi, Ephraim Talyambiri, Philemon Taseula, Rachel Wadaga, Edison Waiswa, Rebecca Waligita, Abnere Wanakomon, Abel Wanzige, and Gertrude Yanga. I also thank Faith Damali Kanyago and Alice Nabirye for working alongside me as research assistants on the project, and Professor Livingston Walusimbi, Professor Grace Bantebya Kyomuhendo, Dr. Nakanyike Musisi, Rose Nkaale Mwanja, and Professor Mahmood Mamdani, for their support and interest in my work.

The staff at various institutions in Uganda, through their professionalism and willingness to help, made research easier than it might have been. These include the Africana Library at Makerere University; the Uganda National Archives in Entebbe; the Department of Land and Surveys in Entebbe; the Church Missionary Society Archives at Uganda Christian University; the Bishop's House Archives and the Cultural Research Centre in Jinja; the Archives of the Kampala Archdiocese in Rubaga; and the Lugwere Bible Translation Project at the Summer Institute for Languages in Entebbe. At the last of these I had the pleasure of meeting Samuel Mubbala who has remained a friend and fount of knowledge since. The

Makerere Institute of Social Research and the Uganda Museum at different times supported my applications for research clearance, which the Uganda National Council for Science and Technology granted with approval from the Office of the President. I extend my thanks to all these institutions for making my research possible.

Elsewhere too, I have benefitted from the professionalism and enthusiasm of librarians and archivists: at the Archives of the Society of Missionaries of Africa (White Fathers) in Rome; the Archives of the Mill Hill Missionaries of the St. Joseph's Missionary Society then held at Mill Hill in London but now in Freshfield, Merseyside; the British Library; the Library and Archives of the School of Oriental and African Studies; and the Library of Africana Studies at Northwestern University.

I owe a deep debt of gratitude to Ron Atkinson, who shared with me his research on Bugwere from some forty years ago and for his enthusiasm throughout. I also thank him for reading a draft and for his comments and suggestions. Another debt of gratitude is to David Cohen for sharing his Collected Texts of Busoga Traditional History and for our conversations. Chris Ehret has consistently supported and encouraged me, while offering valuable criticism and suggestions, for all of which I am grateful.

The Past and Present Society gave me a post-doctoral fellowship for 2008–09 at the Institute of Historical Research, University of London, which allowed me to return to Uganda for additional research and begin the process of turning my dissertation into this book. Teaching at SOAS from 2009 to 2011 was both a pleasurable return to my academic roots and the ideal place to continue writing. I very much benefitted from presenting my work at seminars there, as well as at the University of Sussex, the Institute of Historical Research, the Centre of African Studies at Cambridge University, the University of Birmingham, the Centre d'Études des Mondes Africains at Université Paris I, the former Institute of Languages at Makerere University; and at various meetings of the African Studies Association, the African Studies Association UK, the Third International Conference on Bantu Languages, and the Sixth World Congress of African Linguistics.

During my time back in the United Kingdom, I received support and insightful comments on parts of or the whole manuscript from several people, especially Ceri Ashley, Teresa Bernheimer, Paul Betts, Shane Doyle, Saul Dubow, Graham Furniss, John Giblin, Toby Green, Matthew Hilton, Philip Jagger, Lutz Marten, Tom McCaskie, Henri Médard, John Parker, Derek Peterson, Andrew Reid, Richard Reid, Pauline von Hellermann, and Megan Vaughan. At Columbia University, I have enjoyed the support and friendship of several colleagues in the Department of History and in African Studies. I am particularly grateful to Gregory Mann and Mamadou Diouf for reading the whole manuscript and for their insightful and useful comments. In addition, I received feedback and mentoring from Carol Gluck and Pamela Smith. I would also like to thank the African Studies librarian Yuusuf Caruso for all his efforts in helping me get hold of obscure dictionaries.

I thank Cambridge University Press, especially Eric Crahan (who has now left), Scott Parris, and Kristin Purdy, and the editors of the African Studies Series. I am especially grateful to the anonymous readers who offered valuable suggestions to improve the manuscript. I thank Damien Bovlomov for creating the maps that appear here. Parts of the book were published in different form in "Lineage and Society in Precolonial Uganda," *Journal of African History* 50, no. 2 (2009): 203–221, and in "Birthing Wealth? Motherhood and Poverty in East-Central Uganda, c. 700–1900," *Past and Present* 215 (2012): 235–68. That material is reproduced here with permission from Cambridge University Press and the Past and Present Society, respectively. I am grateful to the Melville J. Herskovits Library of Africana Studies for permission to use an image from The Humphrey Winterton Collection of East African Photographs, 'Native women, Kampala, Uganda,' on the cover of this book, and I am especially grateful to David Easterbrook, Patricia Ogedengbe, and Cassandra Harlan for their help in obtaining the image. I thank Andrea Greengrass for the index.

Unfortunately this book will appear a few months too late for my father Dafydd to read it in print, but it remains inspired by his enthusiasm for studying the past, for dusty books, and for travel to faraway places. My mother Janig's passion for linguistics infected me a long time ago and helped make this research possible, while her encouragement helped get the book done. Jarod Roll has accompanied me since before this project began and while I am grateful to him for all manner of reasons, with regards to this book I am especially grateful that he has been willing to read seemingly countless drafts and always find ways to improve what was written. Finally, Menna's awe that her mother might actually write a book that she could find on a library shelf has inspired me to get it finished.

Note on Language

This book, for the most part, tells the story of people who spoke Bantu languages. In these languages nouns have prefixes that change the meaning of the stem. For nouns describing people, the places they live, and the languages they speak, I have retained those prefixes. So Bagwere, Basoga, Bashana, and Baganda are people who live in Bugwere, Busoga, Bushana, and Buganda and who speak Lugwere, Lusoga, Rushana, and Luganda. Elsewhere, for adjectival purposes, I use only the stem: Gwere, Soga, Shana, and Ganda. But these people did not inhabit a land bereft of people speaking other languages. Some of those they lived alongside spoke Nilotic languages. Where I discuss people from non-Bantu groups, I have retained the forms in those languages as spoken in modern times: Iteso people speak Ateso, Joluo people speak Dholuo, and so on.

Introduction

This book tells the story of the familiar – motherhood – in what, to many readers, is an unfamiliar place, east central Uganda. Motherhood appears regularly in historical studies, but is rarely itself the focus of analysis. Rather, it is invoked as a universal category imbued with relational and emotional significance: motherhood is usually about nurturing, caring, facilitating, and restraining. As such it can be used to explain women's position in society without challenging our ingrained concepts of essentialism and biology. But when the historical lens turns to motherhood itself, its universalism and eternality dissipate almost instantly; motherhood becomes unfamiliar. To write historically about motherhood, it is necessary to expand our understanding of it beyond biological reproduction and practices of nurture and caregiving and think instead about motherhood as a social institution and as ideology. In the area of Uganda that today encompasses the societies of Bugwere, Busoga, and Buganda – all descended from the common ancestral North Nyanza language community – such an approach opens up a wide and complicated history of motherhood that can be traced back to the first millennium and shows it to have been at the heart of most important historical developments in the area, from the organisation and reproduction of lineages and clans to the centralisation of political power into monarchical states (Map 1).

This project started, perhaps rather unfashionably, as a way of exploring women's history in precolonial Uganda. Motherhood is widely recognised as an essential aspect of women's lives in Africa, more important than marriage in terms of identity, social status, and political and

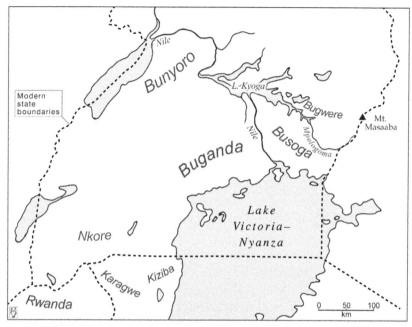

MAP I. Great Lakes Region, including North Nyanza societies and major neighbouring states.

religious authority.[1] It seemed therefore the obvious starting point for a study charting developments in women's lives before the rapid changes of the modern era. Despite the project's initial focus, this book is an exploration of the roles motherhood has played in social organisation, economic activity, and political power rather than a history of mothers per se. To borrow a phrase so effectively used by the historian Lorelle Semley, it is a history of *public motherhood*: of motherhood as social institution and ideology.[2] As such this book speaks to historical research across the

---

[1] For example: "Although wifehood in many African societies has traditionally been regarded as functional and necessary it is at the same time seen as a transitional phase on the road to motherhood. *Mother* is the preferred and cherished self-identity of many African women." Oyèrónké Oyěwùmí, "Family Bonds/Conceptual Binds: African Notes on Feminist Epistemologies," *Signs* 25, no. 4 (2000): 1096. Emphasis in original.

[2] Lorelle D. Semley, *Mother Is Gold, Father Is Glass: Gender and Colonialism in a Yoruba Town* (Bloomington: Indiana University Press, 2011). Semley also uses the phrase 'public mothers,' which she in turn has borrowed from Chikwenye Okonjo Ogunyemi, *Africa Wo/Man Palava: The Nigerian Novel by Women* (Chicago: University of Chicago Press, 1996).

premodern world, not because motherhood is a universal, but because a focus on public motherhood makes possible a fundamentally different way of viewing patrilineal and patriarchal societies.

Motherhood in African history is traditionally seen as having a specifically African form although one that is both unchanging and uniform across different regions and times. The core framework of this depiction works as follows: women who were unable to have children, either through their own infertility or that of their husbands, were socially and economically vulnerable. At best, they faced poverty and, at worst, accusations of witchcraft. After death their spirits were not remembered, except as possible agents of misfortune, and children were not named after them.[3] Although it is rarely explicitly stated, the inverse is thus held to be true: women who were able to reproduce biologically sought to have as many children as possible. Such women were socially included and valued and could look forward to an economically secure future.[4] The high birth rate in twentieth century sub-Saharan Africa is thus generally depicted as a continuation of a subcontinent-wide, precolonial approach to motherhood. There are important exceptions to this generalised depiction, but the dominant vision is of a timeless, and therefore ahistorical, African motherhood.[5]

A History of African Motherhood argues that motherhood in precolonial Africa has a history that is complex and that motherhood is central to our understanding of African history more broadly. A historical perspective enables us to see motherhood as a social institution and as an ideology that both shaped and was shaped by the communities of which it formed such an important part. As those communities changed over time – expanding, diversifying, contracting – so the way in which they constructed motherhood also changed. There was no single trajectory or outcome of motherhood even within individual communities. Some African women may have found economic and social security through their maternity, but many others will not have done so, regardless of the

[3] For a clear summary of this perspective, see Claude Meillassoux, *Maidens, Meal and Money: Capitalism and the Domestic Community* (Cambridge: Cambridge University Press, 1981), 77.

[4] My thanks to Anne Hugon of the Centre d'Études des Mondes Africains, Paris, for our discussion on this question which helped to clarify and sharpen my thinking.

[5] For some of the exceptions, see Steven Feierman, "Struggles for Control: The Social Roots of Health and Healing in Modern Africa," *African Studies Review* 28, no. 2/3 (1985): 73–147; Nancy Rose Hunt, "'Le Bébé en Brousse': European Women, African Birth Spacing and Colonial Intervention in Breast Feeding in the Belgian Congo," *International Journal of African Historical Studies* 21, no. 3 (1988): 401–32.

number of children they had.[6] Some women may have faced isolation and insecurity as a result of infertility, but others were able to acquire ritual authority as mediums precisely because of their infertility.[7] Motherhood also enables us to explore the complexity of social and political organisation by bringing women into the analysis without excluding men. Mothers were wives to husbands, daughters of fathers, and mothers to boys as well as girls. And motherhood, in these societies, could not exist in the absence of fatherhood. As a fundamentally relational institution, all of these relationships shaped both the individual experience of motherhood and its public form. By viewing motherhood as diverse, as culturally specific and as subject to change over time, we can see how people drew on it, as social institution and as ideology, to shape their societies long before the changes wrought by entry into the modern era of long-distance trade, capitalist markets, and colonisation.

Over the past two decades or so, historians and theorists writing about motherhood in Europe and North America have demonstrated it to be both contingent and historical and have posed questions vital for studying motherhood in Africa. "Until quite recently, however," notes the historian of medieval Christianity, Clarissa Atkinson, "motherhood had no history; it was too thoroughly identified with the private sphere and with the 'changeless' biological aspects of the human condition. Women's lives were organized and their capacities defined by their status as mothers, potential mothers, and non-mothers, but motherhood itself was not perceived as an institution shaped by culture and subject to history."[8] To overcome our culturally constrained vision of motherhood as "biological and invariant" and write about it historically, we need to conceptualise motherhood as an institution with an ideology, as Heather Jon Maroney argues.[9] Such an approach enables us to untangle "the social, historical, biological and psychological dimensions of maternity."[10] In viewing

---

[6] Rhiannon Stephens, "Birthing Wealth? Motherhood and Poverty in East-Central Uganda, c. 700–1900," *Past and Present* 215 (2012): 235–68.

[7] See, for example, Iris Berger, "Fertility as Power: Spirit Mediums, Priestesses and the Precolonial State in Interlacustrine East Africa," in *Revealing Prophets: Prophecy in Eastern African History*, ed. David M. Anderson and Douglas H. Johnson (London: James Currey, 1995), 65–82.

[8] Clarissa W. Atkinson, *The Oldest Vocation: Christian Motherhood in the Middle Ages* (Ithaca: Cornell University Press, 1991), 6.

[9] Heather Jon Maroney, "Embracing Motherhood: New Feminist Theory," in *The Politics of Diversity: Feminism, Marxism and Nationalism*, ed. Roberta Hamilton and Michèle Barrett (London: Verso, 1986), 405.

[10] Maroney, "Embracing Motherhood," 399.

motherhood as a social institution, and by writing its history, it becomes possible to demonstrate, in the words of British literary scholar Toni Bowers, that "motherhood, far from a static, 'natural' experience, is a moving plurality of potential behaviors always undergoing supervision, revision, and contest, constructed in particularity."[11] But understanding motherhood to be an institution is only the starting point. "As an institution," asks Atkinson, "how is motherhood constructed? How are its ideologies developed and proclaimed?" Most importantly for our purposes here, we need to ask, "How is the work of mothers related to the political and economic institutions of a society?"[12]

This comes to the fore in the institution of the queen mother, a feature of African monarchical states that has garnered significant scholarly attention.[13] As the historian Sandra Barnes highlights, the commonality of queen mothers, although not all biological mothers to kings, derived from most of them belonging "to the generation senior to the ruler" and occupying "a position in the governmental hierarchy that was equal or complementary to the monarch." Scholars have, furthermore, viewed queen mothers as performing "functions that were derived from 'mothering,' among which protecting and supporting were politically significant."[14] But, argues Semley, "scholars who equate women's political activities primarily with 'mothering' and caretaking present such skills as 'natural.'" In so doing, they obscure "women's leadership and decision making in the ritual, religious, political, and economic well-being of the community."[15] When we approach queen mothers from the perspective of an ideology of public motherhood, as Semley suggests, we can both move beyond culturally determined preconceptions of 'mothering' and place queen mothers effectively in a broader political and ideological context. Queen mothers have long been at the heart of political centralisation in

---

[11] Toni Bowers, *The Politics of Motherhood: British Writing and Culture, 1680–1760* (Cambridge: Cambridge University Press, 1996), 19.

[12] Atkinson, *The Oldest Vocation*, ix.

[13] See, for example, Edna G. Bay, "Belief, Legitimacy and the *Kpojito*: An Institutional History of the 'Queen Mother' in Precolonial Dahomey," *Journal of African History* 36, no. 1 (1995): 1–27; Suzanne Preston Blier, "The Path of the Leopard: Motherhood and Majesty in Early Danhomè," *Journal of African History* 36, no. 3 (1995): 391–417; Flora Edouwaye S. Kaplan, ed., *Queens, Queen Mothers, Priestesses, and Power: Case Studies in African Gender* (New York: New York Academy of Sciences, 1997).

[14] Sandra T. Barnes, "Gender and the Politics of Support and Protection in Precolonial West Africa," in *Queens, Queen Mothers, Priestesses, and Power: Case Studies in African Gender*, ed. Flora Edouwaye S. Kaplan (New York: New York Academy of Sciences, 1997), 2.

[15] Semley, *Mother Is Gold, Father Is Glass*, 39.

east central Uganda, but their history suggests the broader salience of local ideologies of motherhood in social and political life, among royalty and commoners alike.

Viewing motherhood as an ideological concept allows us to reconstruct the historical architecture of its multiple functions, both durable and contingent, as a productive necessity, a cultural form, and a political institution. Some scholars will insist that we should not use the term ideology to discuss the precolonial African context. The term emerged in Europe, apparently in the early nineteenth century, and is closely associated with the European political developments such as communism and fascism. Other scholars, as the political scientist Kathleen Knight notes, have claimed the term is used too often and inconsistently. While competing definitions abound, Knight offers a common definition of ideology that allows for generalisation beyond any specific use or association: "the way a system – a single individual or even a whole society – rationalizes itself." She draws on John Gerring's definition that ideology requires coherence and stability. This is even the case when ideologies are "impractical, or even delusional." As a coherent and consistent social system of meaning, an ideology also requires contrast or opposition, usually in the form of other competing ideologies.[16] In all of these ways, the history of motherhood, in east central Uganda and likely elsewhere, is at heart the history of an ideology. As a cultural form, as a social relationship, and as a key element in political charters, motherhood took an ideological form that was both internally consistent and enduring over generations and at times over centuries. But it was by no means unchanging. People adapted their ideology of motherhood as they faced new challenges and possibilities. As the North Nyanza community expanded and divided, new forms competed with and at times eclipsed older ideologies of motherhood in a complex history of social and cultural change.

To view motherhood as an institution with an ideology is to enable the kind of historical analysis required to replace the universal, timeless conceptions of this common but complicated central feature of human society. It also enables a historical approach to gender in the region. As Joan Wallach Scott so persuasively argued, gender "provides a way to decode meaning and to understand the complex connections among various forms of human interaction. When historians look for the ways in which

---

[16] Kathleen Knight, "Transformations of the Concept of Ideology in the Twentieth Century," *American Political Science Review* 100, no. 4 (2006): 619 (quotes); John Gerring, "Ideology: A Definitional Analysis," *Political Research Quarterly* 50, no. 4 (1997): 957–94.

the concept of gender legitimizes and constructs social relationships, they develop insight into the reciprocal nature of gender and society and into the particular and contextually specific ways in which politics constructs gender and gender constructs politics."[17] A number of historians have demonstrated the truth of Scott's point for twentieth-century Africa, in particular with reference to the role of reproduction in constructing both gender and political relations. Lynn Thomas effectively encapsulated this truth in the phrase, "politics of the womb."[18] In this book, I draw on the insights provided by historians and anthropologists about the centrality of reproduction and gender relations to Africa's colonial and postcolonial experience and set those works in the context of a much longer trajectory of gendered history. In so doing, this fundamental aspect of East Africa's political, cultural, and social history comes more clearly into view.

It can often seem as if the history of much of Africa before the nineteenth century is shrouded in the mists of time. It is true that historians writing about more recent periods have a greater body of material to draw upon. But by taking oral traditions seriously and by exploring the possibilities open to us through interdisciplinary approaches, we now know a good deal about many parts of the continent over the past two thousand years. In the first blossoming of African history, many scholars focused on the precolonial period in a deliberate move away from the then conventional imperial approach in which African history was the history of Europeans in Africa. These works were inspired in part by Jan Vansina's argument that oral traditions, if correctly used, could stand on level ground with written records; perhaps the most famous of these early precolonial studies of East Africa is Bethwell Ogot's *History of the Southern Luo*.[19] This work was also inspired in part by a desire

---

[17] Joan W. Scott, "Gender: A Useful Category of Historical Analysis," *American Historical Review* 91, no. 5 (1986): 1070.

[18] Lynn M. Thomas, *Politics of the Womb: Women, Reproduction, and the State in Kenya* (Berkeley: University of California Press, 2003). The works are too numerous to list, but these three edited volumes include many of the key historians: Jean Allman, Susan Geiger, and Nakanyike Musisi, eds., *Women in African Colonial Histories* (Bloomington: Indiana University Press, 2002); Dorothy L. Hodgson and Sheryl A. McCurdy, eds., *"Wicked" Women and the Reconfiguration of Gender in Africa* (Portsmouth, N.H.: Heinemann, 2001); Lisa A. Lindsay and Stephan F. Miescher, eds., *Men and Masculinities in Modern Africa* (Portsmouth, N.H.: Heinemann, 2003).

[19] Jan Vansina, *Oral Tradition: A Study in Historical Methodology*, transl. H. M. Wright (Chicago: Aldine Publishing, 1965); Bethwell A. Ogot, *History of the Southern Luo: Volume One, Migration and Settlement 1500–1900* (Nairobi: East African Publishing House, 1967). Other East African examples include Gideon S. Were, *A History of the Abaluyia of Western Kenya* (Nairobi: East African Publishing House, 1967);

to write 'authentic' histories of African countries that could be drawn upon as part of the process of building up the new nations that emerged in the 1960s. But by the 1980s the subfield had slowed down. On the one hand, scholars increasingly realised that oral traditions could not be used in the same way as conventional archival material, that they were shaped as much by the tellers of the tales as by the historical events they narrated. On the other hand, the focus of academic historians moved to the colonial and increasingly postcolonial periods as archives opened up, revealing a wealth of material. By grappling with the implications of new understandings of oral traditions, however, scholars have produced nuanced and compelling histories of the deeper past.[20]

Other historians drew on linguistic evidence to write about periods beyond the recall of oral tradition. Among the first proponents of this approach were Roland Oliver and Christopher Ehret.[21] Many of their original arguments have been revised or even discarded as we have learnt more about African languages or as new archaeological evidence has been uncovered. But the underlying premise – that languages can serve as a form of archive giving us insight into past centuries – remains salient. More recently, scholars have combined evidence from multiple sources to write the history of Africa over several centuries and even millennia.[22]

Isaria Kimambo, *A Political History of the Pare of Tanzania c. 1500–1900* (Nairobi: East African Publishing House, 1969); Samwiri Rubaraza Karugire, *A History of the Kingdom of Nkore in Western Uganda to 1896* (Oxford: Clarendon Press, 1971); M. S. M. Semakula Kiwanuka, *A History of Buganda from the Foundation of the Kingdom to 1900* (London: Longman, 1971); David William Cohen, *The Historical Tradition of Busoga: Mukama and Kintu* (Oxford: Clarendon Press, 1972); Godfrey Muriuki, *A History of the Kikuyu, 1500–1900* (Nairobi: Oxford University Press, 1974); William Robert Ochieng', *A Pre-colonial History of the Gusii of Western Kenya: From c. A.D. 1500 to 1914* (Kampala: East African Literature Bureau, 1974); Steven Feierman, *The Shambaa Kingdom: A History* (Madison: University of Wisconsin Press, 1974).

[20] Again for East Africa only this work includes, Steven Feierman, *Peasant Intellectuals: Anthropology and History in Tanzania* (Madison: University of Wisconsin Press, 1990); David Newbury, *Kings and Clans: Ijwi Island and the Lake Kivu Rift, 1780–1840* (Madison: University of Wisconsin Press, 1991); Christopher Wrigley, *Kingship and State: The Buganda Dynasty* (Cambridge: Cambridge University Press, 1996); Jan Vansina, *Antecedents to Modern Rwanda: The Nyiginya Kingdom*, trans. by author (Madison: University of Wisconsin Press, 2004); Neil Kodesh, *Beyond the Royal Gaze: Clanship and Public Healing in Buganda* (Charlottesville: University of Virginia Press, 2010).

[21] Roland Oliver, "The Problem of the Bantu Expansion," *Journal of African History* 7, no. 3 (1966): 361–76; Christopher Ehret, *Southern Nilotic History: Linguistic Approaches to the Study of the Past* (Evanston, Ill.: Northwestern University Press, 1971).

[22] For example, Edda L. Fields-Black, *Deep Roots: Rice Farmers in West Africa and the African Diaspora* (Bloomington: Indiana University Press, 2008); Rhonda M. Gonzales, *Societies, Religion, and History: Central East Tanzanians and the World They Created,*

Taking a broad interdisciplinary approach means that we can draw more complete and accurate pictures, although the remaining gaps in our knowledge are large and so we expect the history presented in these pictures to be challenged and revised. Importantly, through this work we have begun to better appreciate the diversity, complexity, and specificity of African societies, whether the entanglements of food production, culture and identity in the west central African rainforest or the intertwined nature of gender, economy, religion, and political power across the sub-Saharan region.

Some scholars of Africa's older history do have the benefit of written texts, although the texts that are available take a wide range of forms. Those writing about West Africa's place in the trans-Atlantic trade have shown the possibilities of uncovering African history even when using sources produced by outsiders. Since Kenneth Onwuka Dike's seminal *Trade and Politics in the Niger Delta*, they have also shown the value of interpreting a wide range of African sources – written, oral, material – alongside archival ones.[23] Working on areas further inland, historians of the West African Sahel have drawn on the rich materials preserved in the libraries of places such as Timbuktu as well medieval inscriptions from northeastern Mali.[24] Those studying the other side of the continent, whether writing about the Horn of Africa, ancient Nubia, or

c. 200 B.C.E. to 1800 C.E. (New York: Columbia University Press, 2008), Gutenberg e-book, http://www.gutenberg-e.org/gonzales/ (Accessed 2 January 2013); Kairn A. Klieman, *"The Pygmies Were Our Compass": Bantu and Batwa in the History of West Central Africa, Early Times to c. 1900 C.E.* (Portsmouth, N.H.: Heinemann, 2003); Jan Vansina, *Paths in the Rainforests: Toward a History of Political Tradition in Equatorial Africa* (Madison: University of Wisconsin Press, 1990); Jan Vansina, *How Societies Are Born: Governance in West Central Africa before 1600* (Charlottesville: University of Virginia Press, 2004).

[23] K. Onwuka Dike, *Trade and Politics in the Niger Delta, 1830–1885: An Introduction to the Economic and Political History of Nigeria* (Oxford: Clarendon Press, 1956). Some recent examples include, Peter Mark, *"Portuguese" Style and Luso-African Identity: Precolonial Senegambia, Sixteenth-Nineteenth Centuries* (Bloomington: Indiana University Press, 2002); G. Ugo Nwokeji, *The Slave Trade and Culture in the Bight of Biafra: An African Society in the Atlantic World* (New York: Cambridge University Press, 2010); Toby Green, *The Rise of the Trans-Atlantic Slave Trade in Western Africa, 1300–1589* (New York: Cambridge University Press, 2012).

[24] Just a couple of examples from a rich field include, John O. Hunwick, ed. and trans., *Sharī'a In Songhay: The Replies of al-Maghīlī to the Questions of Askia al-Hājj Muhammad* (Oxford: Oxford University Press for the British Academy, 1985); Bruce S. Hall, *A History of Race in Muslim West Africa, 1600–1960* (New York: Cambridge University Press, 2011). On inscriptions see P. F. de Moraes Farias, *Arabic Medieval Inscriptions from the Republic of Mali: Epigraphy, Chronicles and Songhay-Tuāreg History* (Oxford: Oxford University Press for the British Academy, 2003).

the Swahili coast, also have the benefit of documents and inscriptions and chronicles.[25]

This growing body of writing on Africa in times long before the nineteenth century shows just how rich and nuanced that history is, but it also underscores the inadequacy of 'precolonial' as a descriptor for a period of time that stretches over several centuries. The term precolonial is rightly critiqued for privileging the colonial moment, as if all that came before was merely prelude. Equally problematically, it collapses dramatically different episodes of African history into a single, undifferentiated periodisation that intimates a degree of stasis. As yet, however, historians have not developed a new periodisation. Terms such as 'Early Iron Age' and 'Late Iron Age' have fallen out of favour with the archaeologists who first used them. And drawing on the periodisation of European history – ancient, medieval, and modern – risks imposing an external meta-historical narrative that too often makes little sense in the African context. Historians have responded by using specific, albeit broad, dates, a model that works well in individual cases but does not produce a wider generalisation.[26] In the end, we tend to stick with precolonial all the while bearing in mind its serious limitations. What is important is that our work, this book included, demonstrates the dynamism of past African societies and the ways in which people shaped those societies.

The rich and exciting literature on Africa's deeper past sheds light, albeit often indirect, on the history of motherhood. Jan Vansina, for example, writes extensively in *Paths in the Rainforests* about marriage practices and shifts by communities between matrilineal, patrilineal, and bilineal descent.[27] While he does not address it per se in his analysis,

[25] And again, a few examples of the many that exist include, Edward A. Alpers, *Ivory and Slaves: Changing Pattern of International Trade in East Central Africa to the Later Nineteenth Century* (Berkeley: University of California Press, 1975); Derek Nurse and Thomas Spear, *The Swahili: Reconstructing the History and Language of an African Society, 800–1500* (Philadelphia: University of Pennsylvania Press, 1985); Richard Pankhurst, *A Social History of Ethiopia: The Northern and Central Highlands from Early Medieval Times to the Rise of Emperor Téwodros II* (Trenton, N.J.: Red Sea Press, 1992).

[26] Ehret has used 'African Classical Age' for the period 1000 B.C.E. to 400 C.E., in part to highlight the continent's place in world history. See Christopher Ehret, *An African Classical Age: Eastern and Southern Africa in World History, 1000 B.C. to A.D. 400* (Charlottesville: University Press of Virginia, 1998).

[27] Vansina, *Paths in the Rainforests*. This is a very different interpretation from the argument that all ancient African societies were matrilineal (and matriarchal) made by Cheikh Anta Diop and George Murdock, among others. See Cheikh Anta Diop, *L'unité culturelle de l'Afrique noire: Domaines du patriarcat et du matriarcat dans l'antiquité classique* (Paris: Présence Africaine, 1959) and George Peter Murdock, *Africa: Its Peoples and*

marriage and descent are explicitly about motherhood. The decision to follow matrilineal or patrilineal descent was one about whether a woman's children would belong to her and her lineage or to her husband and his lineage. Furthermore, by showing that a social institution such as lineal descent is subject to historical change, Vansina's work undermines the perception that African social institutions are timeless or that their history is unrecoverable.[28] Christopher Ehret's research on the period he terms Africa's 'classical age' shows major shifts in kinship organisation, including between matrilineal and patrilineal descent systems. He also highlights changes in social structures such as age sets that were "central features of the life cycle."[29] Moving beyond kinship and descent, Kairn Klieman's work on relations between Bantu and Batwa people in west central Africa explores how their relationships were mediated through ideology, religion, and social institutions such as initiation ceremonies. She shows how these relations changed as Bantu-speaking people developed what she terms an "Ideology of the Primordial Batwa" and began to claim superior status.[30]

Although a number of works have sought to uncover the dynamic history of African social institutions over the *longue durée*, the study of gender before the nineteenth century remains a very small field. David Schoenbrun's work demonstrated the rich possibilities of using the combined methods of historical linguistics and comparative ethnography to write gender history. *A Green Place, A Good Place* is a history of the Great Lakes region that reflects the centrality of gender relations to economic, social, and political life from c. 500 BCE.[31] In her book on

Their Culture History (New York: McGraw-Hill, 1959). Both were influenced, albeit in different ways, by the older work of Lewis Henry Morgan and Friedrich Engels. See Lewis H. Morgan, *Ancient Society or Researches in the Lines of Human Progress from Savagery through Barbarism to Civilization* (Chicago: Charles H. Kerr, 1877) and Frederick Engels, *The Origin of the Family, Private Property and the State: In the Light of the Researches of Lewis H. Morgan*, ed. Eleanor Burke Leacock, trans. Alec West (New York: International Publishers, 1972).

[28] A. R. Radcliffe-Brown, "Introduction," in *African Systems of Kinship and Marriage*, ed. Alfred R. Radcliffe-Brown and Daryll Forde (London: Oxford University Press for the International African Institute, 1950), 1–2.

[29] Ehret, *An African Classical Age*, 254. On descent systems, see also Per Hage and Jeff Marck, "Proto-Bantu Descent Groups," in *Kinship, Languages, and Prehistory: Per Hage and the Renaissance in Kinship Studies*, ed. Doug Jones and Bojka Milicic (Salt Lake City: University of Utah Press, 2011), 75–8.

[30] Klieman, *"The Pygmies Were Our Compass."*

[31] See in particular, David L. Schoenbrun, "Gendered Histories between the Great Lakes: Varieties and Limits," *International Journal of African Historical Studies* 29, no. 3 (1996): 461–92; David Lee Schoenbrun, *A Green Place, A Good Place: Agrarian Change,*

the Ruvu-speaking people of what is today Tanzania, Rhonda Gonzales builds on Schoenbrun's work on gender, albeit in a very different regional context.[32] The disparities in gender relations between the Great Lakes region and the Ruvu valley serves to highlight the importance of the study of gender in precolonial Africa over the *longue durée*. Most recently, Christine Saidi has published her exploration of matrilineality in east central Africa, highlighting the need to view women historically as inhabiting a wide range of roles, of which wife may have been the least important.[33]

The history of motherhood in the Great Lakes region offers rich answers to the question of its relationship to political and economic institutions. In this region, people developed at least two broad models of motherhood that were very different from each other and yet coexisted in a relatively small area, amongst communities with a shared linguistic and cultural heritage. In the Kivu Rift Valley in the western part of this region, stretching from Lake Mwitanzige Albert in the north to Lake Tanganyika in the south, the ideal form of motherhood was for a woman to have many children. This vision of ideal motherhood, which Schoenbrun has traced back to the late first millennium CE, honoured women who had large numbers of children (seven or more, according to ethnographic evidence from the nineteenth and twentieth centuries[34]). Such women either wore a *rugolí* or crown of maternity or a special bell as a public symbol of their status.[35] At a time when the communities in which they lived "restricted access to land by developing patrilineal idioms of inclusion and exclusion," Schoenbrun argues, women developed "motherhood as an institution for garnering access to land." As mothers "gained standing and political clout," they "engaged with the heart of patriarchal ideology to convert their children into immediate sources of instrumental power and into sources of ease later in life."[36] Women who achieved the ideal form of motherhood, by having many children and laying claim to the

Gender, and Social Identity in the Great Lakes Region to the 15th Century (Portsmouth, N.H.: Heinemann, 1998).

[32] Gonzales, *Societies, Religion, and History*.

[33] Christine Saidi, *Women's Authority and Society in Early East-Central Africa* (Rochester, N.Y.: University of Rochester Press, 2010).

[34] See for example, R. Bourgeois, *Banyarwanda et Barundi: Tome I, éthnographie* Classe des science morales et politiques. Mémoires in-8. N.S. 15 (Brussels: Académie Royale des Sciences Coloniales, 1957), 526.

[35] Schoenbrun, *A Green Place, A Good Place*, 154. The asterisk denotes a reconstructed form of the lexical item.

[36] Schoenbrun, *A Green Place, A Good Place*, 123.

rugolí, held positions of authority in their husbands' households. "By overcoming the risks of childbirth, mothers hoped to increase the amount of domestic labor available to them in order to raise the output of those who lived in the patrilineage *(muryàdngó)* by consolidating their instrumental power over the others in the *muryàdngó.*"[37] This social vision of motherhood, although by no means static and unchanging, was nonetheless durable and meant that women sought to have as many children as possible to achieve the exclusive status of **mugole* which, in the Kivu Rift Valley over the past thousand years, has held the meaning of 'married mother.'[38]

A very different view of ideal motherhood and its place in society emerged at the end of the first millennium CE in North Nyanza – the ancestral community to Bugwere, Busoga, and Buganda and the region that is the focus of this book. Here, motherhood was viewed as an institution for creating networks of relationships and mutual obligation that cut across the dominant patrilineal divides. Success in motherhood rested on being the mother of the heir, whether to the household or the kingdom. A woman's ability to convert motherhood into instrumental power depended on two factors. The first was that she should occupy the position of senior wife in her husband's household because her son would thus be the preferred choice as heir. The second was that she should have the necessary political skills to garner the support of other interested parties in her son's claim. The dominant ideal of motherhood in North Nyanza did not, therefore, reward women for having large numbers of children; it rewarded them for the success of one particular child. In this context, then, there was less reason for women to repeatedly undergo the serious risks of pregnancy and childbirth and more reason to limit the number of children they had in order to nurture them to adulthood and generate the maximum political advantage for one amongst them. These two models of public motherhood, although abstract as ideological systems, had real and varied consequences for people, especially women, in Great Lakes Bantu societies.

Writing the history of this part of Africa beyond two or three centuries ago requires stepping outside of the normal parameters of historical research and drawing on a range of methodological approaches. In Chapter 1, I set out the methodological foundations of the book: historical linguistics, comparative ethnography, and the analysis of oral

[37] Schoenbrun, *A Green Place, A Good Place,* 154.
[38] Schoenbrun, *A Green Place, A Good Place,* 141.

traditions. While beyond the African historian's usual focus on archives and oral history, the use of these approaches is neither new nor limited to African history. I present these methodologies in order to enable non-specialist readers to evaluate the evidence presented in the book. While noting what such sources cannot tell us about the past, the chapter demonstrates how using them makes it possible to write nuanced and detailed history over several centuries. Having set out the sources and methodologies, the book moves on to explore the history of motherhood in the North Nyanza societies from c. 700 CE to c. 1900 over the next four chapters.

Before we can trace continuities and changes in the social institution of motherhood we need a baseline for comparative purposes. What did motherhood look like in North Nyanza society? By exploring who could be a mother and under which conditions, Chapter 2 highlights efforts by North Nyanza–speaking women and men, from c. 700 to c. 1200 CE, to control their own social reproduction as they sought to build sustainable and durable communities. Such efforts focused on marriage and clan taboos. At the same time, the social and political importance of motherhood affected the forms and meanings of marriage. Reproducing the communities speaking North Nyanza involved economic production and political innovation as much as biological reproduction. The chapter's exploration of motherhood during this period thus takes us into the economic history of North Nyanza society, most importantly the gendered nature of food procurement and the rituals surrounding such activities. The rituals that governed farming, hunting, and fishing were informed by North Nyanzan ideologies of motherhood and beliefs about social reproduction. Ideologies of motherhood also worked to shape the contours of early political formations in which queen mothers helped to create and reproduce political authority. Motherhood as a social institution was thus an integral part of efforts by North Nyanza speakers to establish and reproduce sustainable communities.

From the twelfth century we see the descendants of the North Nyanzan community develop two very different ideal forms of motherhood. By this time, people in the area around the North Nyanzan heartland spoke pre- or early Luganda while the communities further to the east spoke South Kyoga. The new linguistic divide was mirrored in other aspects of the lives of early Luganda speakers and their South Kyoga–speaking neighbours and these changes are explored in Chapter 3. The different visions of public motherhood they held shaped the ways in which people organised their communities. South Kyoga speakers emphasised what I term 'social motherhood' where the social position of a woman within her marital home and her kin group was part of what determined her access to motherhood and the material and social benefits it brought. Becoming a mother could depend as much on social position as on biological success; practices of fostering or adoption enabled some women to become mothers in nonphysiological ways. Among early Luganda speakers, by contrast, there was a growing move to emphasise biology over social status so that even marginal women could aspire to be recognised as the mother of the heir on the death of the head of the household. This division was reflected in early polities in both regions and in part grew out of changing economic realities with the move towards more intensive banana cultivation in the early Luganda–speaking areas and the continued importance of millet as the staple crop in the east.

Chapter 4 traces the changes in the institutions and ideologies of motherhood from the sixteenth century to the end of the eighteenth century. By the start of this period, South Kyoga had split into two new speech communities: those of Lusoga and East Kyoga, or early Lugwere. In the west, meanwhile, Luganda speakers were expanding their community. In this period, Luo-speaking people started to move from regions to the north into Busoga and the lands of East Kyoga. This immigration was particularly important in Busoga where Luo speakers and their descendants became the ruling elites of a number of states. These Luo-descendant ruling families, however, predicated their power on older Soga ideologies of social motherhood; intermarriage was key to their maintenance and reproduction of political authority. East Kyoga speakers lived in an environment of even greater linguistic diversity alongside people speaking languages of the Greater Luhyia subgroup of Great Lakes Bantu as well as those speaking Luo languages and other Nilotic languages, such as Ateso. This high level of diversity was increasingly reflected in domestic arrangements and in emerging political structures. In Buganda, the period between the sixteenth and nineteenth centuries was a time of consolidation of power into a single expansionary kingdom by the dominant royal family. This consolidation was justified, in part, by the older ideology of motherhood that continued to prevail within the royal circle. Nonetheless, there were growing challenges during these centuries to the authority of mothers in the governance of the kingdom that reflected the intensification of biological motherhood in Buganda.

The nineteenth century was a turbulent period for much of Africa and particularly so for the Great Lakes region with its growing integration into the wider economic world through the East African coast, and the arrival of traders, European travellers, missionaries, and finally the establishment of colonial overrule. As Chapter 5 sets out, the beginning of the century saw the final breakup of the North Nyanza languages with Lugwere and Rushana emerging from East Kyoga (early Lugwere). This was also a century of dramatic increase in slave-raiding and slave-holding by Buganda in particular which ultimately undermined social stability across the region. In Busoga and further east, slave-raiding and pillaging by Baganda soldiers and armed militias disrupted social reproduction as societies suffered repeated waves of attack. In addition to disrupting patterns of motherhood by removing large numbers of women and girls alongside smaller numbers of men and boys, the growing power of the Buganda kingdom over the Soga polities started to erode the ideology of social motherhood that had been so central to the political legitimacy of Soga ruling families. In Buganda itself, the influx of significant numbers of enslaved women and material plunder also undermined the existing community and political structures. The different historical experiences of people in the eastern communities speaking Lugwere and Rushana, however, offer an important counterpoint to the dominant narrative of Ganda expansionism and show the divergent ways in which an ideology of motherhood remained at the heart of political and social life across the region. The second half of the nineteenth century was a time of great opportunity for some, but a time of fundamental social and economic dislocation for many. In Buganda, in particular, successful chiefs transformed their newfound trade wealth into political capital and challenged the royal family's hold on power. New disease epidemics, warfare, and continued slave-raiding distorted societies and undermined the place of motherhood in community life beyond mere reproduction.

By the end of the nineteenth century Baganda and Basoga elite men had negotiated a new political landscape with the British, a landscape purged of powerful queen mothers and one in which women in general were presented as enslaved by men. This highly gendered political landscape has shaped our understanding of gender relations in precolonial East Africa, but it was new in the nineteenth century and needs to be seen as the outcome of bitter power struggles over political economy. Tracing the history of motherhood in east central Uganda from c. 700 CE demonstrates its centrality to social, political, and economic organisation, while at the same time showing precolonial gender relations to have been dynamic and changing. Motherhood as a social institution and a public ideology is a powerful lens through which to examine the past because it brings together biology, culture, political power, and human relations.

I

Writing Precolonial African History
Words and Other Historical Fragments

How is a history of motherhood in precolonial Uganda possible? The question is two-fold: How can we reconstruct the early history of the East African interior, and how can we reconstruct the history of motherhood in particular? Uganda poses a challenge to historians. While we know that the region it now covers has been inhabited for several millennia, the earliest written sources date only to the 1860s. There are no contemporary documents from the many and varied societies and cultures that inhabited the region that is today Uganda for the period before the nineteenth century. There are no diaries of ordinary people describing their quotidian lives, narrating their experiences of maternity and mothering. Nor are there written constitutions that explain the purpose and meaning of having a queen mother to govern alongside her son in the many kingdoms that existed across the region.

Recovering this history is possible through an interdisciplinary approach that draws on a range of methodologies and evidence. Typically this involves some combination of archaeological data, ecological evidence, comparative historical linguistic reconstructions, comparative ethnography, and analysis of oral traditions. These approaches have been applied in a wide range of contexts ranging from sub-Saharan Africa to Indo-European societies to East Asia and Oceania.[1] Turning to Uganda,

---

[1] For Indo-European history, see, among others, David W. Anthony, *The Horse, The Wheel, and Language: How Bronze-Age Riders from the Eurasian Steppes Shaped the Modern World* (Princeton: Princeton University Press, 2007). For Oceania and Asia, see among others: Peter Bellwood, James J. Fox, and Darrell Tryon, eds., *The Austronesians: Historical and Comparative Perspectives* (Canberra: Australian National University Press, 1995); Jeff Marck, *Topics in Polynesian Language and Culture History* (Canberra: Pacifica

and to east central Uganda in particular, we find that available evidence is of varying quantity and quality across the different disciplines. Although some excellent archaeological work has been conducted in Uganda, it tends to be restricted to the regions most conducive to excavation.[2] The densely populated and humid areas along the northwestern shores of Lake Victoria–Nyanza do not easily yield their buried secrets to archaeologists. In fact, those working there frequently lament that there is "no archaeology" to be found. Stone tools survive well, but bones, plants, metal tools, and even pottery tend to disintegrate, giving a distorted picture of the settlement history of the region. This means we have tantalising fragments such as the Luzira head and the Entebbe figurine – ceramics of human forms made more than a thousand years ago and that are as yet unparalleled in the wider region – but no systematic analysis of settlement patterns in the North Nyanza region.[3] That said, work by Ceri Ashley analysing ceramic finds along the shore of Lake Victoria–Nyanza has recently shed important new light on the communities living there from the mid-first millennium CE. This is discussed in more detail in Chapter 3, but an important insight from Ashley's work is that around the turn of the millennium those communities extended their social horizons beyond the household.[4]

Historical linguistics and comparative ethnography can illuminate the deeper past, and oral traditions give us insights into more recent centuries. The use of comparative ethnography to write precolonial history sits uneasily with many anthropologists and historians, for ethnography is

Linguistica, Australian National University, 2000); Alicia Sanchez-Mazas, Roger Blench, Malcolm D. Ross, Ilia Peiros, and Marie Lin, eds., *Past Human Migrations in East Asia: Matching Archaeology, Linguistics and Genetics* (New York: Routledge, 2008).

[2] See for example, Graham Connah, *Kibiro: The Salt of Bunyoro, Past and Present* (London: British Institute in Eastern Africa, 1996); Andrew Reid, "Ntusi and the Development of Social Complexity in Southern Uganda," in *Aspects of African Archaeology: Papers from the 10th Congress of the PanAfrican Association for Prehistory and Related Studies*, ed. Gilbert Pwiti and Robert Soper (Harare: University of Zimbabwe Publications, 1996), 621–7; Peter Robertshaw, "The Ancient Earthworks of Western Uganda: Capital Sites of a Cwezi Empire," *Uganda Journal* 48 (2002): 17–32; Peter Robertshaw, David Taylor, Shane Doyle, and Rachel Marchant, "Famine, Climate and Crisis in Western Uganda," in *Past Climate Variability through Europe and Africa*, vol. 6, ed. Richard W. Batterbee, Françoise Gasse, and Catherine E. Stickley (Dordrecht, Netherlands: Springer, 2004), 535–49.

[3] Andrew Reid, "Lake Victoria before Buganda," *African Heritage and Archaeology Webpages*, University College London, Institute of Archaeology, http://www.ucl.ac.uk/archaeology/aha/reid/buganda-lakev.htm/ (Accessed 4 January 2013); Andrew Reid and Ceri Z. Ashley, "A Context for the Luzira Head," *Antiquity* 82, no. 315 (2008): 99–112.

[4] Ceri Z. Ashley, "Towards a Socialised Archaeology of Ceramics in Great Lakes Africa," *African Archaeological Review* 27, no. 2 (2010): 135–63.

explicitly the study of the present, even if early writers tended to project their descriptions back into an unchanging past. Ethnography is a rich seam of information, but it cannot be used uncritically. "If pursued by itself," underlines David Schoenbrun, "the comparative study of contemporary cultural practices harbors anachronism."[5] Ethnographic data must be anchored by a different form of evidence; data from historical linguistics is one form, and archaeological evidence is another. Historical linguistics is about reconstructing language and is, as a subdiscipline, largely disinterested in the actions of people. As such it provides us with independent evidence in the form of reconstructed words. While it would be difficult to produce a compelling historical narrative on the basis of lexical reconstructions alone, the comparative ethnographic evidence allows us to understand the contexts in which those words were used in the past.

As each word and its ethnographic context are woven together, a tapestry begins to emerge. It is an imperfect tapestry with many holes and disjunctures and, probably, some mistakes woven into it. Yet it is much richer than many have imagined possible. It depicts a complex and changing world of ideology, kin governance, politics, and economic developments. Writing about how etymologies can tell us about people's reactions to innovations, Jan Vansina notes that, "in the absence of concrete evidence about individuals and their actual doings, it may well be the only way to bring back actors into a record that has erased them."[6] With all its flaws, that is what this is about: not just to write about people who died a thousand years ago because their story is compelling, but also so that people who live in east central Uganda today can reclaim their deeper, shared history, a history that has often been distorted with devastating consequences in the region.

While this is but one of a growing body of studies of the African past that draw on these and other sources (such as palynology, the study of pollen found in layers of sediment), such works remain comparatively rare and so it is still a valuable exercise to set out how this kind of history is written. This discussion is intended to enable readers to evaluate the evidence and analysis presented in the following chapters. What follows is not, however, a comprehensive discussion of the relevant methodologies. For that readers should look elsewhere.[7]

---

5 Schoenbrun, *A Green Place, A Good Place*, 55.
6 Vansina, *How Societies Are Born*, 14.
7 Two good places to start are Christopher Ehret, *History and the Testimony of Language* (Berkeley: University of California Press, 2011); Schoenbrun, *A Green Place, A Good Place*, 19–61, 265–9.

EVIDENCE FROM LANGUAGE

Language is not purely functional. We use words to name and describe our physical environment, but we also use them to talk about our spiritual, intellectual, and ideological worlds. Because of this, the reconstructed vocabularies of now-dead languages enable us to gain insights into the manifold worlds of the speakers of those languages. This is important, for it means that not only can we make historical arguments about when a speech community started to grow millet or adopted a new type of hoe, but we can also trace developments in, for example, religion, politics, and kin governance.

The first step in reconstructing vocabularies is a genetic classification of the languages to establish a historical framework in which to place those words. Genetic classifications establish which languages are descended from the same ancestral or proto-language, an explicitly historical relationship. As speakers of a language move apart in space and time, the languages they speak diverge into dialects and then into distinct languages.[8] Those dialects and languages retain core lexical and grammatical features in common with the others that diverged from the same proto-language. These retentions make it possible to establish the precise relationship of genetically related languages and reconstruct features of the common ancestral language.

The new languages are the children of the proto-language, which in turn has its own parent and siblings. While this kinship metaphor is helpful in mentally mapping the genetic relationships between languages, it is important to note that, in contrast to human reproduction, when a proto-language produces offspring it ceases to exist. This anthropomorphic vocabulary is also problematic in that agency is transferred onto the languages and away from the people speaking those languages. While we speak of language birth and death, what is actually happening is that individual people are making decisions (conscious or not) about the words and grammar they use to talk to each other. That is, languages are spoken by people and it is those speakers who initiate the breakup

---

[8] The boundary between dialect and language is notoriously difficult to establish. In general, dialects have reasonably high mutual intelligibility whereas related languages share common features but have low or very limited mutual intelligibility. In terms of the quantitative classification of genetically related dialects and languages, a threshold of 90 per cent cognation is generally recognised for "closely related dialects." See Sergei Starosin, "Comparative-Historical Linguistics and Lexicostatistics," trans. N. Evans and I. Peiros, in *Time Depth in Historical Linguistics*, ed. Colin Renfrew, April McMahon, and R. Larry Trask (Cambridge: McDonald Institute for Archaeological Research, 2000), 226.

of a language into dialects and then into different languages by changing the words they speak, how they pronounce those words, and the ways in which they are used.[9] It is precisely because of the human agency in language change that we are able to use historical linguistic evidence to write history.

The two most commonly used methods for determining genetic relationships between languages are lexicostatistics and the comparative method. Lexicostatistics is based on the comparison of a more or less fixed set of words or meanings across a number of languages to identify how many are shared. This set consists of meanings that are both most universal and least subject to external influence and is frequently referred to as the Swadesh-list (after Morris Swadesh, the first linguist to work on this systematically). Typically it comprises either one or two hundred items known as core vocabulary.[10] These lists are collected for the set of languages of interest and a number of outlier languages and are then used to establish cognates (i.e., items inherited from a shared ancestral language) between the languages, using regular sound correspondences to do so. Once the cognates have been established, they are counted for each pair of languages to determine percentages of cognation. These percentages can then be arranged in matrix form with the highest numbers at the outside edge, thereby grouping the languages with highest cognation percentages together, enabling the establishment of subgroups. It is thus possible to determine both the boundaries of relatedness and the internal classification of a set of genetically related languages.[11]

The comparative method enables the determination of genetic relationships between languages and the reconstruction of parts of their common ancestral or proto-language. A preliminary determination is made that constituents of a group of languages are likely to have a common ancestor. That determination has typically been based on morphological grounds. For example, linguists recognised strong similarities in the noun class systems of the various Bantu languages. Similarities of these kinds help determine genetic relatedness "because the probability of their

[9] For more on this see, Brian D. Joseph and Richard D. Janda, eds., *The Handbook of Historical Linguistics* (Oxford: Blackwell, 2003), 6–10.
[10] Morris Swadesh, "Lexico-Statistic Dating of Prehistoric Ethnic Contacts: With Special Reference to North American Indians and Eskimos," *Proceedings of the American Philosophical Society* 96, no. 4 (1952): 456–7.
[11] For a more detailed discussion of lexicostatistics and other quantitative methods of genetic language classification, as well as the comparative method, see April McMahon and Robert McMahon, *Language Classification by Numbers* (Oxford: Oxford University Press, 2005).

occurrence by chance in a range of languages is very low."[12] Having made a determination that there is evidence that languages in a given set are related, the comparative method can be applied in a systematic manner, examining all the evidence. This is done by collecting possible cognates for the group, which should include both lexical items and morphological paradigms. The cognates can then be used to identify the regular sound correspondences between the languages in the set. The existence of cognates and regular correspondences demonstrates the relatedness of the group; that is, these demonstrate that the languages form a family descended from a common ancestor.

Once established that the set of languages forms a family, it is then possible to use the regular sound correspondences to work out the phonology of the proto-language because there are rules that govern the kinds and directions of sound changes. Furthermore, the comparative method is premised on the regularity hypothesis, which posits that any sound change should affect all eligible words in the language in the same way, that is, those with the sound in the appropriate context. Once a sound change rule has been identified for a group of languages, it is then possible to use the rule to reverse regular changes and therefore reconstruct the likely forms of lexical items in the ancestral or proto-language. One final stage is determining degrees of relationship within a language family. This is done by examining the morphological patterns and regular sound correspondences to establish which are shared by subgroups of the set of languages and therefore represent innovations at a time when each of those subgroups constituted a single ancestral language at an intermediate stage between the common ancestor and the contemporary languages. It is this last stage that gives us the family tree of the group of languages.[13]

While the comparative method, according to the linguists April McMahon and Robert McMahon, "is typically seen as the gold standard by comparative historical linguists,"[14] most tend to use it in conjunction with quantitative methods, commonly lexicostatistics. For the purposes of classifying the North Nyanza languages, I established the initial classification used here through lexicostatistical analysis and then verified it through the comparative method. The latter was particularly useful in establishing the precise relationship between the North Nyanza

---

[12] McMahon and McMahon, *Language Classification by Numbers*, 6.
[13] McMahon and McMahon, *Language Classification by Numbers*, 9–10.
[14] McMahon and McMahon, *Language Classification by Numbers*, 5.

languages rather than simply demonstrating their genetic unity as a subgroup of Great Lakes Bantu.

The genetic classification of the North Nyanza languages has formed part of a number of studies, although this is the first to focus on the subgroup directly.[15] Before discussing the classification of North Nyanza and its Great Lakes Bantu grandparent, it is worth first setting out the place of Great Lakes Bantu in the larger Bantu family. There are competing classifications of the Bantu languages, although the gaps between them are slowly narrowing. For the purposes of this study, some of the detailed disagreements over the initial divergences of Bantu are not especially relevant. With regards to the more immediate ancestors of Great Lakes Bantu, there is largely consensus, although differences in nomenclature remain. Great Lakes Bantu is descended from Kaskazi Bantu, which is an offspring of Mashariki Bantu. Mashariki, in turn, is descended from a proto-language variously called Eastern Savanna Bantu and East Bantu. Eastern Savanna Bantu, according to Ehret, is descended from Savanna-Bantu. Ehret notes that "Savanna-Bantu emerge[d] as a subsequent offshoot at the southern forefront of the [initial] Bantu advance" into the equatorial rain forest.[16]

Great Lakes Bantu was already being spoken as a language around 500 BCE. According to Schoenbrun, "people speaking proto-Great Lakes Bantu probably settled initially between Lakes Kivu and Rweru. But their speech spread rapidly to as far east as the area around the mouth of the Kagera river" on Lake Victoria–Nyanza.[17] The Great Lakes Bantu speech community diverged, with its descendants speaking five different languages: East Nyanza, Gungu, Luhyia, Western Lakes, and West Nyanza

---

[15] Some of the most important earlier studies include Christopher Ehret et al., "Lacustrine History and Linguistic Evidence: Preliminary Conclusions" (University of California, Los Angeles, n.p. 1973), cited with the kind permission of Christopher Ehret; Martin Joel Mould, "Comparative Grammar Reconstruction and Language Subclassification: The North Victorian Bantu Languages" (PhD diss, University of California, Los Angeles, 1976); Derek Nurse and Gérard Philippson, "The Bantu Languages of East Africa: A Lexicostatistical Survey," in *Language in Tanzania*, ed. Edgar C. Polomé and C.P. Hill (Oxford: Oxford University Press for the International African Institute, 1980), 26–67; David L. Schoenbrun, "Great Lakes Bantu: Classification and Settlement Chronology," *Sprache und Geschichte in Afrika* 15 (1994): 91–152.

[16] Christopher Ehret, "Bantu Expansions: Re-Envisioning a Central Problem of Early African History," *International Journal of African Historical Studies* 34, no. 1 (2001): 32.

[17] Schoenbrun, "Great Lakes Bantu," 105, 106 (quote). This subgroup of languages is variously referred to in the literature as Zone J, Group 9, Lacustrine and Interlacustrine. I use Schoenbrun's Great Lakes Bantu throughout. Please note that the question of dating is discussed in detail in the section on chronology.

```
Great Lakes Bantu
    A. East Nyanza
    B. Gungu
    C. Luhyia
    D. Western Lakes
    E. West Nyanza
            1. Rutara
            2. North Nyanza
                    a. Luganda
                    b. South Kyoga
                            i. Lusoga
                            ii. East Kyoga
                                    α. Lugwere
                                    β. Rushana
```

FIGURE 1.1. The subclassification of the North Nynza languages and their place in Great Lakes Bantu. Underlined languages are currently spoken.

(see Figure 1.1). People spoke proto-West Nyanza in the first half of the first millennium CE and their descendants in turn formed two speech communities, one speaking proto-Rutara and the other proto-North Nyanza. North Nyanza began to be spoken as a language on the northwestern shore of Lake Victoria–Nyanza in the eighth century CE.

By the twelfth century, the descendants of these people were speaking two different languages that had developed out of proto-North Nyanza: early Luganda and proto-South Kyoga. Early Luganda was spoken in the North Nyanza heartland and to the south, west, and north of it, while South Kyoga was spoken to the east, across the Nile (see Map 2). By the sixteenth century, South Kyoga had diverged into early Lusoga and proto-East Kyoga (or pre-Lugwere), with East Kyoga in turn yielding Lugwere and Rushana in the early nineteenth century.[18] Lusoga spread across the region between the Nile and Mpologoma Rivers and Lakes Victoria–Nyanza and Kyoga while proto-East Kyoga was spoken across the Mpologoma River. In the final breakup of the North Nyanza languages, Lugwere continued to be spoken in the East Kyoga heartland while speakers of Rushana settled in the northwestern foothills of Mount Masaaba (Elgon).[19]

Having established the classification, it is possible to move onto reconstructing the words used by people speaking languages ancestral to those

[18] The subclassification of North Nyanza presented here differs from that in Schoenbrun, "Great Lakes Bantu."

[19] Please see Rhiannon Stephens, "A History of Motherhood, Food Procurement and Politics in East-Central Uganda to the Nineteenth Century" (PhD diss., Northwestern University, 2007), 30–58, 239–55, for all the relevant evidence for this classification.

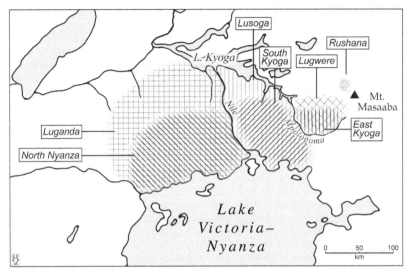

MAP 2. Historical linguistic geography of North Nyanza.

spoken today. The historical reconstruction of vocabulary involves distinguishing cognates, internal innovations, and loan words. Cognates are words with similar meanings and forms in different languages. As noted previously, they are connected by regular sound changes, so while they may look dissimilar, it is possible not only to identify them as cognate, but also to work backwards through the sound changes to posit the original form used by speakers of the proto-language. Internal innovations are words created by a speech community that may then be inherited by its descendants. Sometimes these are entirely new words, but more often it is possible to trace their etymology back in time. Bantu languages are particularly rich in their potential for deriving new words from existing ones and have quite regular mechanisms for doing this.[20] Tracing the etymologies in this way allows us to develop an intellectual history of each word and thus of the attitudes of the people who first used those words. As Vansina recognises, "etymologies tell us something about what the actors imagined about the innovation in question."[21]

Etymology and phonology are also important in establishing that particular words are loan words, or transferred innovations. These are words

[20] For overviews of Bantu derivational mechanisms, see Yvonne Bastin, *Les relations sémantiques dans les langues Bantoues* (Brussels: Académie Royale des Sciences d'Outre-Mer, 1985); Thilo C. Schadeberg, "Derivation," in *The Bantu Languages*, ed. Derek Nurse and Gérard Philippson (London: Routledge, 2003), 71–89.
[21] Vansina, *How Societies Are Born*, 13.

'borrowed' by speakers of one language from another language with whose speech community they have contact and may be from related or unrelated languages. Transferred innovations or loan words are often, but not always, identifiable because their phonology tends to not fit exactly with that of the recipient language, although the words may have been modified to fit in to a certain extent. Such loan words indicate that the institution, concept, or object named is likely to be of foreign origin. This is because people are unlikely to borrow a foreign word to name an indigenous practice or institution unless there are strong social status pressures or a substantial change in the content of the practice or form of the institution.[22] To reconstruct words to various proto-languages, it is necessary to have reflexes (the different iterations of the original word) in at least two of the descendant languages. In addition, the relationship between the reflexes should be "relatable according to a system of regular sound correspondences."[23] Preferably, reflexes should not be from adjoining languages where the possibility of cross-linguistic borrowing is high.[24]

EVIDENCE FROM CULTURE

While the reconstructed vocabularies for proto-North Nyanza and its daughters provide historians with the basis for writing a history, the words alone do not reveal to us the contexts in which they were used. Drawing on the ethnographic record allows us to reconstruct some of those contexts. As we have seen, ethnographic data need to be used carefully in conjunction with independent evidence to avoid anachronism. In addition, we need to take into consideration the authors of such data and the contexts of their production. Vansina has set out several criteria by which to assess the reliability and thus the usefulness of ethnographic data for any given area.[25] Schoenbrun applied this test to the ethnographic material available for Buganda, Busoga, and Bugwere, as part of his larger analysis of material for the Great Lakes region. He determined that the quality of the ethnography for Buganda is excellent, that for

---

[22] Christopher Ehret, "Language Change and the Material Correlates of Language and Ethnic Shift," *Antiquity* 62, no. 238 (1988): 570.

[23] Ehret, *Southern Nilotic History*, 14.

[24] David Lee Schoenbrun, "Early History in Eastern Africa's Great Lakes Region: Linguistic, Ecological, and Archaeological Approaches, ca. 500 B.C. to ca. A.D. 1000" (PhD diss., University of California, Los Angeles, 1990), 130.

[25] Vansina, *Paths in the Rainforests*, 28–9.

Busoga it is very good, but that for Bugwere it is inadequate.[26] While it is true that there is not a wealth of material available for Bugwere, by pulling together various sources and the material from ethnographic interviews I conducted during fieldwork, I have recategorised the quality of material as adequate. There are, on the other hand, virtually no ethnographic data on the Bashana. The little that exist can be found in works on the Sebei (Sabiny) and Bagisu (Bamasaaba) by the Protestant missionary and ethnographer John Roscoe and, later, by the anthropologists Walter Goldschmidt and Robert Edgerton.[27] I conducted some ethnographic interviews with people who identified themselves as Bashana, but without independent (and earlier) sources this remains insufficient. With regard to the ethnography of the Bashana, then, the quantity and quality of the material must be classified as generally inadequate.

Early ethnographic records are particularly rich for writing about Buganda and Busoga in the nineteenth century. For Bugwere, I have often had to rely on ethnographic data gleaned from Ronald Atkinson's oral historical interviews conducted in the 1960s and data from the ethnographic interviews I conducted in 2004 during fieldwork in what was then Pallisa district covering the Lugwere-speaking region.[28] Wherever possible, I have married evidence from my interviews with that from other sources. Given the limited research that has been conducted in Bugwere, there are times when this has not been possible. In these cases, I have tried to winnow out evidence that is clearly influenced by twentieth-century events and also to correlate the evidence with similar practices in Busoga and Buganda. That said, the conclusions that can be drawn from such

[26] Schoenbrun, *A Green Place, A Good Place*, 53.
[27] John Roscoe, *The Bagesu and Other Tribes of the Uganda Protectorate: The Third Part of the Report of the Mackie Ethnological Expedition to Central Africa* (Cambridge: University Press, 1924), 83–5. Roscoe uses the ethnonym Bakama, which is how the Bagisu today refer to the Bashana. However, he argues that the Bakama migrated to Mount Masaaba from Bunyoro along with another group whom he terms the Bagweri. He does not give any linguistic data for the Bakama and notes that they formed a clan among the Sebei. It may be that the groups he refers to as Bakama and Bagweri are two clans of the Bashana. Robert B. Edgerton, *The Individual in Cultural Adaptation: A Study of Four East African Peoples* (Berkeley: University of California Press, 1971); Walter Goldschmidt with Gale Goldschmidt, *Culture and Behavior of the Sebei: A Study in Continuity and Adaptation* (Berkeley: University of California Press, 1976); Walter Goldschmidt, *The Sebei: A Study in Adaptation* (New York: Holt, Rinehart and Winston, 1986). In these latter works, the Bashana are referred to by the Sebei name for them, Bumachek or Bumatyek.
[28] Given the rapidly changing political landscape in twenty-first century Uganda and the proliferation of districts, all references to districts, counties, and subcounties are as they were in 2004.

evidence, especially for earlier periods, have to be seen as more suggestive than those drawn from a deeper and broader evidentiary basis. If
archaeologists or scholars in other disciplines turn their attention to this
corner of eastern Uganda then we will have new evidence to bring to bear
on these questions, which may strengthen the conclusions made here or
undermine them entirely.

Cross-referencing the ethnographic data is important in order to be
as confident as possible that particular cultural practices are not recent
innovations born out of the dramatic events of the nineteenth and twentieth centuries. Because the developments of the past two centuries did not
occur uniformly or simultaneously, it is often possible to detect changes
in cultural practices in individual societies. The example of Ganda marriage practices discussed in Chapter 3 is a case in point. We are, however,
reliant on material that is subject to the context in which it was produced
and that does not date from the time being written about. This means that
there is always an element of doubt. The solution lies in drawing on as
many different sources of evidence as possible and treating that evidence
critically. It also lies in using knowledge about the historical contexts of
the evidence, especially ethnographic data, to sift out anachronisms. As has
been noted for linguistic reconstructions, "we cannot recover every detail,
but we can try to make our reconstructions as realistic as possible."[29]

Having established the quality of the ethnographic material, we can
begin to use it to elaborate the meaning and usage of the reconstructed
vocabulary. By relating ethnographic descriptions to specific words that
we know were used by proto-North Nyanza speakers or one of the speech
communities descended from them, it is possible to develop a richer and
more nuanced picture of the meanings given to those words and thus
develop a greater understanding of the past. It is perhaps easiest to explain
this by illustrating a specific example. The term for a female escort of a
bride in Rushana is *emperekesa*, in Lusoga it is *émperekézí* or *omúgh-
erekézí* depending on the dialect, and in Luganda it is *empélekezê*. In
Lugwere the term is different. Because of the distribution of these cognate
forms, that is, two languages that are farthest apart share the word, we
know that speakers of proto-North Nyanza used this term. It is also easy
to trace the etymology to the proto-Bantu verb **-pédikid-* which has the
meaning 'accompany (someone).'[30] Turning to the ethnographic evidence,

[29] McMahon and McMahon, *Language Classification by Numbers*, 17.
[30] The *mperekezi is discussed in detail in subsequent chapters. Please see No. 36 in
    the appendix. See also Yvonne Bastin and Thilo C. Schadeberg, eds., "Bantu Lexical

however, it is possible to add significant levels of detail to the role played by the *mperekezi*. In Soga and Ganda ethnography we see that she not only accompanied a bride on her wedding day, but also remained with the bride for a considerable period of time, sometimes even becoming a second wife to her husband. Because of the lacunae in the Shana evidence it is harder to be certain that the practices associated with the *mperekezi* also date to the time when proto-North Nyanza was spoken. However, because we know that Lusoga and Luganda are from different branches of North Nyanza and because we can be confident of the antiquity of the term itself, it is reasonable to suppose that these formed part of the practices of the proto-North Nyanza speech community.

EVIDENCE FROM ORAL TRADITIONS

Scholars have been arguing over the use of oral traditions in the writing of African history for a long time now. Despite some fierce arguments against their use, historians have not all abandoned oral sources in their efforts to write the history of African societies before the nineteenth century.[31] Over the past decade, these efforts have frequently centred on reading oral material performatively. With regards to Buganda in particular, historian Neil Kodesh has shown that we can effectively use oral traditions to write about its precolonial history. Furthermore, by incorporating the insights about performance and sites of memory into our approach to what these sources tell us about early events, we can use them to make nuanced and convincing historical arguments.[32] Oral traditions cannot be viewed as straightforward narratives of historical

Reconstructions 3" (Tervuren: Musée Royale de l'Afrique Centrale, online database) http://www.metafro.be/blr/, ID main 2427. (Accessed 4 January 2013).

[31] Among others, see Blier, "The Path of the Leopard"; T. C. McCaskie, "Denkyira in the Making of Asante, *c.* 1660–1720," *Journal of African History* 48, no. 1 (2007): 1–25; Renée L. Tantala, "Verbal and Visual Imagery in Kitara (Western Uganda): Interpreting 'the Story of Isimbwa and Nyinamwiru'," in *Paths Toward the Past: African Historical Essays in Honor of Jan Vansina*, ed. Robert W. Harms, Joseph C. Miller, David S. Newbury, and Michele D. Wagner (Atlanta, GA: African Studies Association Press, 1994), 223–43. For a forcible argument against their use, see Luise White, *Speaking with Vampires: Rumor and History in Colonial Africa* (Berkeley: University of California Press, 2000).

[32] Neil Kodesh, "History from the Healer's Shrine: Genre, Historical Imagination, and Early Ganda History," *Comparative Studies in Society and History* 49, no. 3 (2007): 527–52; Kodesh, *Beyond the Royal Gaze*. It is worth noting that his approach emerged out of insights from both historical linguistics and comparative ethnography, which were initially part of the focus of his research.

events, especially with regards to the deeper past. However, by telling us what people thought important to include and exclude from their oral traditions, such sources give us insights into the political and ideological worlds of past societies. They also provide us with invaluable clues about historical cultural and social practices.

Ganda oral histories differ from the Gwere and Soga materials. In Buganda, the relationship between European interests and Ganda writing is particularly complex with the emergence of a Christian literate elite in the nineteenth century. Early European travellers to Buganda transcribed traditions in a piecemeal fashion. Later in the nineteenth and into the early twentieth century, missionaries and others worked closely with leading Ganda intellectuals to craft a coherent dynastic corpus. Once published – often serially in local papers – this called forth counter-narratives from a variety of different voices among the Ganda intelligentsia.[33] Between the 1860s and the first decade of the twentieth century, Ganda oral historical data had taken on a distinctive, coherent shape, a shape that nevertheless failed to extinguish competing versions, despite its promotion to the status of orthodoxy in the work of Uganda's first generation of academic historians. Neither Bugwere nor Busoga has a similar corpus of oral traditions and it appears that there was less emphasis on retaining such traditions, perhaps due to the fact that their political systems were less centralised than Buganda's. What exist for Busoga and Bugwere are bodies of oral history interviews that address the origins of different clans and the various political formations and are often referred to as 'historical texts.'[34] There are sufficient tie-ins between the texts to substantiate their reliability as sources and make them of central importance not only in establishing events and practices, but also in determining and verifying chronologies.

---

[33] See also Wrigley, *Kingship and State*.

[34] The material for Bugwere consists of Ronald R. Atkinson, ed., "Bugwere Historical Texts," Ronald R. Atkinson Private Collection, collected in the late 1960s and the early 1970s. Ron Atkinson has very generously shared this material with me. The bulk of the material for Busoga is David W. Cohen, ed., "Collected Texts of Busoga Traditional History," David William Cohen Private Collection, collected in the 1960s. David Cohen has also very generously given me access to this complete collection, some of which is available in published form as David William Cohen, *Towards a Reconstructed Past: Historical Texts from Busoga, Uganda* (Oxford: Oxford University Press for the British Academy, 1986). About one hundred texts are available on microfilm, David W. Cohen, ed., "Selected Texts of Busoga Traditional History," (Baltimore, n.p. 1969). An early history of Busoga by a Musoga intellectual narrates several traditions associated with various polities, Y. K. Lubogo, *A History of Busoga*, trans. Eastern Province (Bantu Language) Literature Committee (Jinja: East African Literature Bureau, 1960). The term 'historical

CHRONOLOGY

The genetic classification of languages tells us the order in which proto-languages were spoken. Such classifications are essentially a sequence of language divergences. The subclassification of North Nyanza gives us a relative chronology for these splits. We know that proto-South Kyoga existed at the same time as early Luganda but before proto-East Kyoga and we know that proto-East Kyoga existed at the same time as early Lusoga but before either Lugwere or Rushana. This subclassification means that it is possible to reconstruct lexical items back to the different speech communities that existed at the various stages in the dissolution of North Nyanza and we can make historical arguments on the basis of those reconstructions. However, this chronology does not provide dates and so proves frustrating for the historian.

Glottochronology supplies approximate dates for when proto-languages were spoken in the past and derives from lexicostatistics, the quantitative method set out in the section, 'Evidence from Language,' for classifying languages genetically.[35] Some linguists have noted that while changes in core vocabulary (the part of the lexicon least subject to cultural pressures) are random, the accumulation of those random changes "tends toward a normal distribution."[36] For African languages, that rate of accumulation of random changes has been calculated as a replacement of about twenty-seven words of the one hundred core vocabulary items every one thousand years.[37] This scale can help us map broad dates for the divergence of languages into daughter languages. It is important to emphasize that those dates are approximations that should then be correlated with archaeological evidence wherever possible for further confirmation. Such correlations can be made with evidence of iron-working and vegetation change associated with agriculture as Schoenbrun has done for the Great Lakes region, or with climate change as Kathryn de Luna has done for

texts' was commonly used by historians conducting oral history in the 1960s and 1970s to write about the precolonial past. See, for example, John Lamphear, *The Traditional History of the Jie of Uganda* (Oxford: Clarendon Press, 1976).

[35] For an early overview of the method by its founder, see Morris Swadesh, "Towards Greater Accuracy in Lexicostatistic Dating," *International Journal of American Linguistics* 21, no. 2 (1955): 121–37. For recent expositions of the method, see, among others, Ehret, *History and the Testimony of Language*, 105–32; Fields-Black, *Deep Roots*, 18–22; Klieman, *"The Pygmies Were Our Compass"*, xxvii–xxix.

[36] Ehret, "Language Change and the Material Correlates of Language and Ethnic Shift," 566.

[37] Ehret, *History and the Testimony of Language*, 127, table 9.

south central Africa, or even epigraphic evidence as Ehret has done for northeastern Africa.[38]

There are several critics of this methodology. In their chapter in *Phylogenetic Methods and the Prehistory of Language*, McMahon and McMahon go so far as to argue that linguists should not "do dates," until the methodological disagreements have been resolved.[39] But, as other chapters in the same volume show, some linguists at least do 'do dates.'[40] It is, therefore, worth exploring the concerns some linguists have levelled at glottochronology and the extent to which they remain valid. The most common criticism is that "languages do not always evolve at a constant rate."[41] Languages, in fact, have been shown not to evolve at a constant rate; rather a number of factors can speed up or slow down language change. But glottochronology does *not* assume a "*a regular and predictable* rate of vocabulary change." It is based instead on the "accumulation over time of individual word replacements, each of which is *random and unpredictable*."[42] Thus, Ehret notes, glottochronology "identifies, however imperfectly, a real phenomenon with strong analogues in the natural world – namely, the *patterned accumulation of individually random change among quanta of like properties*." A patterned accumulation which "over long periods tends to form normal distributions."[43]

Another criticism is grounded in the tree model often used to represent language families and that underpins glottochronology in that the method generates approximate dates for each node on the tree. "Languages," as

[38] Schoenbrun, *A Green Place, A Good Place*, 46–8; Kathryn M. de Luna, "Collecting Food, Cultivating Persons: Wild Resource Use in Central African Political Culture, c. 1000 B.C.E. to c. 1900 C.E." (PhD diss., Northwestern University, 2008), 100–9; Ehret, *History and the Testimony of Language*, 119–21.

[39] April McMahon and Robert McMahon, "Why Linguists Don't Do Dates: Evidence from Indo-European and Australian Languages," in *Phylogenetic Methods and the Prehistory of Languages*, ed. Peter Forster and Colin Renfrew (Cambridge: McDonald Institute for Archaeological Research, 2006), 160.

[40] For example, Andrew Garrett, "Convergence in the Formation of Indo-European Subgroups: Phylogeny and Chronology," in *Phylogenetic Methods and the Prehistory of Languages*, ed. Forster and Renfrew, 139–51; and Mark Pagel and Andrew Meade, "Estimating Rates of Lexical Replacement on Phylogenetic Trees of Languages," in *Phylogenetic Methods and the Prehistory of Languages*, ed. Forster and Renfrew, 173–82.

[41] Quentin D. Atkinson and Russell D. Gray, "How Old Is the Indo-European Language Family? Illumination or More Moths to the Flame?" in *Phylogenetic Methods and the Prehistory of Languages*, ed. Forster and Renfrew, 92.

[42] Christopher Ehret, "Writing African History From Linguistic Evidence," in *Writing African History*, ed. John Edward Philips (Rochester, N: University of Rochester Press, 2005), 106. Emphasis in original.

[43] Ehret, *History and the Testimony of Language*, 106. Emphasis in original.

linguists Quentin Atkinson and Russell Gray point out, "do not always evolve in a tree-like manner."[44] Indeed, it is fair to assume that languages almost never evolve in a simple tree-like manner as they are subject to influence from other languages in the form of borrowing, most commonly the borrowing of lexical items but also of phonology and morphology. The tree model is designed to show genetic relationships between languages, not to account for all language change. Furthermore, it is possible in many cases to identify borrowings. This means that they can be excluded from the lexicostatistical calculations and hence too from glottochronological ones in order to account for contact and thus avoid skewed results.

Vansina, who used glottochronology in his work until recently, notes that he became convinced of its fallibility by reading Michael Mann's work, which shows "that different statistical procedures yield different percentages of cognation and hence different dates."[45] This is an issue that certainly requires further exploration and research. But to simply abandoning the endeavour seems a hasty solution. First, as Edda Fields-Black notes, the alternative approach adopted by Vansina involves "estimating that half a millennium elapses between one level of a language's genealogy and the next." But, as she remarks, "these estimates would remain unconfirmed."[46] It is not yet clear that this is a better approach. Second, Ehret and Schoenbrun have demonstrated clear correlations between dates derived from glottochronology and those from archaeological and palynological evidence, with Ehret presenting evidence from twenty-four case studies across the African continent.[47] Such correlations do not address the specific critiques of glottochronology as a method, but serve to strengthen it by demonstrating that it locates speech communities and the physical objects or processes they name in the same place at the same time. These African examples make the case that the evidence demands serious consideration, at the very least.

According to glottochronological calculations, West Nyanza split into North Nyanza and Rutara approximately 1,300 ago, or ca. 700 CE. Luganda began to break away from North Nyanza, leaving South

---

[44] Atkinson and Gray, "How Old Is the Indo-European Language Family?" 92.

[45] Vansina, *How Societies Are Born*, 8, fn. 17. He draws on Michael Mann's work in Yvonne Bastin, André Coupez, and Michael Mann, *Continuity and Divergence in the Bantu Languages: Perspectives from a Lexicostatistic Study*, Annales Sciences Humaines 162 (Tervuren, Belgium: Musée Royal de l'Afrique Centrale, 1999).

[46] Fields-Black, *Deep Roots*, 19.

[47] Ehret, *History and the Testimony of Language*, 105–32; Schoenbrun, *A Green Place, A Good Place*, 32–7, 46–8.

Kyoga about eight hundred years ago, or ca. 1200 CE, while South Kyoga split into Lusoga and East Kyoga some five hundred years ago. Glottochronology cannot give us a date for the emergence of Lugwere and Rushana, but from oral historical evidence it has been possible to establish that it occurred some time in the early nineteenth century.[48] There is very little archaeological data for the North Nyanza region, and what little there is focuses on Buganda. However, these glottochronological dates match those calculated by Schoenbrun for the Great Lakes Bantu region, which have been shown to correlate with the archaeological evidence.[49]

After generating these approximate dates from glottochronology, we can turn to other sources, especially archaeology, for further dates which should increase the accuracy and precision of the dating. We know for example that the Luzira Head in all likelihood dates to the ninth century CE which means that the community to which its creator belonged lived on the northwestern coast of Lake Victoria–Nyanza at that time.[50] While we cannot be certain that people speaking proto-North Nyanza sculpted the Luzira Head – a ceramic sculpture of a head and neck – there are convergences between the broader archaeological record and the linguistic evidence. These convergences centre on "a new scale of social intercourse."[51] Although still not definitive, the fact that the location and dates posited for the proto-North Nyanza speech community and the important historical developments of that period map with a marked shift in the archaeological evidence for that time and place is strongly suggestive. While this talk of approximate dates with ranges of several centuries is not ideal, as historians we must work with the evidence that is available. The upshot is that the various kinds of data that exist with regard to chronology tend to correlate well and so deserve to be taken seriously. Nonetheless, we can only hope that in the course of time new kinds of data and analysis will bring greater chronological clarity.

For the more recent past, we can make use of kinglists and genealogies from Buganda, Busoga, and Bugwere to derive approximate dates for developments after the emergence of centralised polities. This involves counting generations of rulers and assigning an average number of years reign to each, except in the cases where we know the reign was particular brief or where there was sibling succession. Following Roland Oliver's

---

[48] Please see Chapter 5 for a detailed discussion of this final split.
[49] Schoenbrun, *A Green Place, A Good Place*, 46–7.
[50] Reid and Ashley, "A Context for the Luzira Head."
[51] Ashley, "Towards a Socialised Archaeology of Ceramics in Great Lakes Africa," 158.

lead, this generational length is usually taken to be twenty-seven years, although others have followed the Ugandan historian Semakula Kiwanuka in rounding it up to thirty.[52] By combing through multiple sources of evidence and correlating with documented natural phenomena, such as the solar eclipse of 1680, historian Henri Médard has been able to amend and strengthen the chronology of the kings of Buganda. The resulting difference with Kiwanuka's list is a foreshortening of the foundation of the kingdom by about a century.[53] This revision underscores the value of continued research in improving our knowledge of the chronology of the region's history before the mid-nineteenth century. Given the close relationship between the various groups, refined chronologies for one society can improve chronologies in the others by providing better corroborating external evidence. The importance of external evidence is emphasised by the historian David William Cohen, who notes that because of fraternal succession in some of the Soga polities it is necessary to find correlations between them and, where possible, with Buganda.[54]

Again, these dates are approximations and this methodology also has its critics. The most important criticism is that the kinglists themselves are unreliable, having been produced in the context of the arrival of European explorers, missionaries, and officials. David Henige has gone so far as to assert because of this, "that the Ganda kinglist first collected by [Henry Morton] Stanley was an accurate representation neither of the oral resources of mid nineteenth-century Ganda historiography nor of the number of bakabaka [kings]."[55] Christopher Wrigley, again with reference to Buganda, has noted the existence of competing versions of the kinglists and argues that the bulk of all versions is composed of mythic figures.[56] Other historians of Buganda and Busoga, however, have shown greater confidence in the accuracy of the lists with reference to the past

[52] See Roland Oliver, "Ancient Capital Sites of Ankole," *Uganda Journal* 23, no. 1 (1959): 51–63; Roland Oliver, "The Royal Tombs of Buganda," *Uganda Journal* 23, no. 2 (1959): 124–33. Kiwanuka, *A History of Buganda*, 285–6; Henri Médard, *Le royaume du Buganda au XIXe siècle: Mutations politiques et religieuses d'un ancien État d'Afrique de l'Est* (Paris: Karthala, 2007), 570–1.

[53] Holly Hanson helpfully reproduces both lists side by side, Holly Elisabeth Hanson, *Landed Obligation: The Practice of Power in Buganda* (Portsmouth, N.H.: Heinemann, 2003), xvii–xviii.

[54] Cohen, *The Historical Tradition of Busoga*, 62–8.

[55] David Henige, "'The Disease of Writing': Ganda and Nyoro Kinglists in a Newly Literate World," in *The African Past Speaks: Essays on Oral Tradition and History*, ed. Joseph C. Miller (Folkestone: Dawson, 1980), 248.

[56] C. C. Wrigley, "The Kinglists of Buganda," *History in Africa* 1 (1974): 129–39; Wrigley, *Kingship and State*, 20–42.

few hundred years.[57] Some, such as Kodesh, feel that proposed dates for the two hundred years or so of Buganda's history prior to the first written documentation are valid, but that those before the mid-seventeenth century and the expansionist reign of Kateregga are unreliable.[58] Despite the criticisms, we are wrong to dismiss these lists. However abstract they seem, the lists are still a form of historical memory, not random fabrications. While the critiques of them must be taken into account, to dismiss them entirely as a form of evidence about the past (weighted as they are towards a very particular version of that past) would be, to borrow Henige's metaphor, killing the whole because the 'disease of writing' has infected part.[59]

CONCLUSION

Writing precolonial African history is a difficult business. So is the writing of all history, to a greater or lesser extent. The sources available to all historians must always be used critically and with attention to their inherent biases and weaknesses. This is the case whatever period in time and whatever part of the world is being studied. Of course, when the sources do not speak directly to us, as is the case with historical linguistic and ethnographic material, particular problems arise. It is not possible to identify individual actors in these sources and instead we must write about the actions of speakers of a language. At times, the resulting text can seem like the ideological charter of a particular society with little room for dissent. But dissent is present. It is present in the very fact that we can trace changes in social institutions and in the ideologies that surround them. Such changes are the result of conflicts over the meaning and content of those institutions. Oral traditions, too, are complicated sources of evidence, shaped as they are by the moment and authors of their transcription. They cannot be taken as literal descriptions of past

---

[57] Among others, see Cohen, *The Historical Tradition of Busoga*; Kiwanuka, *A History of Buganda*.

[58] Kodesh, *Beyond the Royal Gaze*, 132–3.

[59] Indeed, Vansina notes, with regards to extrapolating political structure from descriptive accounts, that while we should be wary of overenthusiastic extrapolation from very limited data, we "should beware of being hypercritical, and of rejecting all inferences indiscriminately. Otherwise there would be no history left." J. Vansina, "The Use of Process-Models in African History," in *The Historian in Tropical Africa: Studies Presented and Discussed at the Fourth International African Seminar at the University of Dakar Senegal 1961*, ed. J. Vansina, R. Mauny, and L. V. Thomas (London: Oxford University Press for the International African Institute, 1964), 378, fn. 11.

events, but they provide a wealth of detail, sometimes it seems unintentionally, that allows us to see what was important enough to be remembered or forgotten. Therein is a story.

While North Nyanza people and their descendants do not speak to us through writings, they do speak to us in several other mediums. The reconstruction of historical vocabulary allows me to write the history not only of proto-North Nyanza–speaking peoples and Baganda, Basoga, Bagwere, and, to a lesser extent, Bashana, but also of proto-South Kyoga– and proto-East Kyoga–speaking peoples. Comparative ethnography adds depth and complexity to the evidence derived from the reconstructed vocabulary as well as illuminating practices during the nineteenth century. Oral traditions and other oral historical evidence make possible the writing of the history of motherhood in each of the North Nyanza societies. By using the very words that women and men in these societies used to talk about the physical, social, and ideological worlds they inhabited it is possible to navigate around the elite men who transcribed oral traditions and who were most often the informants for ethnographers and for historians in the 1950s and 1960s. When all of these sources are brought together a rich tapestry unfolds to reveal the complex and often surprising social, political, and economic history of North Nyanzan motherhood.

2

Motherhood in North Nyanza, Eighth through Twelfth Centuries

Motherhood as an institution exists only as part of society; it is, however, a dynamic part shaping various aspects of life and social organisation and being shaped by them. To understand the history of motherhood in North Nyanzan times, we must place it within the relevant context of landscape, climate, politics, food production, and kin governance. People speaking proto-North Nyanza lived along the northwestern shore of Lake Victoria–Nyanza from around the eighth century CE (see Map 2). They faced the challenge of establishing a society and moving into new lands as they experimented with new crops and new forms of centralised political authority. To build a sustainable community – one that could reproduce itself biologically and socially – they built broad support networks that not only cut across the lineal and clan divides they inherited, but also embedded those interclan connections in their ritual and social lives. Those networks were founded on matrilateral ties; mothers embodied the connections between clans in a patrilineal context because they belonged to a different clan from that of their children.

Matrilateral ties informed politics in a North Nyanzan society centred on agriculture, which was practised alongside hunting, fishing, gathering wild foods, and keeping small livestock. In this period, people speaking proto-North Nyanza increasingly specialised in the cultivation of bananas for their staple food. The gradual move to intensive banana cultivation placed new value on specific plots of land that were most productive for the fruit, because once established a well-maintained banana grove lasted a generation.[1] A banana grove has a productive capacity up to tenfold

---

[1] For a detailed discussion of these preferences see Hanson, *Landed Obligation*, 38–9.

that of an equivalent sized yam field. This made the rolling hills around the lakeshore that were ideally suited to banana cultivation "attractive places for large communities to settle." The capacity to sustain larger populations through banana cultivation enabled a shift in the scale of political authority.[2] As royal families increasingly controlled leadership, so the ideologies of motherhood that shaped kinship organisation moved into the political realm. This occurred both in the form of queen mothers wielding significant and real authority and in the way in which political power was shored up and transferred between generations.

MOTHERHOOD AND SOCIAL POWER IN NORTH NYANZA

Motherhood – in the moral logics of the North Nyanza society – occurred within marriage. North Nyanza speakers distinguished between what the anthropologist Jennifer Johnson-Hanks has described as the "social category of 'mother'" and the "biological event of giving birth."[3] In other words, to be a mother a woman should do more than conceive and give birth: she should do these in a specified and socially recognised context. For North Nyanzans, the ideal form of that context was marriage marked by the gift of bridewealth. Because North Nyanzan descent followed the male line, children needed a socially recognised father. Recurring themes about the dangers of adultery in the comparative ethnographic record indicate a strong concern that the *pater* and *genitor*, that is, the social and biological father, be the same man.[4] Yet the historical linguistic evidence

---

[2] Schoenbrun, *A Green Place, A Good Place*, 79, 167 (quote).

[3] Jennifer Johnson-Hanks, *Uncertain Honor: Modern Motherhood in an African Crisis* (Chicago: University of Chicago Press, 2006), 2.

[4] Such concerns were reflected in the naming ceremonies and coming-out ceremonies performed across North Nyanza's descendant societies, a significant component of which revolved around testing the legitimacy of the infant or child. See, for example, Atkinson, ed., "Bugwere Historical Texts," Text 24; Cohen, ed., "Collected Texts of Busoga Traditional History," Texts 268, 380, 493, and 515; Julien L. Gorju, *Entre le Victoria l'Albert et l'Edouard: Ethnographie de la partie anglaise du Vicariat de l'Uganda, origines, histoire, religion, coutumes* (Rennes: Oberthür, 1920), 337; L. P. Mair, *An African People in the Twentieth Century* (1934; repr., New York: Russell and Russell, 1965), 56–9; John Roscoe, *The Baganda: An Account of their Native Customs and Beliefs* (London: Macmillan, 1911), 61–4; John Roscoe, *The Northern Bantu: An Account of Some Central African Tribes of the Uganda Protectorate* (Cambridge: University Press, 1915), 215–6; GW-ETH-BUL-F-KJ, interview, 11 November 2004, Bugwere; GW-ETH-IKI-F-KG, interview, 16 November 2004, Bugwere; GW-ETH-IKI-F-MN, interview, 16 November 2004, Bugwere. This emphasis in North Nyanza societies was in contrast with neighbouring regions, for example, among Banyankore by the late nineteenth century at least and almost certainly earlier, the husband of the mother was the

also tells us that North Nyanzans gave women active roles in marriage, in contrast to other speech communities in the Great Lakes region at that time.

North Nyanzan women and girls found themselves, as females in a patrilineal society, in a complicated set of relationships connecting lineages and patriclans. This set of relationships was made all the more complicated by the practice of polygyny in high-status households. Women moved between clans and lineages, creating new networks with their marriages and their children that extended well beyond their immediate families. At birth, a girl belonged to her father's lineage (*ssiga⁵) and to his clan (*-ka (cl. 7/8) [22]),⁶ but her mother's patriclan also had rights in her. As an adult, she was forbidden from marrying a man from either her father's or her mother's clan. When she married and became pregnant, she followed the avoidances and taboos of her husband's clan.⁷ Her children belonged to their father's clan, with her clan retaining strong interests in the form of rights in and responsibilities towards those children. The patrilineage and patriclan, however, were particularly concerned with the children born to their sons. For North Nyanzans motherhood should occur within the confines of matrimony precisely because so many people beyond the biological parents held interests in their children. Bridewealth given by a man's lineage to a woman's embodied those interests.

The ideal form of marriage for North Nyanzans was not a single event but a process involving a number of stages.⁸ A girl's parents, her paternal aunt (*isenga (cl. 1a) [41]), maternal uncle (*koiza [27]), or other guardian would look for a suitable husband for her once they recognised that she had reached physical maturity. At the same time, her *isenga instructed her about married life: how she should behave towards her

father, regardless of who the *genitor* was. See, Shane Doyle, "Sexual Behavioural Change in Ankole, Western Uganda, c. 1880–1980," *Journal of Eastern African Studies*, 6, no. 3 (2012): 490–506.

⁵ David Lee Schoenbrun, *The Historical Reconstruction of Great Lakes Bantu Cultural Vocabulary: Etymologies and Distributions* (Cologne: Rüdiger Köppe Verlag, 1997), 85, root 117.
⁶ The number in square brackets refers to the item in the vocabulary list in the appendix.
⁷ For example, Atkinson, ed., "Bugwere Historical Texts," Text 24; Cohen, ed., "Collected Texts of Busoga Traditional History," Text 41.
⁸ This approach to marriage was common across much of sub-Saharan Africa. In many places the legalistic approach of colonial powers changed marriage to a relationship entered into through a single legal contract at a wedding. See, for example, Jean Allman, "Rounding Up Spinsters: Gender Chaos and Unmarried Women in Colonial Asante," in *"Wicked" Women and the Reconfiguration of Gender in Africa*, ed. Dorothy L. Hodgson and Sheryl A. McCurdy (Portsmouth, N.H.: Heinemann, 2001), 130–48.

husband and her in-laws, including in her sexual life with her husband. As part of this preparation for marriage, the *isenga* would teach her niece the art of 'labia-pulling' which elongated the labia minora (*-fuli* (cl. 9/10) [13]).[9] Once a suitable spouse had been agreed on, negotiations would ensue over the bridewealth he and his family should bring to his future in-laws (*-ko* (cl. 1/2) [26]).

North Nyanzans used a word they had inherited from their Great Lakes Bantu–speaking ancestors to describe the action of the man and his relatives bringing bridewealth to his fiancée's family, *-kwa* [29]. David Schoenbrun posits that the nominal forms of this verb, *-kwánò* (cl. 9) and *-kwé* (cl. 14) – found across the Great Lakes Bantu region – which he glosses as 'brideprice,' are derived from the Savanna Bantu noun, *-kó* (cl. 1/14), 'in-law.'[10] Jan Vansina suggests a proto-Western Bantu origin for *-kó* (cl. 1/2, 14/6) and a proto-Bantu origin for the related verb *-kóéd-*, 'marry.'[11] He rejects the linguist Malcolm Guthrie's etymology for this, who posited that it was derived from 'copulate.' Vansina argues that the derivation is the reverse. Yvonne Bastin and Thilo Schadeberg, both linguists of Bantu languages, draw on a large data set to reconstruct the verb *-kó-* to proto-Bantu with the meaning 'give bridewealth.' In their analysis, the verb *-kóid-*, 'marry, copulate,' is the derivative form.[12] They also see *-kóanò*, 'bridewealth,' as being derived from *-kó-*, 'give bridewealth,' rejecting as they do Guthrie's Common Bantu noun *-kó*, 'relative by marriage.'[13] In brief, according to Bastin and Schadeberg's linguistic reconstruction, the North Nyanza verb *-kwa*, 'give bridewealth,' is derived from the proto-Bantu verb *-kó-* with the same meaning. That is, North Nyanzans retained the same word to talk about giving of bridewealth as their proto-Bantu-speaking ancestors used. This is not surprising: the giving of bridewealth as part of the marriage contract is an ancient practice in very many African communities.

[9] A practice described to me by women as intended to enhance sexual pleasure for both partners: GW-ETH-BUD-F-BA, interview, 30 October 2004, Bugwere; GW-ETH-IKI-F-KG, interview, 16 November 2004, Bugwere; GW-ETH-BUL-F-KJ, interview, 11 November 2004, Bugwere; SO-ETH-KAL-F-NR, interview, 21 January 2005, Busoga.

[10] Schoenbrun, *The Historical Reconstruction of Great Lakes Bantu Cultural Vocabulary*, 94–5, root 132, root 133; 91–3, root 128.

[11] Vansina, *Paths in the Rainforests*, 283–5, nos. 33, 35–7.

[12] Bastin and Schadeberg, "Bantu Lexical Reconstructions 3," ID main 7240, Der. 7250 (Accessed 8 January 2013).

[13] Bastin and Schadeberg, "Bantu Lexical Reconstructions 3," ID Ref. 1857 (Accessed 8 January 2013); Malcolm Guthrie, *Comparative Bantu: An Introduction to the Comparative Linguistics and Prehistory of the Bantu Languages*, vol. 3 (Farnborough: Gregg International, 1970), 287, CS 1092; 304, CS 1175, 305, CS 1177).

For North Nyanza speakers, marriage marked by the gift of bride-wealth was the ideal context for motherhood because it created a physical connection between all those with an interest in the children who should ensue. As David William Cohen has noted for nineteenth-century Busoga, "the goods paid over as brideprice would have been circulated through the lineage of the bride, with the understanding – in fact it is a highly durable contract – that if the marriage should break up a reasonably equivalent mix of goods would be returned to the lineage of the husband."[14] While this analysis is for a time several centuries after North Nyanza ceased to be spoken, the linguistic evidence suggests that Cohen's argument holds true for this earlier period. Through the distribution of the bridewealth among the lineage of the bride and the understanding that they should return it (or its equivalent) should the marriage fail, the two patrilineages became enmeshed in economic as well as social relationships.[15] In his analysis of the relations of reproduction in Africa, Claude Meillassoux asserted that the "kinship relations resulting from marriage" are "relationships that form around the reproduction of individuals." While kinship relationships also result from birth, birth is subsumed within marriage because it is "only an event regulated by rules fixed at marriage."[16] For Cohen, by contrast, the relationship between "kinship relations resulting from marriage" and those resulting from birth is more complicated because the latter outlive the former. So long as children had been born, even if a marriage broke up, the *bako* or in-law relations formed would continue through the interests of the two lineages in those children.[17] This reflects the importance of relationships formed through the mother, relationships that shaped North Nyanzan kin – as well as political – governance.

As part of the marriage process, a bride's mother was singled out for special recognition. This came as a gift, which may have been in the form of a goat, and was known as *-síímo* (cl. 12/14) [43], a noun derived from a proto-Bantu verb *-cìim-* with the meanings 'admire, love,

---

[14] David William Cohen, *Womunafu's Bunafu: A Study of Authority in a Nineteenth-Century African Community* (Princeton: Princeton University Press, 1977), 51.

[15] A similar, rather more detailed, point is made for contemporary Joluo communities in western Kenya in Parker Shipton, *The Nature of Entrustment: Intimacy, Exchange, and the Sacred in Africa* (New Haven, Conn.: Yale University Press, 2007), 120–57. Shipton uses the evocative phrase 'Marriage on the Installment Plan' to illustrate the often prolonged nature of bridewealth payments.

[16] Meillassoux, *Maidens, Meal and Money*, 38.

[17] Cohen, *Womunafu's Bunafu*, 99. See also Radcliffe-Brown, "Introduction," 49, 51.

delight.'[18] This verb also existed in North Nyanza in the form *-síímá [42] with the meanings 'approve, thank, be pleased with, like.' The gift of *-síímo marked an appreciation of the work of mothering. It may also have marked the start of relationships of avoidance between the groom and his mother-in-law.[19] Furthermore, the *-síímo reflected the reality that the new network of relations created through the marriage extended beyond the immediate patrilineages of the bride and groom to include their matrilateral kin.

Once the bridewealth had been transferred from the man's lineage to the woman's, she was taken by her paternal aunt and a companion, usually a younger sister, to her marital home. This may have been her actual sister, but could just as likely have been a younger female lineage or clan member.[20] North Nyanzans used the word *-perekezi (cl. 1a) [36] to describe the bride's companion, as noted in Chapter 1. This noun has reflexes in all the languages descended from North Nyanza except Lugwere and was derived, probably by Mashariki speakers, from the older verb *-perekera meaning 'accompany, escort.' A North Nyanzan *-perekezi escorted her sister, but it was the *isenga [41] or paternal aunt who gave the bride to her husband. The *-perekezi was part of the public performance of the creation of the wider relationships that resulted from the marriage. These relationships were formed through the 'giving' of the bride to her husband and his family in return for the gift of bridewealth. As an assistant to a new wife, and perhaps later as her junior wife, the *-perekezi both embodied a woman's wider social support network – that of her maternal and paternal kin – and physically helped with the labour a wife was expected to perform in her marital home. Once she became a mother, a wife could expect the help of her children in that labour; as a new bride, the burden fell to her and her *-perekezi. Thus, while the ideal form of marriage served to mark publicly the new social relations between lineages and clans and – through the payment of bridewealth – to compensate a lineage for the loss of one of its members, the assistance

---

[18] Bastin and Schadeberg, "Bantu Lexical Reconstructions 3," ID main 609, see also ID main 576, ID Var. 608, ID Der. 5515 (Accessed 8 January 2013).

[19] GW-ETH-BUL-F-KJ, interview, 27 October 2004, Bugwere; Gorju, *Entre le Victoria l'Albert et l'Edouard*, 320; Mair, *An African People in the Twentieth Century*, 82–4; Roscoe, *The Baganda*, 89.

[20] Gertrude Logose, "Eirya lye Kigwere," Lugwere Bible Translation Project, Summer Institute of Languages, Entebbe, Uganda; Mair, *An African People in the Twentieth Century*, 84–5; Roscoe, *The Baganda*, 90; SO-15-BUG-F-KJ, interview, 20 January 2005, Busoga.

a woman received from her *-perekezi* meant that she, too, benefited from following the moral order of North Nyanzan society.

People speaking the grandparent language of North Nyanza, Great Lakes Bantu, innovated a new verb to describe the act of a man marrying a woman, *-túèr(er)-.*[21] We know that this word was inherited by West Nyanza speakers because people speaking Rutara and its daughter languages also used it to talk about marriage. North Nyanzans, however, dropped this word from their vocabulary and coined a series of words to describe the process of marriage. They replaced *-túèr(er)-* with the verb *-gasa* [15], glossing as 'marry (of a man).' Drawing on the anthropologist Lucy Mair's assertion that the Luganda reflex of this verb, *-wasa* is the causative form of *-wata*, 'peel (bananas, potatoes, etc.),' scholars have argued that this demonstrates the centrality of banana cultivation to Ganda society.[22] The verb 'peel' in Luganda, however, has a long vowel and is more accurately represented as *-waata* and the causative form ('make someone to peel') as *-waasa*. Given the distribution of the reflexes of the verb *-gasa* in North Nyanzan and Rutaran languages, a more reliable etymology suggests that it derives from a West Nyanza verb with the meaning 'mate, copulate.'

Women's acts of marrying, however, were described with a new verb – *-bayira* [3] – by speakers of North Nyanza. It is unusual for Bantu languages to have an active verb glossing as 'marry' (of a woman). The common practice is to use the passive counterpart of the verb for 'marry' (of a man), thus yielding the meaning 'be married' (by a man).[23] Indeed West Nyanzans used the passive form *-túèr(er)w-* when talking about women getting married.[24] As Schoenbrun notes, this reflected the West Nyanzan social reality that a woman's lineage identity was complicated at marriage as she, and any children she had, became part of her husband's lineage while her husband retained his existing lineage identity.[25] Although North Nyanzan women also faced a situation in which their

---

[21] Schoenbrun, *The Historical Reconstruction of Great Lakes Bantu Cultural Vocabulary*, 104, root 150.

[22] L. P. Mair, *Native Marriage in Buganda* (London: Oxford University Press for the International Institute of African Languages and Cultures, 1940), 13. On other scholars, see, for example, Hanson, *Landed Obligation*, 29.

[23] In Swahili, for example, the verb *-oa* describes the act of a man marrying a woman, while its passive counterpart *-olewa* translates as 'to be married' and describes the act of a woman being married by a man.

[24] Schoenbrun, *The Historical Reconstruction of Great Lakes Bantu Cultural Vocabulary*, 104, root 150.

[25] Schoenbrun, *A Green Place, A Good Place*, 101.

husbands and children had a lineage different from their own, the importance placed on relationships forged through mothers shifted the emphasis. Through their marriages, these women stood to become the mothers of children who would be of enduring importance to their own lineages and clans as well as to their husbands' patriclans. As a result, North Nyanzans viewed women as active participants in the process of their marriages. The creation of a new active verb, *-bayira*, in place of the more conventional passive construction reflected this worldview.

Women's marriages created alliances between established lineages in North Nyanzan society and were a primary means of integrating newcomers, whether from another part of North Nyanza or from outside the linguistic and cultural group altogether. In such situations, the woman's brother or her father often retained significant control over her children. This appears to have worked in two ways. First, while a newcomer would have had few alliances in the immediate region and thus little social authority, he may nonetheless have been prestigious and could make use of his connection with his *bako* or in-laws to establish himself or his children in the new locale. *Bakungu*, or chiefs, of neighbouring societies perhaps, wishing to extend their sphere of influence could marry local women or send sons to marry local women in this way.[26] Second, a newcomer with no particular prestige could marry a local woman with a well-established lineage to improve his situation or that of his descendants.[27] The coining by North Nyanzans of the verb *-bayira* [3] to describe women's acts of marriage may indicate that these kinds of relationships that emphasised women's integrative roles became more important at this time.

North Nyanzan innovations in the semantic field of marriage included the way they described the state of being married. This was particularly the case for words that were specific to women. North Nyanza speakers did this by using the noun *-rya* (cl. 5/6) [39], with the meaning 'marriage'

[26] *Bakungu* initially referred to hereditary chiefs when the term was innovated by Great Lakes Bantu speakers but sometime around the turn of the second millennium CE as North Nyanza was breaking up into pre-Luganda and South Kyoga it came to refer to appointed chiefs as new forms of kingship and chiefship emerged. See Schoenbrun, *A Green Place, A Good Place*, 104, 184–9; Schoenbrun, *The Historical Reconstruction of Great Lakes Bantu Cultural Vocabulary*, 139–42, roots 208–10.
[27] Atkinson, ed., "Bugwere Historical Texts," Text 1; Cohen, ed., "Collected Texts of Busoga Traditional History," Text 71; Cohen, *The Historical Tradition of Busoga*, 14, 17; Cohen, *Womunafu's Bunafu*, 28, 117–18; Schoenbrun, *A Green Place, A Good Place*, 184; Renée Tantala, "Gonza Bato and the Consolidation of Abaisengobi Rule in Southern Kigulu" (paper presented at the Department of History Research Seminar, Makerere University, Kampala, Uganda, 21 August 1972), 10, 13–4, Cohen Private Collection.

or 'married state' (applied only to a wife). They derived this noun from the proto-Bantu verb *-dí-* 'eat.'[28] This etymology suggests that they saw marriage as a social institution in which women ate, both literally and metaphorically. The reason for this view of marriage lies in women's control of food production within the household. When she married, a woman left her childhood home, in which she worked in her mother's garden, and moved to her husband's household. There she gained control of food production on entering motherhood. She cultivated for herself, her husband, and her children, whose labour she would in turn control until they left home. She also controlled the preparation and distribution of food within the household, at least in the matrifocal unit if it was a polygynous or multigenerational home. In this way, a wife and mother, in all likelihood, was able to have greater control over her own access to food. If she had several children who lived until they were old enough to work in the fields alongside her, then this would shore up her immediate economic security, so long as her husband and his lineage gave her access to enough land to feed them all. The new word *-rya* reflected this change in status. This organisation of food production is not unique to North Nyanzan society, but the word *-rya* is. Marriage may have become more important for women as a means of securing access to land as patrilineages sought greater control over it once banana cultivation came to the fore and changed the way North Nyanza speakers thought about both land and wealth.

Although the ideal form of marriage for North Nyanza speakers followed the format outlined in this chapter, not all relationships between men and women would have conformed to social expectations. This was neither new nor unique to North Nyanza. Indeed, North Nyanzans inherited from their West Nyanza–speaking ancestors their paired verbs for the act of eloping. Those verbs, *-hambuka* (intr.) (for a woman) and *-hambula* (tr.) (for a man) [18], were derived from a much older verb *-pamba* meaning 'seize.'[29] The derivation of the new verbs from the older one makes use of the *-ul-* and *-uk-* 'separative' suffixes. These are most commonly described as 'reversive' suffixes, but, as Schadeberg notes, "only some of the verbs with these extensions have a 'reversive' meaning. The two other most frequently recurring senses are 'intensive'

---

[28] Bastin and Schadeberg, "Bantu Lexical Reconstructions 3," ID main 944 (Accessed 8 January 2013).
[29] David Schoenbrun, personal communication, August 2007; Bastin and Schadeberg, "Bantu Lexical Reconstructions 3," ID (no label) 8401 (Accessed 8 January 2013).

and 'repetitive.'"[30] A reversive meaning of 'unseize' is unlikely in this context, but the 'intensive' meaning gives a plausible reading of the verbs. It is also of note that while the female form of the verb *-hambuka* is intransitive, it is not in the passive mood. That is, the etymology of this verb does not suggest an interpretation in which women were seized by men. Rather, it has a more nuanced meaning. Although West Nyanzan and, later, North Nyanzan women may not have seized men in order to elope, they did 'seize themselves' into elopement. The etymology of *-hambuka* and *-hambula* thus suggests that they were acts of violence. While the violence may have been in male acts of 'intensively seizing' women, the active – though intransitive – *-hambuka* does not lend itself easily to this analysis.[31] Whether or not physical violence occurred as part of *-hambuka*, elopement was a socially violent act for members of the woman's lineage; bridewealth was not paid and so the contractual bond between *bako* or 'in-laws' that it signified was not formed. Not only did the woman's lineage not receive compensation for losing her, but the ongoing relationships formed through her and her marriage were also not created. For the woman, too, elopement had a violence that went beyond any physical violence during the act itself. In a marriage ensuing from elopement, a new wife would not have the companionship and assistance of a *-perekezi* (cl. 1a) [36] and so faced greater hardship and isolation in her new home.

After the marriage process had been completed, North Nyanzans had different ways of naming the newly married woman. The general noun for 'wife' – *-kádí* (cl. 1/2) [23] – was inherited from proto-Bantu speakers. This noun had the dual meanings of woman and wife, indicating a continuing moral logic in which to be a woman, that is to achieve adult female status, one also needed to be a wife. North Nyanza speakers also gave a new meaning to a word they inherited from their West Nyanzan ancestors: *-gólé* (cl. 1/2) [16]. Schoenbrun has reconstructed

---

[30] Schadeberg, "Derivation," 78. In making this point, Thilo Schadeberg draws on E. Dammamm, "Inversiva und Repetitiva in Bantusprachen," *Afrika und Übersee* 43 (1959): 116–27.

[31] Henri Le Veux's translations of the two terms reflect a vision of male agency and female passivity, but this would appear to result from his cultural construction of these acts, rather than from the words themselves: *-wambuka* "Partir avec son séducteur," *-wambula* "Débaucher une femme et l'emener. Ravir." Père Le Veux, *Premier essai de vocabulaire luganda – français d'après l'ordre étymologique* (Maison Carrée, Algeria: Imprimerie des missionaires d'Afrique (Pères Blancs), 1917), 998*. Note that page numbers higher than 959 are repeated up to three times in the dictionary. Please refer to the alphabetical word entry for the correct page.

this word back to Great Lakes Bantu with the meaning 'maternal power.'[32]
In the Kivu Rift Valley in the western part of the Great Lakes region,
people speaking proto-Kivu, which came into being slightly before North
Nyanza in the mid-first millennium, gave *-gólé (cl. 1/2) the meaning
of 'married mother.' They placed great emphasis on a high fertility rate,
with women who succeeded in bearing and raising large numbers of children earning the right to wear a *rugolí or crown of maternity.[33] Rhonda
Gonzales's recent historical work on the Ruvu peoples of Tanzania has
shown the term to be older than was previously thought. Speakers of proto-Ruvu gave it a slightly different meaning by placing it in the diminutive
ki- noun class (cl. 7/8) and using it to refer to girls whose breasts had
developed, signalling them as almost ready to marry. Gonzales writes that,
the people speaking Kaskazi, the parent language of both proto-Ruvu
and proto-Great Lakes Bantu, coined the term to designate 'woman,'
perhaps referencing those who had achieved their maternal potential.[34]
North Nyanzans, however, used *-gólé to refer to the maternal potential
of brides and newly married women, with an emphasis on the 'newcomer'
status of such women. From the late nineteenth century onwards, Catholic
missionaries in Buganda used the noun mùgòlê to describe a newly baptised person, apparently in reference to the spiritual marriage between
the baptismal candidate and Christ.[35] However, this remained separate
from its original and continued use by North Nyanza speakers and their
descendants to refer to brides and newly married women.

Assuming the marriage process had more closely followed the ideal
form than its counterpart of elopement, there was a specified social category of senior wife within the household. The senior wife in a North
Nyanzan household was called *kaidu (cl. 12) [19]. This noun underscores the existence of polygyny in North Nyanzan society, although it
is reasonably safe to assume that many, even most, marriages were not
polygynous. The innovation of *kaidu indicates a new importance for the
role of senior wife, as opposed to say the wife who had borne the most
children or the wife who had borne the first son in the household. This

---

[32] Schoenbrun, The Historical Reconstruction of Great Lakes Bantu Cultural Vocabulary,
83–4, root 114. For the various meanings and mobilisations of the concept of *-gólé
across the Great Lakes Region, see Schoenbrun, A Green Place, A Good Place, 138,
140–1, 151–4.

[33] Schoenbrun, A Green Place, A Good Place, 154.

[34] Gonzales, Societies, Religion, and History, Chapter 4, paragraphs 27–32 (Accessed 8
January 2013).

[35] Le Veux, Premier essai de vocabulaire luganda – français d'après l'ordre étymologique,
215.

interpretation is significantly strengthened by the fact that this innovation coincided with the change in meaning of the noun *-góló* [16]. What is less clear is the etymology of *kaidu*. In their dictionaries, both the linguist R. A. Snoxall and the Catholic missionary Père Le Veux connect its Luganda reflex to the word for a male slave in Luganda: *omuddu*.[36] The implication is that all wives in Buganda, senior or not, were no more than slaves. It is important to recall that this interpretation was developed against an antislavery, pro-imperialist backdrop in which all women in Buganda were regularly described as slaves as part of the justification for colonial overrule.[37] Schoenbrun argues that the original meaning of *-iru* (cl. 1/2) (the underlying form of *omuddu*) was most likely 'peasant' or 'farmer' and that the meaning 'male slave' was given to the noun only after the dissolution of North Nyanza in the twelfth century or even much more recently.[38] In this case *kaidu* may have had the affectionate, diminutive meaning 'little farmer' and thus referred to a senior wife's role in managing food production.

The innovation of *kaidu* also gives us some insight into the potential of motherhood to improve the social status of individual women. In polygynous households during the time that North Nyanza was spoken, the comparative ethnographic evidence indicates that the heir was ideally a son of the senior wife or *kaidu*.[39] On her son's accession as head of the household, a *kaidu* could thus expect to be looked after until her death. This meant that a woman who attained the position of senior wife could expect a relatively secure future, especially in comparison to her co-wives, who faced considerable uncertainty as widows. The evidence suggests that the first wife to marry into a household did not necessarily hold the position of senior wife. The most convincing explanation of how a woman secured the position of *kaidu* is that her natal lineage and clan negotiated this at the time of her marriage and ensured she remained the senior wife despite more women marrying into the household. Becoming

---

[36] R. A. Snoxall, *Luganda-English Dictionary* (Oxford: Clarendon Press, 1967), 211; Le Veux, *Premier essai de vocabulaire luganda – français d'après l'ordre étymologique*, 118, 643.

[37] Nakanyike Beatrice Musisi, "Transformations of Baganda Women: From the Earliest Times to the Demise of the Kingdom in 1966," (PhD diss., University of Toronto, 1992), 172–7.

[38] David Schoenbrun, "Violence, Marginality, Scorn and Honour: Language Evidence of Slavery to the Eighteenth Century," in *Slavery in the Great Lakes Region of East Africa*, ed. Henri Médard and Shane Doyle (Oxford: James Currey, 2007), 43–4, 62–3, no. 10.

[39] Roscoe, *The Northern Bantu*, 200; SO-15-BUG-F-KJ, interview, 20 January 2005, Busoga; SO-ETH-NAU-F-ME, interview, 21 January 2005, Busoga.

a *kaidu*, then, would have required a woman to come from a lineage of sufficiently high social status to successfully make such demands.

The usual way for a woman to become a mother in North Nyanza was through pregnancy and childbirth. North Nyanza speakers used the same word to describe giving birth as their proto-Bantu–speaking ancestors some four thousand years earlier: *-bịád-* [4]. This verb could also be used to describe the begetting of children by men, although the primary meaning does appear to be that applied to women. Some women, however, faced difficulties in becoming a mother through this most conventional of ways: they or their husbands might be infertile or their pregnancies might not result in live births. In the case of infertile women, North Nyanza–speaking people again used the same word as their proto-Bantu ancestors, *-gumbà* [17], and it is self-evident that childlessness was neither a new phenomenon nor one peculiar to North Nyanza society. While infertility or barrenness in a woman could have many causes, ranging from the physical to the spiritual, the North Nyanza speech community did not innovate new words to describe these various forms. It was the consequence of an absence of pregnancies and children that mattered most to them, not the cause of that absence.

The noun that North Nyanza speakers coined to describe an impotent man suggests that manhood was as intimately connected to reproduction for them as was womanhood. They derived the noun for 'impotent man,' *-fiirwa* (cl. 1/2) [10], from the passive form of the verb *-fa* 'die,' giving a literal meaning of 'one who is bereaved.' The bereavement suffered by such a man was both the loss of anticipated children and the ending of his lineage.[40] Furthermore, a man with no children would have no one to tend to his spirit after his death. If a woman's husband was impotent, the comparative ethnographic evidence suggests that she was socially sanctioned to leave him and find another husband.[41] The main reason for this, we can surmise, was that his impotence was an impediment to her becoming a mother, although her right to sexual fulfilment was presumably also a factor. If a wife remained with an impotent man, not only did her husband's lineage not gain the children it expected, but her patrilineage also did not gain the nephews and nieces it anticipated from the marriage of its daughter. Her husband's impotence threatened the social reproduction

---

[40] Miss Laight and Y. K. Lubogo, "Basoga Death and Burial Rites," *Uganda Journal* 2, no. 2 (1934/1935): 126.
[41] GW-ETH-KAD-F-ZK, interview, 17 November 2004, Bugwere; SO-ETH-NAU-F-ME, interview, 21 January 2005, Busoga.

of both lineages and so broke the contract made between them through marriage. It is noteworthy that the comparative ethnographic data do not reveal the taking of a lover as a solution to the dilemma caused by a husband's impotence. This may reflect the growing anxiety that *pater* and *genitor* be the same man in North Nyanza, in contrast to some other societies wherein marriage, not biology, created paternity.

A woman who found herself in a childless marriage faced a difficult and lonely life and a double death, for most North Nyanza clans would not name children after a barren woman and so she would not be remembered after her demise.[42] She suffered from a lack of status in her marital home with, in all likelihood, access to less land for cultivation and little or no labour to assist her; she could also expect a lonely and poverty-stricken old age.[43] An important possibility available to such women emerged from the social institution of **-perekezi* (cl. 1a) [36] discussed previously. After accompanying the bride to her new household, the **-perekezi* could stay with the new wife for a prolonged period and, should she become pregnant by the husband, would become one of his wives.[44] Because of her relationship with the **-perekezi*, the wife could lay some claim to her **-perekezi's* children if she did not conceive. Alternatively, if a woman's **-perekezi* did not remain with her, an infertile wife could go to her lineage or the wider clan to ask for a young woman to join her in her marriage. She could then lay claim to one or more of the children who issued from the new union.[45] The issue of extant social status and access to the benefits of motherhood is again relevant here. The junior wife could not benefit from her biological motherhood until she had provided a child (or perhaps more) for her senior co-wife. This was not an egalitarian sisterhood, but rather a power structure from which women of higher social status were able to co-opt the reproductive ability of those of lower standing.

Adoption and fostering served several purposes in North Nyanza society, only one of which was to provide a son for a senior wife. It was also a way of marking the rights various kin – maternal and paternal – held

[42] Laight and Lubogo, "Basoga Death and Burial Rites," 127; GW-ETH-BUL-F-KJ, interview, 11 November 2004, Bugwere; GW-ETH-IKI-F-MN, interview, 16 November 2004, Bugwere.
[43] Meillassoux, *Maidens, Meal and Money*, 77.
[44] Mair, *An African People in the Twentieth Century*, 85.
[45] Roscoe, *The Northern Bantu*, 200; GW-ETH-BUL-F-KJ, interview, 27 October 2004, Bugwere; SO-ETH-NAU-F-ME, interview, 21 January 2005, Busoga; SO-ETH-NAU-F-YG, interview, 20 January 2005, Busoga.

in the children. More basically, it was a means of redistributing children to balance labour and food among members of the lineage and of the society in general.[46] Speakers of North Nyanza made a clear distinction between the acts of giving a child out of the household and of taking a child into the household. The North Nyanza verb for 'entrust a child to' was *-wereka* [49], which was derived through semantic extension from an older verb used by speakers of Great Lakes Bantu, namely *-pereka*, 'entrust, hand over temporarily.'[47] This verb was in turn derived from *-pédik-*, 'hand over,' which is an ancient Bantu word.[48] Speakers of North Nyanza's sister language, Rutara, had the different but related meaning of 'entrust cattle' for *-hereka*, their reflex of the verb. North Nyanzans and Rutarans inherited the verb from their West Nyanza–speaking ancestors who had used it to describe the entrusting of a valuable life, without specifying between humans and cattle.[49] We will see this connection between entrusting children and cattle recurring again during the time that South Kyoga was spoken and again among Lugwere speakers. This suggests a long-standing association between these practices, dating to West Nyanzan times. It is well established in the historiography of the wider Great Lakes region that cattle loans were used to create patron–client relationships, both between individuals and between lineages.[50] The etymologies of these verbs indicate that the movement of children between households similarly involved unequal relationships of power. What is not clear is how exactly such dynamics worked,

---

[46] Because "individual procreative capacity is not linked to productive capacity," the balance is redressed "through redistributing offspring rather than produce." Meillassoux, *Maidens, Meal and Money*, 58.

[47] There is some uncertainty whether this was the proto-North Nyanza verb for 'foster a child out' because of the distribution of the reflexes. The only reflex in the North Nyanza languages that I have been able to identify is in Luganda, which is the North Nyanzan language closest to Lunyoro and Runyankore, the Rutaran languages that have the reflexes meaning 'entrust cattle.' However, the antiquity of the underlying verb and its prevalence throughout Great Lakes Bantu language subgroups is evidence in favour of the innovation in meaning having occurred first in West Nyanza and then narrowing in North Nyanza.

[48] Bastin and Schadeberg, "Bantu Lexical Reconstructions 3," ID main 2427 (Accessed 8 January 2013).

[49] It may be that this was a proto-Great Lakes Bantu verb, but given the potential for independent innovation and the fact that I have been able to identify only a single iteration outside of West Nyanza (in Olunande), we must assume that it was innovated by speakers of proto-West Nyanza.

[50] See, for example, Catharine Newbury's discussion of *umuheto* relationships centred on cattle in nineteenth-century Rwanda. Newbury, *The Cohesion of Oppression: Clientship and Ethnicity in Rwanda, 1860–1960* (New York: Columbia University Press, 1988).

for it seems it was women with high social status and chiefs who took children from those of lower standing in an inversion of the practice with cattle.[51]

The other side of fostering and adoption – that of taking a child into the household rather than entrusting a child to another household – was talked about using the verb *-fuura* [12]. North Nyanzans inherited *-fuura* – 'adopt a child' – from their West Nyanza–speaking ancestors who created it by expanding the meaning of an older verb. In Great Lakes Bantu *-fuura* had two meanings: 'pour' and 'bend a bow.' West Nyanza speakers gave this verb two new and related meanings: 'change' and 'adopt.' They may have done so in the face of the challenges posed to their communities by *-cweke*, the condition of being childless or heirless.[52] As North Nyanzans developed strategies to avoid *-cweke*, such as through shifting inheritance practices, so the need for men to adopt children appears to have fallen away. The rise in importance of the senior wife or *kaidu* [19] of a household and the preference for her to be the mother of the heir, however, meant that practices of adoption and fostering continued.

While biological reproduction was not in itself sufficient for a woman to be a mother, for all North Nyanza–speaking women biological reproduction within marriage would have been the most common route into the social category of mother. But biological reproduction was not somehow isolated from culture. As the historian Nancy Demand notes with reference to Classical Greece, "birth is a natural physiological process, but for human beings it is also a social event. Culture intervenes in countless ways to shape and structure the experience." "Giving birth," therefore, "is not so much a 'natural' event as a 'cultural construction.'" According to Demand, this means that "the study of the way in which a particular society perceives and manages childbirth reveals fundamental aspects of its cultural and social values."[53] To ensure successful biological reproduction, a North Nyanzan woman who was pregnant, *-ba nda* [1], had to follow several avoidances and social restrictions. These were known by the same name as the food avoidance totems of clans, *-ziro*

[51] Parker Shipton discusses the overlaps and profound differences between entrustments of children and livestock in contemporary Luoland, western Kenya in *The Nature of Entrustment*, 81–98.

[52] Schoenbrun, *The Historical Reconstruction of Great Lakes Bantu Cultural Vocabulary*, 180–1, root 275.

[53] Nancy Demand, *Birth, Death, and Motherhood in Classical Greece* (Baltimore: Johns Hopkins University Press, 1994), 1.

(cl. 3/4) [52].[54] The word is of proto-Bantu origin; taboos and avoid-ances, like bridewealth, are an ancient feature of Bantu societies.[55] Among the speech communities descended from North Nyanza, many of these avoidances were specific to individual clans and so we can be reasonably confident that this was also the case for North Nyanzans. The avoidances were wide-ranging, from not eating specific foods to prohibitions on shaking hands, particularly with men.[56] By imposing these *-ziro* on the women who had married into their clan, a man's kin marked the pregnancy, and thus the future child, as belonging to their lineage and their clan.

After a woman had given birth, clan customs also dictated the manner in which the placenta should be disposed of. North Nyanzans innovated a new noun for placenta, *-tani* (cl. 7) [46], and saw it as the twin of the newborn infant. The comparative ethnographic evidence associated with *-tani* suggests that they understood the placenta to have its own *-zimu* (cl. 3/4) or spirit that could bring misfortune to the family of its infant 'twin' should it not be properly placated. To avoid any such misfortunes, the *-tani* or placenta had to be correctly disposed of and respected according to clan custom. The placenta was buried inside the house or by its doorway. Reflecting the growing importance of banana cultivation to the North Nyanzan economy, some clans started to placate the *-zimu* by burying the placenta at the base of a banana plant.[57]

---

[54] For the history of clans in the region, see Cohen, *The Historical Tradition of Busoga*; Kodesh, *Beyond the Royal Gaze*; Newbury, *Kings and Clans*.

[55] For food prohibitions during pregnancy in some other Bantu societies, see Gonzales, *Societies, Religion, and History*.

[56] Atkinson, ed., "Bugwere Historical Texts," Text 24; Mair, *An African People in the Twentieth Century*, 39–40; GW-ETH-IKI-F-KG, interview, 16 November 2004, Bugwere; GW-ETH-BUL-F-KJ, 27 October 2004, Bugwere; SO-ETH-NAU-F-ME, interview, 21 January 2005, Busoga.

[57] Cohen, ed., "Collected Texts of Busoga Traditional History," Texts 14, 41, 287, 380, 468, and 515; Mair, *An African People in the Twentieth Century*, 42; Roscoe, *The Baganda*, 52–7; Roscoe, *The Northern Bantu*, 214; GW-ETH-IKI-F-KG, interview, 16 November 2004, Bugwere; SO-ETH-KIT-F-NM, interview, 19 January 2005, Busoga; SO-ETH-NAU-F-ME, interview, 21 January 2005, Busoga; SO-15-BUG-F-KJ, interview, 20 January 2005, Busoga. On *-zimu*, see Schoenbrun, *The Historical Reconstruction of Great Lakes Bantu Cultural Vocabulary*, 182–3, root 278. Across the world, in Papua New Guinea, similar ideas about placentas being members of the clan and the need to treat them appropriately also prevailed. Leanne Merrett-Balkos, "Just Add Water: Remaking Women through Childbirth, Anganen, Southern Highlands, Papua New Guinea," in *Maternities and Modernities: Colonial and Postcolonial Experiences in Asia and the Pacific*, ed. Kalpana Ram and Margaret Jolly (Cambridge: Cambridge University Press, 1998), 225.

We can posit from the comparative ethnographic evidence that, among speakers of proto-North Nyanza, a new mother and her baby remained secluded in the house in which she had given birth until the stump of the infant's umbilical cord had dried and fallen off. When they emerged from seclusion, a ceremony was performed to establish the legitimacy of the child and therefore his or her membership in the father's clan. As with the placenta, the dried stump of the umbilical cord was treated according to clan customs: in some clans it was discarded along with other rubbish swept out of the house, whereas in others it was preserved, most likely in barkcloth. The umbilical cords of twins, however, were always preserved; at some point they started to be kept in elaborate barkcloth and shell wrappings. The widespread nature of this practice suggests it may date to North Nyanzan times. All of the aforementioned rituals were more elaborate if a woman gave birth to twins with further additional ceremonies performed.[58] Twins were both feared and respected in North Nyanza society, and special precautions and rites were performed at their birth. Having survived the ritual dangers of bearing twins (and, for the mother, the physical dangers of doing so), their parents were granted special respect and awarded honorific titles. Given the distribution of these practices among the descendant societies of North Nyanza, we can again be confident that they date to the period during which North Nyanza was spoken, although we do not know, for example, the titles North Nyanza speakers gave to the mothers and fathers of twins.[59]

Becoming a mother in North Nyanza thus enmeshed a woman in a network of clan and lineage relations. Establishing the lineage and, hence, the clan of the child was important, both to the patrilineage to which she or he would belong and to the kin of the mother, because the children of a female lineage member had an important – in fact, vital – role in the social reproduction of her clan and lineage. That role could be performed safely only by children whose paternity, and hence whose clan, was well established. One way of controlling the paternity of children was through marriage. Another was by enforcing the respecting of clan *-ziro* (cl. 3/4)

[58] See, for example, the description in: Apolo Kagwa, *The Customs of the Baganda*, transl. Ernest B. Kalibala, ed. May Mandelbaum (Edel) (1934, repr. New York: AMS Press, 1969), 105–8.

[59] Mair, *An African People in the Twentieth Century*, 43–53; Roscoe, *The Baganda*, 61–4, 69–70; Roscoe, *The Northern Bantu*, 217–9; GW-ETH-IKI-F-KG, interview, 16 November 2004, Bugwere; GW-ETH-BUL-F-KJ, interview, 11 November 2004, Bugwere; GW-ETH-IKI-F-MN, interview, 16 November 2004, Bugwere; SO-15-BUG-F-KJ, interview, 20 January 2005, Busoga; SO-ETH-KIT-F-NM, interview, 19 January 2005.

[52] by pregnant wives. If she followed the *-ziro of a clan other than that of the *genitor* of the foetus, a pregnant woman risked miscarriage or stillbirth and thus the failure to achieve motherhood.

MOTHERHOOD AND LINEAGE POLITICS IN NORTH NYANZA

Speakers of North Nyanza organised their communities along patrilineal lines, but gave continued and renewed importance to the connections formed by and through mothers. A woman's children were known as *-ihwa (cl. 1/2) [20] by the people in her clan and lineage. Her brother had a particular interest in his sister's children, as did her father: both had specific rights in and responsibilities towards them. The people who spoke proto-North Nyanza did not follow bilateral descent nor were there matrilineal clans. It is quite clear that all their clans and lineages were patrilineal. Nonetheless, North Nyanzans maintained a more complicated form of social organization than such labelling suggests. The existence of matrilateral relationships cutting across patrilineal social organisa- tion was recognised in many African societies by the earliest anthropolo- gists, who focused on explaining the function of this relationship.[60] More recently, Wyatt MacGaffey has highlighted the importance of historicis- ing these social institutions of kinship.[61] Matrilateral ties in the North Nyanza speech community were not merely a relic of matrilineal descent or a long-lost matriarchal society. They were a strategy for creating cross-lineal networks at a time when the community needed the broadest possible support base in order to ensure its survival and prosperity.[62]

The renewed importance of matrilateral ties and networks formed by and through mothers, cutting across patrilineal descent groups, was reflected in linguistic innovations and in specific social and cultural prac- tices. North Nyanzans placed motherhood at the heart of their social organisation in response to the challenges they faced in building sus- tainable societies, despite following patrilineal descent. As they did so, they created seriated networks of kinship and obligation that reached

---

[60] For an overview of these, see Jack Goody, "The Mother's Brother and the Sister's Son in West Africa," *Journal of the Royal Anthropological Institute of Great Britain and Ireland* 89, no. 1 (1959): 61–88.

[61] Wyatt MacGaffey, "Changing Representations in Central African History," *Journal of African History* 46, no. 2 (2005): 189–207. See also Vansina, *Paths in the Rainforests*, 113–14, 152–5.

[62] See also Rhiannon Stephens, "Lineage and Society in Precolonial Uganda" *Journal of African History* 50, no. 2 (2009): 203–21.

outside of the patrilineage and the patriclan. This was by no means a static form of social organisation. Indeed, as we see in the following chapters, the relationship between a woman's children and her kin group changed in quite distinct ways among the communities descended from people speaking proto-North Nyanza. At the same time, that relationship remained a central feature of those communities, nowhere more so than in political life.

The word that North Nyanzans used to talk about their sisters' children, *-ihwa* (cl. 1/2) [20], can be traced back to proto-Bantu. According to Schoenbrun, for Great Lakes Bantu speakers the noun *-jIpùà* described "the new member of the group, lost to the group which gave the wife and gained by the group which received the wife."[63] In North Nyanza, *-ihwa* were 'lost' to their mother's patrilineage in that they belonged to their father's lineage, but the relationship between a mother's kin and her children suggests their continued connection. It was *-ihwa* who washed the bodies of their maternal kin in preparation for burial and who assisted in the special ceremonies for twins and at other ritual occasions.[64] If an *-ihwa* succeeded to political office his maternal kin could expect to benefit from their new connection to power.[65] So while *-ihwa* did not belong to their mother's lineage or clan they were not entirely 'lost' to their maternal kin group either. It was precisely because *-ihwa* belonged to another lineage and another clan that they could carry out these ritually dangerous duties.

The continued connection between a mother's kin and her children was thus a strong feature of North Nyanzan social and political life. For people speaking proto-North Nyanza, the most important person

[63] Schoenbrun, *The Historical Reconstruction of Great Lakes Bantu Cultural Vocabulary*, 86–7, root 120 (quote p. 86); Schoenbrun, *A Green Place, A Good Place*, 97. *-jIpùà* is the proto-Great Lakes Bantu form of *-ihwa*.

[64] Atkinson, ed., "Bugwere Historical Texts," Texts 37, 47, and 48; Laight and Lubogo, "Basoga Death and Burial Rites," 120–44; Mair, *An African People in the Twentieth Century*, 46–8; SO-15-BUG-F-KJ, interview, 20 January 2005, Busoga. Banyoro *baihwa* were also expected to undertake ritually dangerous tasks for their maternal uncles, Renée Louise Tantala, "The Early History of Kitara in Western Uganda: Process Models of Religious and Political Change" (PhD diss., University of Wisconsin-Madison, 1989), 297. For the rights and responsibilities of *baihwa* and their maternal uncles in Bunyoro, see J. M. Beattie, "Nyoro Marriage and Affinity," *Africa: Journal of the International African Institute* 28, no. 1 (1958): 19–22.

[65] Roscoe, *The Baganda*, 191; Renée Tantala, "Community and Polity in Southern Kigulu," (paper presented at the Department of History Research Seminar, Makerere University, Kampala, Uganda, 27 November 1972), Cohen Private Collection; Tantala, "Gonza Bato and the Consolidation of Abaisengobi Rule in Southern Kigulu."

or persons among a mother's kin with regard to her children – as across many sub-Saharan African communities – was her brother or brothers. Speakers of proto-East Bantu (the great-great-great-grandparent of North Nyanza) innovated a word for 'maternal uncle,' *máá-dú̧ mè*, which had the literal meaning of 'male mother.'[66] North Nyanza speakers inherited this term, but they changed its meaning to refer to 'male in-laws.'[67] This important shift in meaning may have been a reflection of tensions between patrilineal descent and ongoing matrilateral ties or it may have been connected with the new ideas about women's active participation in marriage seen in the innovations in verbs and nouns associated with acts of marriage, as discussed in the previous section. Having changed the meaning of *máá-dú̧mè*, speakers of North Nyanza coined a new noun, *koiza* (cl. 1a/2) [27], to name the mother's brother. The etymology of this noun is unclear. There is a verb in Lunyoro (spoken in the area neighbouring Buganda today) that means 'be greedy or gluttonous': -*koija*. It is possible therefore that there was a West Nyanza verb *-koiza* with a similar meaning from which North Nyanza speakers derived the noun for maternal uncle and that reflected the right of the maternal uncle to make demands of his nephews and nieces. But the verb is found only in Lunyoro and so a more likely possibility is that Lunyoro speakers coined it as a result of their contacts with people speaking languages descended from proto-North Nyanza. The Lunyoro verb may thus reflect the perceived greed of maternal uncles among a neighbouring people. This would fit with changing perceptions of matrilateral rights over time, particularly during the eighteenth and nineteenth centuries.

Whatever the etymology, that North Nyanzans innovated a new noun to name the maternal uncle suggests either a change in their views of him or an evolution in his role during this time. Ethnographic evidence indicates that it was not only the maternal uncle who had rights in his sister's children, for maternal grandfathers could also make claims to them. It appears that, at least initially, it was the latter who could demand compensation from his son-in-law for some of the children born to his daughter. This right may well have passed on to the *koiza* (cl. 1a/2) [27] on the

---

[66] East Bantu is also referred to as Eastern Savanna Bantu.

[67] Jeff Marck and Koen Bostoen, "Proto-Oceanic Society (Austronesian) and Proto-East Bantu Society (Niger-Congo) Residence, Descent, and Kin Terms, ca. 1000 BC," in *Kinship, Language, and Prehistory: Per Hage and the Renaissance in Kinship Studies*, ed. Doug Jones and Bojka Milicic (Salt Lake City: University of Utah Press, 2011), 86, table 8.1; Schoenbrun, *The Historical Reconstruction of Great Lakes Bantu Cultural Vocabulary*, 97, root 136.

maternal grandfather's death.[68] Nonetheless, North Nyanzans created a
new name only for the maternal uncle. One explanation for this renam-
ing of the maternal uncle lies in the political developments of the period
that opened up new possibilities for power. North Nyanzans continued
a political evolution initiated by their West Nyanza–speaking ancestors,
namely a move towards "instrumentally powerful kingship": a kingship
with at least some control over land.[69] This political evolution led to
the consolidation of power by royal families. As we will see, it is most
likely that the institution of the queen mother was part of early states in
North Nyanza, placing ideologies of motherhood at the heart of political
complexity. A woman's son relied on his maternal kin to support claims
to power and, reciprocally, a maternal uncle benefited from his *-ihwa*'s
(cl. 1/2) [20] political success. The *koiza* of a politically successful man
would have wielded considerable authority in the region's early polities.

Ceri Ashley's recent analysis of ceramics found on the north and
northwestern shore of Lake Victoria–Nyanza suggests that, from the
ninth century CE, the communities living there enlarged the scope of their
social and political lives. The people who composed those communities
changed the types and functions of the ceramics that they produced. Small,
high-quality pots and jars – Urewe Ware – that were used in homestead
settings, primarily for cooking but also for ritual purposes, are replaced
in the archaeological record by "large to very large spherical or hemi-
spherical bowls with bulbously thickened rims, sometimes enlarged as
much as five times the thickness of the body." Ashley notes that the scale
and shape of these new ceramics (dating from the 9th to 13th centuries),
"suggests a quite narrowly defined function, which, given the size of the
ceramics, indicate that they were probably linked to large-scale communal events."[70] When placed in the broader archaeological and historical
context, this shift in scale suggests that social focus moved away from
the homestead during this period and towards the communal level. This
social and political change is also apparently represented by the ceramics

---

[68] Cohen, *Womunafu's Bunafu*, 27–8; Père Le Veux, *Manuel de langue luganda comprenant la grammaire et un recueil de contes et de légendes* (Maison Carrée, Algeria:
Imprimerie des Missionaires d'Afriques (Pères Blancs), 1914), 456; W. H. Long, "Notes
of the Bugwere District," c.1933, 459, from J. R. McD. Elliot Papers, Atkinson Private
Collection; Roscoe, *The Northern Bantu*, 217; Tantala, "Community and Polity in
Southern Kigulu," 12; Tantala, "Gonza Bato and the Consolidation of Abaisengobi Rule
in Southern Kigulu," 15.

[69] Schoenbrun, *A Green Place, A Good Place*, 184–95 (quote p. 185).

[70] Ashley, "Towards a Socialised Archaeology of Ceramics in Great Lakes Africa," 154 (first
quote), 155 (second quote).

known as the 'Luzira head' and 'Entebbe figurine.' These, along with a
number of other fragments of human figurines found alongside them, are
the only archaeological finds of figurines in the wider region, and Andrew
Reid and Ceri Ashley have recently used contextual dating to place their
manufacture in the ninth century.[71] This was a time of significant development in both political ideology and healing practices, in the creative and
instrumental aspects of power along the Lake Victoria–Nyanza littoral.

Political centralisation was not a new phenomenon in the Great
Lakes region at the end of the first millennium. It is easy, nonetheless, to
envisage a situation in which people speaking proto-North Nyanza and
establishing themselves in a new environment along the northwestern
lakeshore and its hinterland in the eighth century focused first on building and consolidating households before turning to communal level politics. Archaeologist Peter Robertshaw's research on second millennium
polities in western Uganda has emphasised elite men's efforts to control
women's reproductive labour in a context of low fertility and high infant
mortality. He concludes that the struggle over women was central to state
formation throughout this period.[72] The emphasis on reproduction lay
at the heart of political centralisation in the North Nyanzan community
too, but women – as mothers in particular – were at the heart of these
processes. Successful North Nyanzan leaders converted their positions
into hereditary ones, thereby creating royal families, continuing a process
that emerged during the time that proto-West Nyanza was spoken. The
consolidation of political power into royal families meant that the form
of polities reflected the successful social reproduction of the whole society. For the royal family to maintain its hold on power by transferring

---

[71] Reid and Ashley, "A Context for the Luzira Head."

[72] Peter Robertshaw, "Women, Labor and State Formation in Western Uganda,"
Archeological Papers of the American Anthropological Association 9, no. 1 (1999):
51–65. In making this argument, Robertshaw builds on a substantial body of Marxist
and feminist scholarship, including, Engels, *The Origin of the Family, Private Property
and the State*; Christine Ward Gailey, *Kinship to Kingship: Gender Hierarchy and State
Formation in the Tongan Islands* (Austin: University of Texas Press, 1987); Eleanor
Leacock, "Interpreting the Origins of Gender Inequality: Conceptual and Historical
Problems," *Dialectical Anthropology* 7, no. 4 (1983): 263–84; Reyna Rapp, "Gender and
Class: An Archaeology of Knowledge Concerning the Origin of the State," *Dialectical
Anthropology* 2, no. 4 (1977): 309–16; Karen Sacks, *Sisters and Wives: The Past and
Future of Sexual Equality* (Westport, Conn.: Greenwood Press, 1979). More recently
Robertshaw has emphasised women's harnessing of creative power in the face of their
"arduous and humble lot," in particular in association with Cwezi shrines in Bunyoro.
See Peter Robertshaw, "Beyond the Segmentary State: Creative and Instrumental Power in
Western Uganda," *Journal of World Prehistory* 23, no. 4 (2010): 255–69 (quote p. 263).

leadership from one generation to the next, it had to produce that next generation. Royal families were thus an embodiment of successful reproduction, and the importance of this was made manifest in the office of the queen mother.

In the middle part of the first millennium, people speaking West Nyanza and its dialects – what would become North Nyanza and Rutara – changed their political system. The "revolutionary innovation" of this period, according to Schoenbrun, "lay in the invention of concepts of hereditary nobility and the link that was created between nobility and the institutions of instrumental control over people."[73] In other words, kings, queens, and other members of royal families were able to assert their control over chiefs by making chiefships, such as *-kungu* (cl. 14) and *-tongore* (cl. 14), appointed rather than hereditary offices, in theory at least if not always in practice.[74] This development was marked by West Nyanzans' innovation of two terms related to hereditary power: *-kama* (cl. 1/2), 'king,' and *-langira* (cl. 1/2), 'hereditary royal.'[75] The noun *-kama* (cl. 1/2) was derived from an older verb, *-kama*, with the meaning 'milk, squeeze' and points to West Nyanzans' conviction that the king had the "responsibility for 'feeding' his people," and the symbolic importance of pastoralism at the heart of political authority.[76] It also highlights the extractive nature of political leadership. The etymology of *-langira* (cl. 1/2) speaks to a different aspect of power. West Nyanza speakers derived it from the verb *-lánga*, which has a range of related meanings: 'report, announce, foresee future, prophecy.' Thus the status of *-langira* (cl. 1/2) embodied the 'creative' as opposed to (or perhaps in addition to) the 'instrumental' side of power and governance.[77] This etymology appears to have reflected a reality in which at least some *-langira* (cl. 1/2) were mediums for deities.[78] The term *-langira* (cl. 1/2)

[73] Schoenbrun, *A Green Place, A Good Place*, 185.

[74] Schoenbrun, *The Historical Reconstruction of Great Lakes Bantu Cultural Vocabulary*, 141–2, root 210; 169–70, root 257.

[75] See Schoenbrun, *A Green Place, A Good Place*, 189–95, for an extensive discussion of the emergence of these two terms and the offices they named, as well as for a discussion of the broader implications of this change in the political organisation of West Nyanzan societies.

[76] Schoenbrun, *A Green Place, A Good Place*, 213, fn. 76.

[77] Schoenbrun, *The Historical Reconstruction of Great Lakes Bantu Cultural Vocabulary*, 146–7, root 217; 211–2, root 324; Schoenbrun, *A Green Place, A Good Place*, 12–13 and varia.

[78] Gorju, *Entre le Victoria l'Albert et l'Edouard*, 223–4; Apolo Kaggwa, *The Kings of Buganda*, trans. M. S. M. Kiwanuka (Nairobi: East African Publishing House, 1971), 18;

encompassed all hereditary royals, male and female, in West Nyanzan society in the mid-first millennium.

Speakers of North Nyanza, by contrast, divided their hereditary royals along gender lines, assigning the original term to male royals or princes while innovating a new term, *-mbeeza* (cl. 1/2) [31], for their female counterparts. The division of hereditary royals into gendered groups and the innovation of a new term for female royals suggests developments in the category of princess in North Nyanza. The basis for these developments with regard to *-mbeeza* (cl. 1/2) may lie in their connections to an alternative locus of power in North Nyanza, namely the shrines of deities. In both Buganda and Bugwere, princesses could be wives for deities and it is likely that this was also the case in North Nyanzan times.[79] Shrines were centres of healing and as such of creative power that could be, and on occasion was, wielded against the instrumental power of the political state. Kodesh has argued that the practice of Baganda princesses marrying deities stemmed from efforts by the king to control their reproductive power and to "direct the collective energies and authority associated with shrine complexes toward the royal center."[80] Once married to deities, princesses could not become mothers in the conventional sense for North Nyanzans, but, as was the case for female mediums more generally, they were able to channel their reproductive capacity as women into creative power. In the early North Nyanzan polities *-mbeeza* (cl. 1/2), through their marriages to powerful deities, would have created networks of connections that ran between deities, their mediums and their followers, and the royal family, and, ultimately, to the king and queen mother. Naming princesses, and thus marking them as distinct from princes, may have been part of an attempt by state players to co-opt the standing of female royals as intermediaries between these two centres of authority.

One of the most important political roles in North Nyanza was played by someone who was not a member of the royal family, the queen mother, that is, the commoner wife of the former king who was mother to the new king. The office of the queen mother exemplifies the mobilisation by North Nyanzans of their ideology of motherhood in the political arena as well as more broadly throughout society. This office embodied both

---

Roscoe, *The Baganda*, 74, 303, 307, 308; Laurence D. Schiller, "The Royal Women of Buganda," *International Journal of African Historical Studies* 23, no. 3 (1990): 468.

[79] This is implied rather than explicitly stated in Atkinson, ed., "Bugwere Historical Texts," Text 44. It is explicitly stated in Kagwa, *The Customs of the Baganda*, 120; Kagwa, *The Kings of Buganda*, 84; Roscoe, *The Baganda*, 74, 303, 307, 308.

[80] Kodesh, *Beyond the Royal Gaze*, 157.

the connection between a woman's clan and her children and afforded power to a commoner on the basis of her maternity. The ethnographic and linguistic evidence do not allow a definitive statement of the age of the institution of queen mother. In the nineteenth century, queen mothers existed across the Great Lakes region, pointing to a great historical depth for this aspect of royal power. They were to be found in Rwanda, Nkore, and Buhaya, amongst others, as well as in Buganda, Busoga and Bugwere. Yet, the titles given to the office varied across the region, suggesting more recent, independent innovation. In many of these societies, as Schoenbrun tells us, "people made the words for queen mother with the same word-building artistry. They added the relevant term for adult woman to the corresponding term for king."[81] This model, however, was not used by those speaking North Nyanzan languages. Luganda speakers innovated the term *nnàmasòle* (cl. 1a) [33] to name the office and people in Busoga, or at least in the kingdom of Bugabula, used the term *nakazaire* (cl. 1a).[82] These two terms not only differ from each other, but also break from the model of word-building used in naming the office elsewhere in the region. The linguistic evidence thus indicates later independent innovations of the office. Schoenbrun notes that the distinct Luganda term "suggests quite strongly that these innovations all occurred after the break up of the most recent subgroups of Great Lakes Bantu – West Highlands, Rutara, and North Nyanza – and that they all referred to different political processes in those royal domains, processes that unfolded after the sixteenth century." However, he is aware of the tension in the available evidence and concludes that, "it is certainly fair to argue that the office of the queen mother came into existence virtually simultaneously with the named position of king."[83] In Busoga, the king of each state had a different title. Several, but not all, of these titles derived from the eponymous founders of the states. The ruler of Busambira, for example, was referred to as *Kisambira*, that of Busiki as *Kisiki*, of Buzaaya as *Muzaaya*, of Bukono as *Nkono*, and of Bukooli as *Wakooli*.[84] There

---

[81] Schoenbrun, *A Green Place, A Good Place*, 192. See also Schoenbrun, *The Historical Reconstruction of Great Lakes Bantu Cultural Vocabulary*, 114, root 163; 151, root 225.

[82] The evidence for Busoga is extremely thin and I have attestations for this term only in reference to Bugabula: Cohen, ed., "Collected Texts of Busoga Traditional History," Text 125. I have not found a Lugwere term; it may be lost or may never have existed.

[83] Schoenbrun, *A Green Place, A Good Place*, 192–3. Hanson, in contrast, draws on this evidence to argue that the office must have emerged after 1500. See *Landed Obligation*, 49.

[84] Cohen, *Towards a Reconstructed Past*, 90, fn. 127.

is no suggestion that each of these micro-states independently innovated the institution of hereditary ruler. Despite the linguistic evidence for the institution of queen mother, then, there is little reason to view it as a more recent invention than kingship. Indeed, the view that queen mothers are as old as kings in this region is further strengthened once it is placed in the broader context of the emphasis on motherhood in social organisation.

The queen mother was appointed to her office at the same time as her son was made king. In the polities that emerged among people speaking proto-North Nyanza it is likely that the queen mother was ideally the senior wife or *kaidu* (cl. 12) [19] of the deceased king.[85] Succession would not always have been uncontested, especially when the maternal kin of princes stood to gain from the accession of their *-ihwa* (cl. 1/2) [20], and so we must recognise the potential for dissonance between ideal succession and the contested realities. Drawing from more recent practices in Busoga and Buganda, we can surmise that part of the North Nyanza polities would probably have been under the queen mother's direct control in the form of estates.[86] The extent of such estates would in all likelihood have varied according to the power of the royal family and the influence individual queen mothers were able to wield within it. Aside from her own estates, the queen mother's power would have lain in her ability to influence others in power, including her son and the chiefs. It would also have depended on the relative strength of her lineage and clan and their ability to support her when disputes arose. In addition to her kin group benefiting in general from their proximity to power, the queen mother's brother (real or classificatory) would be appointed to an important chiefship or *-kungu* (cl. 14).[87]

The queen mother had, of course, first been a wife to the king. Polygyny was likely to have been practised by kings in North Nyanza and one of his wives was appointed as the senior wife or *kaidu* (cl. 12) [19].[88] The

---

[85] Atkinson, ed., "Bugwere Historical Texts," Text 41; Cohen, ed., "Collected Texts of Busoga Traditional History," Text 917; Lloyd A. Fallers, *Bantu Bureaucracy: A Century of Political Evolution among the Basoga of Uganda*, 2nd ed. (Chicago: University of Chicago Press, 1965), 135.

[86] Cohen, ed., "Collected Texts of Busoga Traditional History," Text 125; Kagwa, *The Customs of the Baganda*, 95; Roscoe, *The Baganda*, 244–6; Schiller, "The Royal Women of Buganda," 459.

[87] Cohen, *The Historical Tradition of Busoga*, 14; Kagwa, *The Kings of Buganda*, 104; Schiller, "The Royal Women of Buganda," 460; Wrigley, *Kingship and State*, 190.

[88] Atkinson, ed., "Bugwere Historical Texts," Texts 11, 41, and 46; Cohen, ed., "Collected Texts of Busoga Traditional History," Texts 719, 759, and 917. Note that two texts are

kaidu of a North Nyanzan king could expect to become queen mother, whether through her son inheriting from his father or through the social construction of maternity. In other words, she was recognised as the mother of the king because of her position in the household and it was not necessary for her to be his biological mother.[89] The *kaidu* was able to wield some power: through her influence over the king as his senior wife, through her position as head of the royal household and her rank in the court, and through her anticipated power as the future queen mother.[90] Motherhood – social, ideological, and biological – was therefore at the heart of authority in North Nyanza; it helped to determine which son would succeed the king and granted political power to his mother.

THE ECONOMICS OF MOTHERHOOD IN NORTH NYANZA

Successful social and political reproduction require more than effective biological reproduction within moral codes; they also need economic production, particularly of food. The lands in which North Nyanzans and their descendants lived and worked ranged from swamps and lakesides to drier plateaus.[91] While drought was a perennial threat and medium-term climatic variation an ongoing challenge, agricultural crops tended to thrive in these areas of relatively high rainfall. During the time that North Nyanza was spoken, bananas became more important alongside the grain crops of sorghum and millet and the yams and legumes that supplemented these staples. North Nyanzans and their descendants associated a range of food procurement activities with healthy social reproduction and political centralisation. Their agricultural practices contributed to the nourishment and ritual well-being of social life and, in turn, their

labelled 917. James F. Cunningham, *Uganda and Its Peoples: Notes on the Protectorate of Uganda Especially the Anthropology of Its Indigenous Races* (London: Hutchinson, 1905), 125; Fallers, *Bantu Bureaucracy*, 83; Kagwa, *The Customs of the Baganda*, 67–8; Roscoe, *The Baganda*, 84; Schiller, "The Royal Women of Buganda," 469; GW-ETH-KAA-M-MY, interview, 2 December 2004, Bugwere.

[89] Atkinson, ed., "Bugwere Historical Texts," Text 41; Cohen, ed., "Collected Texts of Busoga Traditional History," Texts 670 and 917; Roscoe, *The Northern Bantu*, 200.

[90] Atkinson, ed., "Bugwere Historical Texts," Text 11; Cohen, *Womunafu's Bunafu*, 23–5; Kagwa, *The Customs of the Baganda*, 67–8; Roscoe, *The Baganda*, 84; Schiller, "The Royal Women of Buganda," 469.

[91] Schoenbrun, *A Green Place, A Good Place*, 165–6. See also Peter Robertshaw and David Taylor, "Climate Change and the Rise of Political Complexity in Western Uganda," *Journal of African History* 41, no. 1 (2000): 19–24. For palynological data see David Schoenbrun, "Treating an Interdisciplinary Allergy: Methodological Approaches to Pollen Studies for the Historian of Early Africa," *History in Africa* 18 (1991): 323–48.

moral and social constructs, including their ideology of motherhood, determined who performed various economic tasks, most important of which was food procurement.

The lands that became Buganda and Busoga are renowned for banana cultivation, and the move to intensive banana farming has frequently been used to explain the emergence of the Buganda kingdom and of gendered patterns of labour within it. There are clear limits to the usefulness of bananas as an explanatory tool; nonetheless, the increasing reliance on bananas as the primary staple crop had an impact. It both led to shifts in ideas about wealth during the time that proto-North Nyanza was spoken and, later, facilitated changes in the division of productive work. Tracing the growth in the importance of bananas to the North Nyanzan community and its descendants enables us to explore the ways in which the fruit came to be incorporated into the public performance of social reproduction. As we have seen, the comparative ethnographic evidence suggests that North Nyanzans started to use banana plants in practices surrounding the birth of infants. As bananas came to dominate the economic and physical landscape after the breakup of proto-North Nyanza, so they came to play a much greater role in the performative acts that marked the reproduction of the community.

Bananas (*Musa*, sp.) are not an indigenous species in Africa, and debates are ongoing about their antiquity in the Great Lakes region, and how they reached there from south Asia. Recent work suggests that people may have been cultivating bananas in these lands as early as the fourth millennium BCE, but the evidence on which this is based has been challenged.[92] What is clear is that significant further archaeobotanical

---

[92] B. Julius Lejju, Peter Robertshaw and David Taylor, "Africa's Earliest Bananas?" *Journal of Archaeological Science* 33, no. 1 (2006): 102–13. This is significantly earlier than the working hypothesis proposed by De Langhe et al., who argue that plantains were brought to Africa "more than three thousand years ago" and that they "would have entered the rainforest [of central Africa] at least 2000 years ago." Other banana varieties, however, arrived significantly later. E. De Langhe, R. Swennen and D. Vuylsteke, "Plantain in the Early Bantu World," *Azania* 29–30 (1994–1995): 152. The evidence and conclusions presented by Lejju et al. are challenged in Katharina Neumann and Elisabeth Hildebrand, "Early Bananas in Africa: The State of the Art," *Ethnobotany Research and Applications* 7 (2009): 353–62. A competing argument by Gerda Rossel sees plantains being introduced to the East African coast between the 4th century BCE and the 6th century CE. In which case, "the establishment of the plantain as a food crop in the area would probably not have taken place before the 8th century." The East African Highland banana (the most common beer banana) "arrived or spread later." The evidentiary basis for this argument is diverse, but relies heavily on written texts for the dating of the arrival of bananas in Africa. Gerda Rossel, *Taxonomic-Linguistic Study of Plantain in Africa* (Leiden, Netherlands: CNWS Publications, 1998), 220–1.

research is required before any firm conclusions can be drawn on their antiquity. While bananas may have been present in the region for several millennia, their systematic cultivation is certainly a more recent development. Speakers of West Nyanza in the early to mid-first millennium CE innovated a term for a bill-hook used to prune banana plants, suggesting that they were developing specialised skills arising from an increase in intensity of cultivation.[93] The highly diverse and intensive banana cultivation encountered by European travellers to the region in the late nineteenth and early twentieth centuries is likely to have developed less than a thousand years ago. Drawing on the "large number of completely unique terms for varieties of both AAA *Musa* (East African beer bananas, and by far the most numerous) and AAB *Musa*," in the various Great Lakes Bantu languages, Schoenbrun argues that the development of intensive banana farming began in the fifteenth or sixteenth century.[94] He does, nonetheless, recognise the possibility that near Lake Victoria–Nyanza the transition to such an agricultural system may be a few centuries older.[95] Christopher Wrigley, while noting the need for further research, argues that this development began "well into the millennium's second half," pointing to a royal decree by King Ssemakookiro of Buganda in the late eighteenth century regarding the maintenance of banana groves.[96] The vast number of banana varieties present in Buganda in the nineteenth and twentieth centuries and the detailed taxonomy that accompanied them do suggest that Buganda was unique among its neighbours as a centre of extensive innovation in banana cultivation.[97] At the same time, the linguistic evidence suggests that the move to intensive banana cultivation occurred somewhat earlier than previously posited.

Using the evidence then available, Schoenbrun reconstructed two proto-North Nyanza terms for cooking banana varieties: *-kono and *-wogolowa.[98] Drawing on new data, I have reconstructed five further terms: *-fuba [11], *-subi (cl. 7) [45], *-njaaya (cl. 6) [32], *mbwa-zirume (cl. 9) [7], and *-kago (cl. 9) [24]. Of these, one is a beer banana (*-subi), while *-fuba, *-njaaya, and *mbwazirume are varieties of

---

[93] David L. Schoenbrun, "Cattle Herds and Banana Gardens: The Historical Geography of the Western Great Lakes Region, ca AD 800–1500," *African Archaeological Review* 11, no. 1 (1993): 50.

[94] Schoenbrun, "Cattle Herds and Banana Gardens," 52.

[95] Schoenbrun, *A Green Place, A Good Place*, 82.

[96] C. C. Wrigley, "Bananas in Buganda," *Azania* 24 (1989): 69.

[97] It is possible to list well over 60 varieties. In addition there is a detailed Luganda taxonomy for the parts of the banana plant.

[98] Schoenbrun, "Cattle Herds and Banana Gardens," 71, table 3, root 42 and root 44.

cooking bananas. These are substantially fewer in number than the varieties later developed and named by Luganda speakers. All the same, they attest to the growing importance of banana farming in the economy of North Nyanzans. Most significantly, *-kago is a generic term for cooking bananas. "The development of taxonomies distinguishing generics reflects the increased importance of Musa as an item of both nutritional and social value."[99] This new evidence, then, suggests that the transition on the northwestern shores of Lake Victoria–Nyanza to an agricultural economy giving a substantial role to banana cultivation dates to the late first millennium.[100] The innovation by proto-North Nyanza speakers of two other terms related to banana cultivation further indicates the importance of bananas at this earlier time. North Nyanzans coined a new noun that specifically described a banana plantation (rather than another cultivated area): *-suku (cl. 11). In so doing they marked the land on which bananas were grown as distinct and as requiring its own label.[101] It is likely that this marking of land was connected with shifting notions of wealth and property as lineages and clans sought control over the most fertile plots. The second innovation was a verb for 'harvesting bananas': *-juunja.[102] The innovation of a specific verb for harvesting bananas as opposed to other crops both underlines the specific agricultural techniques needed to grow and harvest bananas and suggests the growing importance, social and economic, of bananas in North Nyanzan times.

North Nyanzans inherited knowledge of banana cultivation from their West Nyanza ancestors, but they expanded significantly on those skills and their application. By exploiting the suitability of the environment in which they lived for banana cultivation they were able to propagate new varieties of brewing and cooking bananas. The more varieties available to them, the less the risk posed by events such as disease on the banana plants.[103] Because North Nyanzans innovated new terms not only for

---

[99] Schoenbrun, "Cattle Herds and Banana Gardens," 51.

[100] The dating of banana agriculture would benefit greatly from further archaeological evidence, but the significant difficulties in conducting archaeological work in Buganda does not make this a very likely prospect. For a summary of these difficulties see, Andrew Reid, "Bananas and the Archaeology of Buganda," Antiquity 75, no. 290 (2001): 811–2.

[101] Schoenbrun, "Cattle Herds and Banana Gardens," 71, table 3, root 43.

[102] This verb has reflexes in Luganda and Lugwere clearly pointing to its innovation by speakers of proto-North Nyanza. Schoenbrun, "Early History in Eastern Africa's Great Lakes Region," 530, table 4.14 IIA.

[103] Research on the history of banana diseases and pests in the region would be invaluable in developing a deeper understanding of banana cultivation and place the current crisis of banana wilt in historical perspective.

banana varieties but also for a banana grove and for harvesting bananas, we can be confident about the increased importance of banana cultivation at this time. This growing emphasis on bananas in the agricultural economy must have led to more permanent settlements around the lands best suited to banana cultivation and increased competition for control of that land.[104] This in turn facilitated the development of small, politically centralised units ruled by royal families. Banana cultivation thus played a role in the development of political complexity in the region.[105]

Banana cultivation is frequently labelled women's work in the historical literature on the Great Lakes region, especially with reference to Buganda. This analysis is based on an argument that the maintenance of banana gardens required only light levels of labour – as opposed to the cultivation of yams, for example, where the soil must be dug each year – and so the work could be undertaken by women and children.[106] In addition, the preparation of food from bananas is also seen as requiring relatively light labour, in contrast to the pounding of yams or the grinding of millet. Because of the lighter labour requirement, argues Wrigley for Buganda, "women were able to take over nearly all the labour of food production apart from the clearance of land."[107] The comparative ethnographic evidence strongly indicates, however, that during the time that banana cultivation began to be practised more intensively by proto-North Nyanza speakers, it was not the work of women alone.[108] We should also be hesitant in labelling the work of banana cultivation, harvesting, and cooking as 'light,' even if we do so in relative terms.[109] One of the nouns that North Nyanzans innovated to describe a variety of cooking banana,

[104] Schoenbrun, *A Green Place, A Good Place*, 180–1.
[105] Jean-Pierre Chrétien, *The Great Lakes of Africa: Two Thousand Years of History*, trans. Scott Strauss (New York: Zone Books, 2003), 64; Hanson, *Landed Obligation*, 37; Conrad P. Kottak, "Ecological Variables in the Origin and Evolution of African States: The Buganda Example," *Comparative Studies in Society and History* 14, no. 3 (1972): 355–6; Médard, *Le royaume du Buganda au XIXᵉ siècle*, 63; Wrigley, *Kingship and State*, 234–6.
[106] Médard, *Le royaume du Buganda au XIXᵉ siècle*, 63. Médard argues that one woman could produce sufficient bananas to feed 10 people. Roscoe uses the number 3 or 4 men, which may approximate to 10 people, depending on his precise meaning. Roscoe, *The Baganda*, 431.
[107] Wrigley, *Kingship and State*, 60 (quote); Wrigley, "Bananas in Buganda," 64.
[108] Cunningham, *Uganda and Its Peoples*, 120; Roscoe, *The Bagesu and Other Tribes of the Uganda Protectorate*, 111; GW-ETH-IKI-F-MN, interview, 16 November 2004, Bugwere; GW-ETH-BUL-F-KJ, interview, 27 October 2004.
[109] "It is certainly not clear that bananas were as easily produced as has been suggested." Richard Reid, *Political Power in Pre-Colonial Buganda: Economy, Society and Warfare in the Nineteenth Century* (Oxford: James Currey, 2002), 25.

-fuba [11], may caution against such labelling, for this word is derived from the verb *-fuba*, meaning 'work hard, put out effort.'

Even though North Nyanzans increasingly emphasised bananas in their agriculture and diet, both millet (*Eleusine*) and sorghum continued to be important crops. We know from the linguistic record that these crops were cultivated in the Great Lakes region before speakers of Great Lakes Bantu lived there. Speakers of Central-Sudanic, Sog Eastern Sudanic, and Tale Southern Cushitic all cultivated either sorghum or millet or both.[110] By the time proto-North Nyanza was spoken, Great Lakes Bantu languages dominated the region's linguistic landscape. North Nyanzan communities and their descendants, however, constituted a northern borderlands area of profound multilingual interactions. Their interactions with people speaking other languages led to continued cross-cultural borrowings related to the cultural and economic aspects of food procurement.

Speakers of North Nyanza inherited from their West Nyanza–speaking ancestors a new term for 'dense porridge made of millet flour': *-(y)ita*.[111] In addition to its nutritional value, *-(y)ita* had a central cultural role in North Nyanzan life. The ceremonial eating of the first porridge from the newly harvested millet was an important ritual event that helped ensure the social reproduction of the community by guarding against future crop failure.[112] Sorghum too continued to be cultivated, although its primary function was in beer brewing. To that end, North Nyanzans retained *-weemba* but limited its meaning to 'millet or sorghum for brewing beer.'[113] This restriction of meaning does not imply a reduced importance, for the cultural and ritual value of *-lwa* (cl. 6) [30] or 'millet beer' would have been great – in marking important events, in prestations to chiefs and royalty, and in socialising. Indeed, the narrowing of meaning may have served to highlight the importance of brewing and drinking beer. Another North Nyanzan innovation was a noun for a granary raised on stilts: *-(y)agi* (cl. 7/8) [50]. Because rain fell throughout the year in the lands near Lake Victoria–Nyanza, farmers growing grain

---

[110] For a detailed discussion of early farming in the Great Lakes region, see David L. Schoenbrun, "We Are What We Eat: Ancient Agriculture between the Great Lakes," *Journal of African History* 34, no. 1 (1993): 9–22; Ehret, *An African Classical Age*, 88–92.

[111] Schoenbrun, "Early History in Eastern Africa's Great Lakes Region," 527, table 4.12, II.

[112] Atkinson, ed., "Bugwere Historical Texts," Texts 13, 44, 45, and 46; Roscoe, *The Northern Bantu*, 235.

[113] Schoenbrun, "Early History in Eastern Africa's Great Lakes Region," 530, table 4.14, IIA. *-weemba* is the proto-North Nyanza reflex of *-pémbá*.

crops that had to be stored from harvest to harvest needed to keep the grains clear of the ground to prevent destruction from excessive moisture. A *-(y)agi* (cl. 7/8) consisted of a large basket with a thatch roof raised on a tripod.[114] While North Nyanzans did shift towards greater cultivation of bananas, these innovations regarding grain crops demonstrate their ongoing importance – nutritionally and culturally – at the turn of the first millennium.

Economic diversity would have remained essential because bananas have a lower relative nutritional value than other staples, particularly millet. As the anthropologist Conrad Kottak has noted, the "caloric value of the banana is inferior per unit weight to that of wheat, rice, millet, maize, and the major grain staples of the world, and to manioc or cassava flour."[115] Where bananas make up the bulk of the diet, they must be supplemented by protein- and vitamin-rich foodstuffs such as meat, fish, and legumes. During the time that North Nyanza was spoken, both bananas and millet would have been consumed as staples. However, fish and meat were also important components of the diet, even if they may have been consumed less regularly than other foodstuffs. Many scholars view the work of hunting and fishing as entirely the realm of men. Other scholars have argued both that we should be hesitant to assume that hunting in the deep past was uniformly a male activity and that we should recognise that the English gloss 'hunting' covers a multiplicity of activities. The latter was surely the case for North Nyanzans. Different animals were hunted using different methods: some, such as elephants, were hunted by small groups of highly skilled men whereas others, such as small mammals, required the participation of large groups who corralled the quarry.[116] A wide range of methods were also applied in fishing, depending on the fish sought and the particular water environment.[117] North Nyanzan women performed certain types of fishing, particularly

---

[114] GW15-KAI-M-MPM, interview, 29 October 2004, Bugwere; GW-15-BUD-F-KH, interview, 15 November 2004, Bugwere; SO-15-BUG-F-KJ, interview, 22 January 2005, Busoga; SO-2-WAI-F-NH, interview, 8 March 2005, Busoga; SO-15-BUE-M-KR, interview, 10 March 2005, Busoga.

[115] Kottak, "Ecological Variables in the Origin and Evolution of African States," 356. In his analysis, in order to get the "minimum daily requirement of 55 grams of protein and 2,500 calories, one would have to consume 5.5 kilograms of bananas (for the protein) or 2 kilograms for the calories alone."

[116] Atkinson, ed., "Bugwere Historical Texts," Text 46; Kagwa, *The Customs of the Baganda*, 133; Roscoe, *The Baganda*, 445–51; Roscoe, *The Northern Bantu*, 238–40.

[117] Kagwa, *The Customs of the Baganda*, 149–51; Roscoe, *The Baganda*, 391–9; Roscoe, *The Bagesu and Other Tribes of the Uganda Protectorate*, 118; Roscoe, *The Northern Bantu*, 237–8.

in inland areas, but were, the comparative ethnographic record suggests, excluded from the chase. Trapping small animals, especially those that encroached on cultivated fields, was likely also an important means of adding protein to the North Nyanzan diet and may well have been performed by women.[118] Trapping would not have had the same prestige associated with it as hunting; as the historian Eugenia Herbert has noted, when "women kill small animals or children snare birds, it usually isn't even defined as hunting."[119] Despite this, trapping can be assumed to have been a more reliable method of food collection than hunting large prey.[120] The linguistic evidence for trapping, however, indicates little innovation by North Nyanza speakers and does not clearly point to the gendering of the practice.[121] Neither does the comparative ethnographic record tell us much in this regard. It is not possible, therefore, to make a definitive statement on who performed these tasks.

Whereas the potential for hunting and trapping would have varied according to local environments, fishing was a much more restricted practice. Yet, even quite far from Lakes Victoria–Nyanza and Kyoga, or from the smaller lakes such as Wamala and the major rivers, fish would have been an important part of the diet and of certain ritual events. North Nyanzans used proto-Bantu verbs to describe 'fishing,' *-vuba, and 'fishing with a line,' *-loba.[122] For speakers of North Nyanza and its descendant languages, fishing, like hunting, appears to have been divided into two main types. For some it was an activity that formed part of

---

[118] In the forest regions to the west of the Great Lakes, "Certain crops attracted certain animals: thus bushpigs love root crops and antelopes vegetable leaves. Such observations were used to tie trapping directly to farming. The fields were protected by traps especially [sic] designed for the major predators expected... Thus a yam field also produced bushpigs and beans produced antelopes." Vansina, *Paths in the Rainforests*, 90.

[119] Eugenia W. Herbert, *Iron, Gender, and Power: Rituals of Transformation in African Societies* (Bloomington: Indiana University Press, 1993), 165. This lack of prestige may well explain the lack of ethnographic evidence for the practice. Early ethnographers largely interviewed male informants and were themselves restricted by their own perceptions of prestigious behaviour and gendered activities.

[120] "Trapping achieved two things which hunting did not, in that it caught all sorts of animals which hunters did not get and it gave a much more regular supply with less expenditure of energy than hunting." Jan Vansina, *The Tio Kingdom of the Middle Congo: 1880–1892* (London: Oxford University Press for the International African Institute, 1973), 124, cited in Herbert, *Iron, Gender, and Power*, 165.

[121] Schoenbrun, *The Historical Reconstruction of Great Lakes Bantu Cultural Vocabulary*, 242–3, root 370; Vansina, *Paths in the Rainforests*, CE: 287, no. 48.

[122] The proto-Bantu forms are *-dùb- and *-dób-. Bastin and Schadeberg, "Bantu Lexical Reconstructions 3," ID main 1244 and ID main 1088 (Accessed 8 January 2013); Guthrie, *Comparative Bantu*, vol.3, 196, CS 731; 174, CS 638.

food procurement activities for the household and was performed mainly using special basket fish-traps. According to the comparative ethnographic record, women dominated this form of fishing and they practised it in nearby swamps. The second form of fishing was a specialised activity dominated by men who lived in villages on the lakeshores. The fish caught by specialist fishermen was dried and traded to communities further inland. The archaeological evidence on the flourishing of lakeshore communities around the turn of the first millennium suggests a viable lacustrine economy at the time proto-North Nyanza was spoken. Fish were also given in prestation to chiefs and royal families, helping to shore up emergent polities and establishing the importance of lakeside people in political centralisation.[123]

The procurement and consumption of food in North Nyanza was shaped by the environment in which North Nyanzans lived and the varieties of foodstuffs available to them. It was also shaped by cultural factors: which foods of those available were preferred, whose labour went into their acquisition, and the ways in which North Nyanzans understood them to interact with issues of fertility and social reproduction. While gender played a role in the organisation of economic activities, the evidence strongly suggests this was in less deterministic ways than historians have previously argued. Yet the intimate relationship between production and reproduction was of central importance. It affected the ways in which speakers of North Nyanza procured foodstuffs and luxury items and it structured the consumption of particular foods at key points in the life-cycle.

Social reproduction was, of course, essential to the viability of communities speaking proto-North Nyanza. They sought to regulate it through marriage, through taboos, and through ceremonies marking its various stages. Efforts to regulate social reproduction do not, however, appear to have centred on men controlling women's reproductive labour. Rather, women played active roles in the creation and maintenance of their marriages and the interlineal networks that they created through their maternity. These broader ideas about the role of motherhood in social organization were reflected in emerging polities and embodied in the royal families that came to dominate political leadership at this time. The North Nyanza ideology of motherhood was salient across society from elite politics to ordinary household economies.

[123] GW-15-KAI-M-MPM, interview, 17 November 2004, Bugwere; Roscoe, *The Baganda*, 391.

3

Consolidation and Adaptation

The Politics of Motherhood in Early Buganda and South Kyoga, Thirteenth through Fifteenth Centuries

The people who spoke proto-North Nyanza gradually built households and settlements further away from their ancestral lands. By the end of the twelfth century, their descendants had expanded across the region around the northwestern shores of Lake Victoria–Nyanza. As they did so they began to speak new languages: Luganda and proto-South Kyoga. Those who moved furthest east from the North Nyanza homeland, and who spoke South Kyoga, were again faced with the challenge of building sustainable communities in new environments. To those settling beyond the North Nyanza area the lands along the shoreline of the Victoria-Nyanza would have resembled their ancestral home, but further north the topography was less familiar. Instead of the marked distinctions between swampy valleys and fertile hills that were to be found around the lake, the interior landscape transitioned more gradually from ridge to valley. And in contrast to the relatively regular rainfall around the lake, in the north precipitation could fall heavily and violently, eroding the hillsides.[1] As South Kyoga speakers settled in these new lands, they reshaped their ideology of motherhood in order to create broad networks of mutual obligation and support in more uncertain surroundings.

Over time, as they built their homesteads across the landscape, the people who spoke North Nyanza changed the way they talked until after several generations they came to speak different dialects. Those dialects continued to change until they had diverged into separate languages. Change was not limited to language, however. The people speaking proto-South Kyoga instituted important shifts in their ideology of

[1] Cohen, *Womunafu's Bunafu*, 41.

74

motherhood and in how they mobilised that ideology in the organisation of their social, political, and economic lives. For the South Kyoga speech community, motherhood can be seen to have become increasingly social: it was about a woman's status in each of her natal, marital, and, ultimately, maternal homes. Elite motherhood, in particular, was as much a product of social contracts as it was the outcome of biological reproduction. Such social contracts became ever more important towards the end of the fifteenth century when the expanding and diversifying South Kyoga community came into increasing contact with people speaking unfamiliar Nilotic languages. At a time of expansion, these communities would have sought to bring new members into their households; networks of marriage and motherhood were the most effective way of doing so. In this eastern borderlands area, a new form of social motherhood served to facilitate contacts between people with different languages and cultures and to integrate newcomers into the South Kyoga communities.

In the lands closer to the North Nyanza heartland, where people spoke early-Luganda, expansion had different implications for its inhabitants. Here people did not have to deal with unfamiliar environments or new people; rather they faced the challenge of competition for control of the most productive and fertile plots. Living in what was a more linguistically and culturally homogeneous environment meant that the incorporation of newcomers was less of a priority and questions of lineage and legitimacy became more dominant. In these communities, biological constructions of motherhood started to emerge as the central ideology of reproduction. The people in what was becoming Buganda thus employed a very different construction of motherhood to address the particular challenges that they faced as they consolidated their communities and centralised political authority. Biological reproduction challenged social motherhood as households and lineages sought tighter controls on access to land and the distribution of wealth. Nonetheless, the older ideology of motherhood continued to hold significance, both in the new polities founded and reproduced in royal families and in kin governance.

During this period after the breakup of North Nyanza, then, we see the emergence of two distinct ideologies of motherhood. Speakers of South Kyoga made use of the flexibility of a social understanding of motherhood as they worked to establish their communities in unfamiliar terrain and, later, alongside unfamiliar people. While they inherited this from their ancestors who spoke North Nyanza, they remodelled it for their own ends, emphasising the need for certain women to be mothers, regardless of physiological processes. In early Buganda, it was precisely those physiological processes that came to dominate constructions of motherhood. In a context of consolidation and nascent struggles over the most productive land, biological descent grew in importance.

STATUS AND SOCIAL MOTHERHOOD IN SOUTH KYOGA AND EARLY BUGANDA

Just as in the North Nyanza–speaking community, a woman's maternity in both South Kyoga and early Ganda society was predicated on her social status, including her marital status and her status within her own kin group. But important differences emerged in the two communities about who could make claims to be a mother, especially in the face of biological or social impediments. These differences had implications for women's potential economic security in addition to the social status they could achieve through motherhood. If economic success was marked, as across sub-Saharan Africa, through 'wealth-in-people,' the phrase coined by Suzanne Miers and Igor Kopytoff "for the well-appreciated fact that interpersonal dependents of all kinds – wives, children, clients and slaves – were valued, sought and paid for at considerable expense in material terms in pre-colonial Africa," then economic failure was surely marked by its inverse.[2] This relationship between wealth and access to household labour was symbiotic. Without children or other dependents to help her cultivate her fields, a woman's chances of economic security were marginal, but without economic security both social motherhood and biological motherhood would have proved elusive.[3]

South Kyoga speakers built on the innovations of their North Nyanza–speaking ancestors with regard to their ideal forms of motherhood and the ways in which women could achieve status and influence as mothers. We have seen that North Nyanzans narrowed the meaning of the noun *-gólé* (cl. 1/2) [16] to 'bride' or 'newly wed woman' from its older reference to women who had achieved their maternal potential. At the same time, they innovated a new noun, *kaidu* (cl. 12) [19], to name the senior wife in a household. Acquiring the status of *kaidu* (cl. 12) helped a woman secure social motherhood, even if she did not have a

---

[2] Jane I. Guyer and Samuel M. Eno Belinga, "Wealth in People as Wealth in Knowledge: Accumulation and Composition in Equatorial Africa," *Journal of African History* 36, no. 1 (1995): 92 (quote). See also Suzanne Miers and Igor Kopytoff, eds., *Slavery in Africa: Historical and Anthropological Perspectives* (Madison: University of Wisconsin Press, 1977).

[3] See also, Stephens, "Birthing Wealth?"

biological son to be heir to his father. This situation was significantly strengthened in South Kyogan households, where the practice of fostering children continued to be an option for otherwise childless women. In South Kyoga, as in North Nyanza, the ideal inheritance passed from the male head of household to a son of his *kaidu (cl. 12) – in chiefly and royal households as well as in commoner or *-kopí (cl. 1/2) [28] ones. This would have been the ideal and presumably not followed in all cases since succession was fundamentally a political event and there was the possibility of collateral succession. There were, however, processes in place to ensure the social motherhood of South Kyoga *kaidu (cl. 12) who were not biological mothers. These processes centred on fostering and adoption. Speakers of South Kyoga stopped using the North Nyanza verb *-werèka [49] to describe the act of giving a child to be fostered; instead they used the general verbs *-wâ [48], meaning 'give,' and *-gábá [14], meaning 'distribute.'

The innovation of a new South Kyoga verb for fostering-in a child, however, gives us the most insight into these acts: *-píítá [38] referred to the fostering of both children and calves. Speakers of South Kyoga borrowed it from their neighbours speaking Nilotic languages. This loan becomes evident when we trace the distribution of this verb in the languages descended from those spoken at the same time as South Kyoga. The Southern Luo branch of Nilotic languages has the following range of meanings for the root verb: in Dholuo *pidho* (tr.) glosses as "foster," while in Acholi *pitto* (tr.) holds the meanings "rear, breed cattle; feeding children, nourishing baby, bringing up children."[4] And in Ateso, from the Teso-Turkana branch of Nilotic languages, *ai-pit* glosses as "breed; rear."[5] Christopher Ehret has reconstructed the root *pīt to proto-Nilo-Saharan with the meaning "to rise."[6] The antiquity of this verb in the Nilo-Saharan language phylum demonstrates that the direction of borrowing must have been from the Nilotic languages to the Great Lakes Bantu languages and not the inverse. The verb *-píítá has reflexes in Lugwere and Lusoga, but not, as far it has been possible to ascertain, in Rushana.

---

[4] Asenath Bole Odaga, *English-Dholuo Dictionary* (Kisumu, Kenya: Lake Publishers & Enterprises, 1997), 75; Alexander Odonga, *Lwo-English Dictionary* (Kampala: Fountain Publishers, 2005), 217.

[5] J. H. Hilders and J. C. D. Lawrance, *An English-Ateso and Ateso-English Vocabulary* (Nairobi: Eagle Press, 1958), 51.

[6] Christopher Ehret, *A Historical-Comparative Reconstruction of Nilo-Saharan* (Cologne: Rüdiger Köppe Verlag, 2001), 384–5, no. 581. Please note that the 't' is a dental, voiceless, plosive rather than the English alveolar, voiceless, plosive.

South Kyoga speakers' ancestral speech community, North Nyanza, had its own words to describe processes of fostering, as we have seen. That speakers of South Kyoga borrowed and adapted this new verb – *-píítá* – therefore suggests two things: first, that there was a change in the meaning or practice of fostering and, second, that fostering occurred cross-culturally between the South Kyoga speech community and Nilotic-speaking groups. With regards to the latter point, while not surprising, it is worth emphasising that interactions between Bantu and Nilo-Saharan speech communities are both long-standing in this region and extended well beyond the domain of politics and the palace to which they are frequently relegated by scholars.[7] This was a borderlands area inhabited by people speaking South Kyoga and other Great Lakes Bantu languages of the Luhyia subgroup as well as people speaking completely unrelated Nilotic languages, with all the rich linguistic and cultural diversity this suggests. Both the Nilotic and the Great Lakes Bantu speech communities in this area followed exogamous marriage practices. As a result, a significant proportion of households are likely to have been composed both of people speaking proto-South Kyoga and Southern Luo or Teso-Turkana languages. As women married into Bantu-speaking households, they brought their language with them. From the ethnographic record, we know that when women fostered children into their husbands' households they tended to foster children from their natal kin groups.[8] A Nilotic-speaking woman in a Bantu-speaking household thus would likely have turned to her Nilotic-speaking kin should she want to foster a child. This helps us make sense of why a Nilotic term came to be used to describe the practice of fostering-in. That the term was adopted by proto-South Kyoga speakers and has undergone what appear to be regular phonological changes (such as vowel lengthening) also suggests that such interlinguistic marriages were reasonably common.

An important feature of *-píítá* in proto-South Kyoga is that it referred to both the fostering-in of children and the 'fostering-in' of calves. As is

---

[7] For more recent such contacts see David William Cohen, "The Cultural Topography of a 'Bantu Borderland': Busoga, 1500–1850," *Journal of African History* 29, no. 1 (1988): 57–79; David William Cohen, "The Face of Contact: A Model of a Cultural and Linguistic Frontier in Early Eastern Uganda," in *Nilotic Studies: Proceedings of the International Symposium on Languages and History of the Nilotic Peoples, Cologne, January 4–6, 1982*, part II, ed. Rainer Vossen, and Marianne Bechhaus-Gerst (Berlin: Dietrich Reimer Verlag, 1983), 339–55.

[8] Roscoe, *The Northern Bantu*, 200; GW-ETH-BUL-F-KJ, interview, 27 October 2004, Bugwere; GW-ETH-IKI-F-MN, interview, 16 November 2004, Bugwere; SO-ETH-NAU-F-ME, interview, 21 January 2005, Busoga; SO-15-BUG-F-KJ, interview, 20 January 2005.

clear from the reflexes in the Southern Luo languages and in Ateso, this was an existing feature of the verb when speakers of South Kyoga borrowed it.[9] The association of *-piítá* with both the fostering of children and of calves indicates that this type of fostering may well have involved the creation of relationships of obligation, in the same way that the giving of young livestock created such relationships among North Nyanza peoples.[10] The kind of fostering described by *-piítá* would thus have been less about caring for needy children than it was about creating social relationships between families and lineages. When a senior wife in the South Kyoga speech community fostered a child into her husband's household this served two important purposes. First, if she were childless, or rather more crucially son-less, the fostering-in of another child enabled her to maintain her social position as *kaidu* (cl. 12) [19] by making it possible for her to be the mother of the heir in her widowhood.[11] Second, and the two are closely related, it meant that a senior wife could shore up her status within the household through social motherhood. It seems most likely this new verb, *-piítá*, referred to the fostering-in of children by senior wives unable to fulfil their maternal potential through biological means. As the role of *kaidu* became more important in South Kyoga, particularly with reference to a senior wife's social motherhood, fostering in this specific context became more clearly defined through this new verb.

At the same time, however, the kind of fostering that involved taking in orphans or children with no other kin to care for them also existed. South Kyoga speakers extended the meaning of an existing verb *-yámbá* ('help') to create a second verb describing the act of fostering-in. That this referred to a form of fostering involving the care of those without kin is suggested both by its etymology and the later Lusoga noun *katééyámba* or 'orphan.' Importantly, *-yámbá* [51] applied only to human children. This further indicates that it was used in reference to situations in which the care of children was the focus, rather than the establishment of relationships of obligation or the fulfilment of the social position of senior

---

[9] Parker Shipton, however, notes that in contemporary Luoland the same word is not used to describe the fostering of children and entrustment of livestock: "It is not polite in East Africa to compare human beings to animals too explicitly without explanation." Shipton, *The Nature of Entrustment*, 83.

[10] Roscoe describes Baganda chiefs creating relationships of clientship with peasants through goats. Roscoe, *The Baganda*, 422. Cohen describes how patron–client relationships worked (and failed) in Busoga. Cohen, *Womunafu's Bunafu*, 80–1.

[11] On son-infertility in a modern African context, see Amal Hassan Fadlalla, *Embodying Honor: Fertility, Foreignness, and Regeneration in Eastern Sudan* (Madison: University of Wisconsin Press, 2007).

wife. As such it was a pragmatic approach to ensure the survival of orphaned or abandoned children, rather than a means of enabling social motherhood. The use of two etymologically and phonologically very different verbs strongly indicates that speakers of South Kyoga viewed these two forms of fostering as distinct.

In contrast to the innovation in vocabulary around child-fostering by speakers of South Kyoga, early Luganda speakers were quite conservative in this semantic field. They maintained both the North Nyanza verb **-werèka* [49] to describe the act of fostering a child out and the North Nyanza verb **-fúúra* [12] to talk about fostering a child in. At the same time, Luganda speakers stressed the temporary nature of fostering. This is reflected in the proverb: *Mperese: efa waaboyo mirembe* ('If a foster child dies at home there will be peace [but if she or he dies at the foster home there will not]').[12] Thus, the birth parents of a child fostered-out retained a strong interest in the child and her or his well-being. While they may have been conservative in the language they used to talk about fostering, Luganda speakers significantly changed the nature and meaning of fostering. Most strikingly, fostering was not a means of achieving social motherhood. It did, however, work to shore up the interlineal networks formed through mothers. These changes mirrored the different histories of South Kyogans and Baganda after the twelfth century, in particular their approaches to the social institution of motherhood. By the late nineteenth century, noted the missionary and ethnographer John Roscoe, "No woman could receive the guardianship of a child; she might, indeed, nurse and tend a small child, cook for it, and in a general way watch over it, but she could not take it away from the father's relations, and it was these latter who were directly responsible to the clan for its care."[13]

It is very difficult to date the timing of these changes, but they were widespread and apparently deeply embedded in Ganda society in the nineteenth century. It is significant that at least one type of fostering – that done by maternal uncles – formed part of the Ganda origin charter, the story of Kintu and Nnambi. In this narrative, Walumbe, Nnambi's brother, lay claim to some of Kintu and Nnambi's children as his 'share' or *èndóbòló* by virtue of being their maternal uncle. When Kintu refused him, Walumbe ('Death') vowed to kill the children, thereby introducing

[12] Le Veux, *Premier essai de vocabulaire luganda – français d'après l'ordre étymologique*, 1025*, under the entry for *-wereka*; Ferdinand Walser, *Luganda Proverbs* (Berlin: Reimer Verlag, 1982), 252, no. 2798. My translation.
[13] Roscoe, *The Baganda*, 12.

death to the Baganda.[14] In the Luganda speech community, fostering shifted away from enabling the motherhood of senior wives and instead centred on both patrilineal and matrifocal networks. Women who were not biological mothers could not adopt a child in order to become social mothers in the way that their South Kyoga–speaking neighbours could. Instead, the people who fostered were paternal aunts (*bassenga*), maternal uncles (*bakòjjâ*), and grandparents. Children were also sent to the households of chiefs and to the royal palaces as dependents.[15] In spite of Roscoe's statement that "no woman could receive the guardianship of a child," it is clear that women could foster children; they could not, however, acquire the status of mother by so doing, even if they acted as guardians. That is, a paternal aunt who fostered her brother's child remained a *ssenga*, rather than becoming that child's mother. This tension is captured in folk literature through the proverb, *Omwana tabukutira mu nda bbiri* ('A child does not rumble in two bellies'), that is, a child is not born of two wombs.[16]

The change in fostering from enabling social motherhood to marking kin networks through *bassenga* and *bakòjjâ* co-occurred with a change in inheritance patterns. Among Baganda, the son of any wife could be selected as heir, whether to a king, a chief, or a commoner (*òmùkopí*).[17] This shift had important consequences for the selection of a new king, queen mother, and queen sister. It also had contradictory consequences for wives in the polygynous households of wealthy men and chiefs. While this change in inheritance preference meant that wives of lowly backgrounds had a chance at becoming the mother of the heir and acquiring the influence within the household that this brought, it emphasised biological, rather than social, motherhood. The success of individual women in acts of biological reproduction determined their potential to be the mother of the heir, not their social position within the household. It is not clear whether this change originated in commoner households or in the royal household, but it would have served to free the royal family to adjust its choice of preferred heir according to the changing fortunes of the clans of the royal wives.

---

[14] Le Veux, *Manuel de langue luganda comprenant la grammaire et un recueil de contes et de légendes*, 456.

[15] Mair, *An African People in the Twentieth Century*, 59–64; Roscoe, *The Baganda*, 76.

[16] Ferdinand Walser, *Luganda Proverbs*, 397, no. 4441. Note that this is my translation, which differs significantly from the one provided by Walser.

[17] There was also the possibility of fraternal or collateral succession, but the relevant point here is that when a son succeeded his father he could have been born to any of his father's wives.

So while motherhood held the potential of social mobility and future economic security for some Baganda women, there were two crucial constraints. One was that there was only one heir, and in a polygynous household such mobility was afforded to only one among the wives. The second was that the recognition of biological reproduction over social motherhood severely limited the present and future prospects of women who suffered infertility or the death of their children. The move away from fostering as a mechanism for enabling motherhood reinforced this, and barrenness (*obugumba*) in a woman came to be closely associated with poverty.[18] The associations among barren women, poverty, and social disdain are clear in Luganda proverbs. For example, *Ekisa ky'omugumba: kijja emmere eggwawo* ('The generosity of a barren woman: comes when the food is nearly finished'). The Mill Hill missionary who collated the proverbs, Ferdinand Walser, explicated this as meaning that a barren woman "eats her fill and only then remembers others."[19] A mother, the proverb implies, would always feed her children first. The sharpness of the proverb for any *omugúmba* who heard it must surely have been intensified through the second meaning of *ekisá*: labour pains. Similarly dismissive of infertile women is the proverb: *Nnantaganyula: ng'omunafu omugumba* ('A useless person: like a barren, lazy woman').[20] And the association between infertility and poverty for women is explicit in the Luganda noun `*ngujuubà* (cl. 9), which primarily means either a 'carefree, irresponsible person' or a 'completely destitute person,' but was also used to refer to a 'woman without children.'[21] This usage can be seen in the proverb, *Ngujuuba: bw'agabega bw'agalya* ('A woman without children: what she dishes up, she eats').[22] Individual Baganda women's

---

[18] Jan Kuhanen, *Poverty, Health and Reproduction in Early Colonial Uganda*, University of Joensuu Publications in the Humanities 37 (Joensuu, Finland: University of Eastern Finland Electronic Publications, 2005) http://urn.fi/URN:ISBN:952-458-898-6/ (Accessed 9 January 2013), 34.

[19] Walser, *Luganda Proverbs*, 124, no. 1364. Note that this is my translation, which differs from that given by Walser. Cited in Kuhanen, *Poverty, Health and Reproduction in Early Colonial Uganda*, 34, fn. 95. Walser was born in Austria and worked as a Mill Hill Father in Uganda between 1923 and 1959. See Robert O'Neil, *Mission to the Upper Nile: The Story of St Joseph's Missionary Society of Mill Hill in Uganda* (London: Mission Book Service, 1999), 232.

[20] Walser, *Luganda Proverbs*, 294, no. 3272. My translation, which differs slightly from Walser's.

[21] Snoxall, *Luganda-English Dictionary*, 240.

[22] Le Veux, *Manuel de langue luganda comprenant la grammaire et un recueil de contes de de légendes*, 354. Cited in Walser, *Luganda Proverbs*, 279, no. 3112. Again the literal translation is mine and differs from Walser's.

social status suffered significantly in the face of infertility. Dating such a development is of course almost impossible, but in the broader context of the other changes set out in this chapter we can assume it to have occurred well before proverbs like these were first written down in the nineteenth century.

Although we have no way of knowing the precise extent of infertility or infant mortality rates in Uganda between the twelfth and sixteenth centuries, it is possible to make some educated assumptions on the basis of much more modern evidence. In 1948, 40 percent of Baganda children died before the age of puberty. Shane Doyle argues that it is likely that pre-colonial child mortality would have been substantially higher. But even if we assume that child mortality in this earlier period was only 50 percent, statistically this would have left one in four women who had two live births with no living children.[23] For a childless woman, the consequences for her old age (should she live that long) would have been the same regardless of whether her children died in infancy or she failed to deliver any children. What mattered was keeping those infants alive into adulthood. Any woman who failed in this endeavour faced a poverty-stricken life, most especially if she outlived her husband.

The historian Henri Médard has written about the social, as well as biological, reasons for low total fertility rates in Buganda. He highlights two factors. The first was the practice of delaying recognition of children as belonging to their father's clan until the completion of a ceremony that established their legitimacy. The second was the very common practice in Buganda of children being raised by people other than their parents. Médard also argues that commoner women in Buganda may have emulated the low fertility of aristocratic women in a context where princesses were not permitted to become mothers and where royal wives, who numbered in the tens, hundreds, and even thousands, rarely had large numbers of children.[24] Other reasons may also have shaped women's decisions to limit the number of children they had. Success in motherhood rested on being the mother of the heir, and as such, a woman's ability to convert motherhood into instrumental power required political skills to garner the support of interested parties in her son's claim. The dominant ideology of motherhood did not reward women for having large numbers of children; it rewarded them for the success of one particular child. In this

---

[23] Uganda Protectorate, Annual Medical Report 1953 (Entebbe, 1954); pers. comm. Shane Doyle. I am grateful to Shane Doyle of the University of Leeds for sharing both the original information and this analysis with me.

[24] Médard, *Le royaume de Buganda au XIXe siècle*, 81.

context there was less reason for women to undergo repeatedly the serious risks of pregnancy and childbirth and more reason to limit the number of children they had in order to nurture them to adulthood and generate the maximum political advantage for one amongst them. Baganda named a specific disease that affected a child, causing her to weaken, if her mother fell pregnant while she was still nursing. This was *omusánà* and it suggests that Baganda recognised a connection between birth-spacing and reduced infant and child mortality.[25]

SHIFTING RELATIONS OF MARRIAGE AND MOTHERHOOD

As the South Kyoga speech community established itself across the Nile from the North Nyanzan heartland, marriage and the social networks and social contracts it created remained a central part of building social stability. As such, the ideal form of marriage strongly resembled that of North Nyanzan times, although there were undoubtedly changes in the details. But speakers of proto-South Kyoga do not appear to have changed the language they used to talk about marriage and the relationships it created. Bridewealth was given by the man's lineage and clan to the woman's, in an act called *-*kwa* (tr.) [29], and this created networks of social and economic obligation between in-laws or *-*ko* (cl. 1/2) [26]. South Kyogans also saw women as active participants in marriage and used the North Nyanza verb *-*bayira* [3] to describe a woman's act of marrying. South Kyoga brides also took a companion or *-*perekezi* (cl. 1a) [36] with them to their marital homes who would have helped them with the work of establishing new gardens, as had done their North Nyanzan mothers. Should the need arise these companions could also be called

---

[25] Jennifer Tappan discusses this with reference to modern Buganda and notes that a Ugandan doctor she interviewed in 2004 made the argument that monogamy had decreased birth spacing as each household sought nonetheless to have large numbers of children. See Tappan, "'A Healthy Children Comes From A Healthy Mother': Mwanamugimu and Nutritional Science in Uganda, 1935–1973" (PhD diss., Columbia University, 2010), 68–75. Modern studies suggest that infant and child mortality may decrease by 8 percent if women have fewer than four children and that birth spacing of at least two years may reduce infant mortality by 10 percent and child mortality by 21 percent. See James Trussell and Anne R. Pebley, "The Potential Impact of Changes in Fertility on Infant, Child, and Maternal Mortality," *Studies in Family Planning* 15, no. 6 (1984): 267–80. It is, however, very difficult to measure the precise impact of a reduction in the fertility rate on infant and child survival because it does not occur in isolation of other factors, such as socioeconomic change. See John Bongaarts, "Does Family Planning Reduce Infant Mortality Rates?" *Population and Development Review* 13, no. 2 (1987): 323–34.

upon to enable the social motherhood of a wife. As we saw in Chapter 2, a *-perekezi* might be obliged to give her children to the bride she accompanied should the latter fail to have her own biological children. It is not likely that all marriages followed the social ideal. Nonetheless, South Kyogans did not innovate new words to talk about elopement, but rather continued to use the terms of their North Nyanza–speaking ancestors. This apparent conservatism with regards to the language of marriage and elopement contrasts with the situation in the Luganda speech community to the west.

Luganda speakers developed a new vocabulary to talk about marriage; nonetheless they retained some North Nyanza terms. There were also important continuities in meaning and form, alongside the innovations. Bridewealth remained a central and essential component of marriage. Again, this is not to suggest that bridewealth was transferred for every relationship that resembled marriage, but that the ideal form of marriage was established through bridewealth. Baganda innovated various new words to describe the bridewealth itself. The most common of these new terms were *òmwandù* (cl. 3) and *òmùtwâlo* (cl. 3). The term *òmwandu* is the older and etymologically richer of the two. Schoenbrun has reconstructed it to Great Lakes Bantu in the form *-jàandu* (cl. 3/4), with the gloss 'wealth, property (often reckoned in women or concerning the transfer of women).' In North Nyanza the meaning of *-jàandu* was extended to include widows who could be inherited by their deceased husband's heir.[26] By the late nineteenth century, the most important meanings for *òmwandu* in Luganda were 'royal store for loot; loot of women, slaves and goods; harem; and wealth.'[27] The primary meanings of *òmùtwâlo* are 'load (of cowry shells); ten thousand,' and it is derived from the verb *-twâla*, 'take; carry.'[28] The ethnographic record shows that by the nineteenth century, at least, bridewealth in Buganda was in large part paid in the form of cowries.[29] Both these nouns and the payment in cowries rather than livestock suggest a change in the meaning of bridewealth and in the role and perception of women in marriage.

[26] David Schoenbrun, personal communication, August 2007.
[27] Le Veux, *Premier essai de vocabulaire luganda – français d'après l'ordre étymologique*, 12.
[28] Snoxall, *Luganda-English Dictionary*, 228, 323.
[29] Père Le Veux, "Au temps jadis: Le mariage des Baganda (au Victoria Nyanza)," Archives of the Kampala Archdiocese, Rubaga, Uganda; Mair, *An African People in the Twentieth Century*, 135–6.

Overall these changes proved negative for women's social position. The North Nyanza verb *-kwa (v.tr.) [29] had strong semantic associations with the relationships created through the giving of bridewealth, namely relationships 'in-law' or *-ko (cl. 14) [26]. The move by Baganda to instead use the noun òmwandu to describe bridewealth suggests a change in emphasis in the role of marriage from creating new social networks (through in-law relations and the matrilateral connections to the children born into it) to one in which wives were acquired by men primarily as markers of social status. The adoption of òmùtwâlo as an alternative noun for bridewealth and payments in the form of cowry shells indicate that women's active participation in their marriages was reduced. Whereas the giving of livestock symbolised the reproductive function of marriage, cowry shells marked it more as a financial transaction. This shift was undoubtedly a gradual process, with cowries, especially in the tens of thousands, an innovation of the eighteenth century at the earliest and most likely a product of the extensive engagement in the long-distance trade that expanded rapidly in the nineteenth century. However, as explored later in this section, other evidence pointing to a growing emphasis on patrilineal ties over all others suggests that this change in women's roles in marriage pre-dates the eighteenth century and was connected to efforts to retain control over land, especially as banana cultivation became an ever more significant economic activity. The raiding expeditions by Ganda armies of the late eighteenth and nineteenth centuries, as we see in Chapters 4 and 5, and the importation of vast numbers of women captives into Buganda led to a more pronounced devaluation of the role of women in social networks created through their marriages and their maternity.[30]

There is a wealth of Luganda words to talk about marrying, marriage, and married people, and their etymologies indicate that their innovation was symptomatic of growing restrictions on women over the long term. Some of these – such as -wáyírá and -wásá – were inherited from North Nyanza. Others were innovated by Luganda speakers. Among these innovations were a set of related words all derived from the proto-Bantu verb *-tùmb- (tr.), 'burn; roast, boil' and that has the form –fúmbá, 'cook, boil' in Luganda: -fúmbírwá (intr.), 'marry (of a woman)'; -fúmbízá (tr.), 'cause to espouse, marry'; obufúmbó (cl. 14), 'the marriage state'; and

---

[30] On these raids, see Reid, Political Power in Pre-Colonial Buganda, 116–23; and for the impact on women's social status in particular, see Wrigley, Kingship and State, 176–7, 236.

omufúmbó (cl. 1/2), 'married person.'[31] Taken by themselves, we would be hard-pressed to make an argument about changes in marriage from the derivation of these terms from the verb 'cook.' When they are placed in the context of the more pronounced division of labour along gender lines in Buganda set out in the next section and other changes we have already seen, the direct association between cooking and marriage further suggests a narrowing of women's social roles. The etymology of these verbs is not, however, altogether straightforward. The verb *–fumbírwá*, 'marry (of a woman),' is the passive, dative (or applicative) form of *-fúmbá*. That is, a literal translation would be 'to be cooked for.' So while women's marriages are semantically associated with cooking in Luganda, the verb 'marry (of a woman)' does not suggest that men married women so that they would cook. As with the North Nyanzan noun *-rya* (cl. 5/6) [39], 'marriage' or 'married state' (applied to a woman), there is an implication that marriage was understood as a social institution in which women ate. However, *-fumbírwá* has the particular implication that a wife who entered into this form of marriage benefited from the assistance of lower-status people in the household who cooked for her. Those people may have been poor dependents, slaves, or wives of lower rank.

Baganda had several words to describe different kinds of 'marriage,' only very few of which constituted what the White Fathers missionary Julien Gorju referred to as *"le mariage proprement dit"* ('proper marriage').[32] A woman who entered a relationship with a man through the processes described by the verbs *-wayira*, *-fumbirwa*, *-wasibwa*, and *-ogerezwa* became an *omuwase*, 'wife'; those who entered a relationship with a man through the other processes were labelled differently and had a lower status in the marital household. For example, a woman who was given by her father, brother, or master to a client in return for his labour (*-wumirizibwa*) was known as an *òmùwumirizè*.[33] The verb

---

[31] Bastin and Schadeberg, "Bantu Lexical Reconstructions 3," ID main 3113 (Accessed 9 January 2013); Snoxall, *Luganda-English Dictionary*, 78–9. While some or all of these words are found today in Lusoga, Lugwere and Rushana, they are recent areal spreads: their reflexes have not undergone the relevant sound changes. This makes sense because Christian missionaries, who were located first in Buganda and used a Luganda translation of the Bible in Busoga and Bugwere, adopted these words to exclusively describe Christian marriage.

[32] Gorju, *Entre le Victoria l'Albert et l'Edouard*, 303. Gorju was born in Brittany, France, and served as a priest for the Missionaire de l'Afrique (Pères Blancs) between 1892 and 1922, when he was ordained as a bishop and served as Vicar Apostolic of Urundi until 1936.

[33] Audrey Richards, "Field notes, 16.VI.54 (Mawokola)," file 6/2, 13, Audrey Isabel Richards Collection, London School of Economics Archives.

-wumirizibwa also applied to the process of a father giving a woman to his pubescent son as a "second order wife" until he made his own choice about who to marry formally. Père Le Veux explicitly sets out the social distinction between these kinds of marriage when he notes, "in common opinion, these 'waiting' or 'fortune' unions, did not result in *'justae nuptiae'*, real marriage, free and firm; and the wife [*compagne*] *'muwâse'* was counterposed by – the *muwumîrize*, the *mugule*, the *munyage*, the *nvuma*, the *ndobolo*, the *musikire*, etc."[34] We can safely assume that relationships in which the woman was described as *mugule*, 'the bought one'; *munyage*, 'the seized one'; and *nvuma* (low ranked female slave) either emerged or became dramatically more common after the inception of the Ganda expansionary wars in the early eighteenth century. On the other hand, relationships in which the woman was described as *ndobolo*, 'the share'; *muwumîrize*; *èndola* (woman given for labour); and *musikire*, 'the inherited one' were most likely of greater antiquity, fitting as they did into earlier social practices.[35]

There was, then, a shift in the role and meaning of marriage in Buganda away from using it to create social networks through women's maternity. All the same, it was not a clean break between two discrete models. The changes in bridewealth and in the vocabulary for marriage are markers of this shift, but other evidence points to continuities with older traditions inherited from North Nyanzans that centred on the role of mothers in their daughters' marriages. One of these continuities was the practice of giving a specific gift to the mother of the bride known as *akasíímó* (cl. 12/14) in Luganda. As in proto-North Nyanza there was a strong ongoing semantic association with the verb *-síímá* (tr.) 'be pleased with, approve,' from which it was originally derived.[36] By the nineteenth century, as with the bridewealth, this gift was generally paid in cowries, although anthropologist Lucy Mair's informants in the early twentieth century reported that the *akasíímó* included clothing in recognition of the taboo of avoidance that existed between mother and son-in-law.[37] The role of the mother in making new alliances between patrilineages possible continued to be recognised in Buganda, despite the changes to marriage.

---

[34] Le Veux, *Premier essai de vocabulaire luganda – français d'après l'ordre étymologique*, 1054*, fn. 1, under the entry for *-wumiriza*. My translation. One person interviewed by Audrey Richards in 1954 noted that: "Kuwumiriza marriage was a bad custom because if the girl refused to marry the man she was forced to and beaten and if she persisted her ears were cut off." Richards, "Field notes, 16.VI.54 (Mawokola)," 16.

[35] Snoxall, *Luganda-English Dictionary*, 238.

[36] Snoxall, *Luganda-English Dictionary*, 285.

[37] Roscoe, *The Baganda*, 89; Mair, *An African People in the Twentieth Century*, 82.

As well as receiving the *akasíímó*, Baganda mothers were prominent in the preparations and rites of marriage. The bride's mother, for example, was the one to wash her before she left her prenuptial seclusion.[38] It was also the bride's mother who performed the cleansing rite known as *kùkuzà* with the bride's father both immediately after the bride left her parental home and on her first return visit with her husband. Mair noted that historically, "only her actual parents could do this, and to this day if the mother has left her husband she is expressly fetched back for it."[39] In order to perform *kùkuzà*, a man stepped over the outstretched legs of his wife, an act that symbolised sexual intercourse.[40] The act of *kùkuzà* was performed in several other contexts, including some related to fishing and hunting practices, and marked moments of both danger and creation. In the context of a daughter's marriage, it marked the creation of a new set of relationships between the bride's parents and their lineages and clans and the parents, lineage, and clan of their son-in-law. The preference that the biological mother of the bride be the one to perform *kùkuzà* reflects the broader shift amongst Baganda to an emphasis on biological rather than social motherhood, a shift that we saw earlier with reference to practices of fostering. At the same time, however, the rite points to a continued recognition of the importance of mothers in connecting their natal kin, their children, and their daughters' marital kin. It also points to Cohen's argument about the enduring nature of *obukô* or in-law relationships after the failure of marriage if children had been born.[41] The mother of the bride remained the central nexus of those relationships and so she was the one to perform the rite because her daughter's marriage created a new layer of *obukô* relations. Indeed, Le Veux asserted that should an unmarried young woman fall pregnant, her birth mother had to be present at the ceremonies to lift the taboo that prevented her from eating with her parents and kin. "If the mother has deserted the conjugal residence, it is necessary to fetch her. If she is dead, they call for her replacement (*omusika* [lit. heir]) or the mistress of the house."[42] Thus even if the new layer of relations were being created through the violation

---

[38] Mair, *An African People in the Twentieth Century*, 84.

[39] Mair, *An African People in the Twentieth Century*, 88–9, quote p. 89.

[40] Mair, *An African People in the Twentieth Century*, 247–8; Roscoe, *The Baganda*, 357, fn. 1.

[41] Cohen, *Womunafu's Bunafu*, 99. See Chapter 2.

[42] "Si la mère a déserté le domicile conjugal, il la faut aller quérir. Si elle est morte, on requiert sa remplaçante (*omusika*) ou la maîtresse de maison." Le Veux, *Premier essai de vocabulaire luganda – français d'après l'ordre étymologique*, 1019*, under the entry for *-wémuka*. My translation.

of social norms, the birth mother or her heir was required to attend the ceremonies to assuage the damage caused by such violation.

The final continuity in marriage between North Nyanza and Buganda that is relevant here is the existence and role of the *empérékézê* (cl. 9) or 'companion' to the bride. In North Nyanza, the **-perekezi* (cl. 1a) [36] both supported the bride in the transition to married life and offered the possibility of social motherhood should biological reproduction be unsuccessful. In Buganda, the latter role fell away with the move away from fostering as a means of achieving motherhood. The former role, by contrast, remained an important part of the marriage process. "One young girl, who was decorated, with ornaments and well-dressed, went with the bride; she was either her sister, or a near relative." Roscoe specifically noted that, "she was not an orphan or slave." He continued, "this girl was called: 'The one who accompanies' (mperekezi); she stayed with the bride for some days after her marriage, it might be for a week, or as long a period as three months, to let the bridegroom's family understand that his wife had relations who cared for her."[43] Mair concurred with Roscoe that the minimum stay was for a few days, but went on to note that the *empérékézê* "was described as the husband's 'second wife,' and if he wanted actually to marry her this was taken as a compliment by her family. It seems to have been quite common for her to become pregnant by him, and such an event was not attended with the disgrace which customarily attached to it."[44] Should the *empérékézê* stay in her sister's marital home she would be a junior wife to her sister.

Speakers of both Luganda and South Kyoga retained the North Nyanzan noun **kaidu* (cl. 12) [19] or 'senior wife,' but in Luganda it came to have a narrower meaning than in South Kyoga. The role that the term described was also somewhat different in the two speech communities. For South Kyogans, **kaidu* referred to the senior wife in any household. The **kaidu* was the preferred wife to be the mother of the heir on her husband's death. In that role, she could, as we have seen, adopt a son from a co-wife in order to fulfil the expectations of motherhood should she not have a biological son. For Baganda, the North Nyanzan term came to be limited to the senior wives of the king and chiefs and they innovated a new noun, *nnálúgóngó* (cl. 1a), for the senior wife of a commoner. As this semantic narrowing of **kaidu* occurred, speakers of Luganda made an important modification to the noun by suffixing

[43] Roscoe, *The Baganda*, 90.
[44] Mair, *An African People in the Twentieth Century*, 85.

lubáále (cl. 1a/2), 'god, deity,' giving *káddúlúbáále* (cl. 1a/2), which has the literal meaning 'senior wife of a deity.'[45] Historians have recognised the interdependence – complex and fraught as it was – between the 'creative power' held by the mediums of the *balubáále* and the 'instrumental power' wielded by the rulers of the Buganda kingdom.[46] By naming the senior wives of the king and chiefs *káddúlúbáále*, Baganda made them the embodiment of the connection between political or instrumental power and religious or creative power in the households of kings and chiefs wielding the former. The power of the senior wife herself, however, was limited to the life of her husband, as she was unlikely to be the mother of the heir.

Along with the innovation of *káddúlúbáále* from the North Nyanzan noun **kaidu*, Baganda innovated terms for the wives who followed her in the household hierarchy. The two wives immediately below the senior wife were the *kabéjja* (cl. 1a) and *nnásázá* (cl. 1a).[47] Pointing to her power and influence over the Ganda king, it was the *nnamásolé* (cl. 1a) [33] or queen mother who selected all three of the senior wives for her son.[48] Despite the pronounced shift away from the role of motherhood as an ideology in Ganda social organisation, the *nnásázá* was selected from the clan of the king's paternal grandmother (though not from her direct lineage), marking the continued importance of maternal kin connections across generations. This was also the case for chiefs and, possibly, for commoners.[49]

South Kyoga speakers extended the major shift in meaning for the noun **-gólé* (cl. 1/2) [16] that the North Nyanza speech community had

---

[45] Snoxall, *Luganda-English Dictionary*, 181.

[46] I take these terms from Schoenbrun, *A Green Place, A Good Place*, 12, 195–206. See also Kodesh, *Beyond the Royal Gaze*, 138–43; Médard, *Le royaume du Buganda au XIXe siècle*, 345–67.

[47] There is some disagreement over whether *kabéjja* was the title of the second wife and *nnásázá* that of the third (Le Veux, *Premier essai de vocabulaire luganda – français d'après l'ordre étymologique*, 274, 713; Snoxall, *Luganda-English Dictionary*, 249, 251; Schiller, "The Royal Women of Buganda," 469) or vice versa (Roscoe, *The Baganda*, 83; Abasi Kiyimba, "Gender Stereotypes in the Folktales and Proverbs of the Baganda" [PhD diss., University of Dar es Salaam, 2001], 69). Kagwa does not label them as either second or third, but he does list *kabéjja* before *nnásázá*. See Kagwa, *The Customs of the Baganda*, 68. A likely explanation for the confusion is that they ranked jointly immediately below the *káddúlúbáále* and above all the other wives.

[48] Schiller, "The Royal Women of Buganda," 468, citing Tor V.H. Irstam, *The King of Ganda: Studies in the Institutions of Sacral Kingship in Africa*, trans. Donald Burton (Lund: H. Ohlssons boktr., 1944).

[49] Kiyimba, "Gender Stereotypes in the Folktales and Proverbs of the Baganda," 69; Roscoe, *The Baganda*, 83.

made. As we saw in Chapter 2, North Nyanzans used the noun to refer
to the maternal potential of brides and newly married women. South
Kyoga speakers dropped the gendered nature of the noun as they used it
to refer to both brides and bridegrooms. In so doing they also dropped
the association with maternity or maternal potential that had been the
core meaning of the noun in North Nyanza and its ancestor languages.
Because they emphasised social over biological motherhood in the
reproduction of households, this shift in the meaning of *-góle* reflects a
different importance given to marriage. It is essential to stress that I am
not arguing that reproduction was not important to the people speaking
proto-South Kyoga; it was essential. But the way that importance manifested itself was somewhat different to its manifestation among their
neighbours speaking Luganda, where biological motherhood was given
more weight. It also differed among other Great Lakes Bantu people
further to the southwest, such as in Burundi, where emphasis was placed
on bearing large numbers of offspring, with special titles and diadems
for those women who were mothers to seven children.[50] In South Kyoga,
the social motherhood of the senior wife, rather than the number of
children, was an essential part of the ideal social reproduction of the
household.

  The social reproduction of households was part of the larger process
of reproducing lineages and clans. In both Buganda and South Kyoga,
clans sought to mark the pregnancies of in-marrying women as belonging to them, continuing the practice of their North Nyanza ancestors.
Through clan-specific taboos, members of the patriclan both publicly
marked the unborn child as theirs and reminded the future mother that,
although she was not of her husband's clan, the fruits of her reproductive labour belonged to it. As with the North Nyanzan speech community, it is difficult to precisely reconstruct these clan-specific practices for
speakers of South Kyoga but, on the basis of the taboos in later Soga,
Gwere, and Shana society, we can presume that they centred on avoiding
certain foods and avoiding contact with men who were not relatives. In
Buganda, by the nineteenth century, there were a number of general food
avoidances that all pregnant women were supposed to follow, regardless
of which clan they had married into. Given their distribution in North
Nyanzan societies these taboos are likely of some antiquity and included

[50] Bourgeois, *Banyarwanda et Barundi*, 526; Schoenbrun, *A Green Place, A Good Place*,
159; Schoenbrun, *The Historical Reconstruction of Great Lakes Bantu Cultural
Vocabulary*, 83–4, root 114.

abstention from eating rock salt (as opposed to salt from reed ashes) and the sweet *gonjâ* bananas.[51]

There were also general behavioural avoidances for pregnant women in Ganda households, including not passing a man in a doorway or stepping over his feet, not sitting on a man's bed or washing from the same water pot as him. The latter two approximated adultery, presumably because they were most unlikely to occur unless a woman was in an intimate relationship with a man. Breaking these taboos was said to have the same negative consequence as being adulterous, namely suffering from the disease *-kíro* (cl. 6) [25].[52] *Amakíro* afflicted women throughout North Nyanzan societies and was always associated with adultery during pregnancy, either by the expectant mother or her husband. If left untreated, its most extreme symptom was said to be that the mother would attempt to eat her baby immediately after it was born.[53] *Amakíro* was then the physical representation of broader social anxieties about the need for the *pater* and the *genitor* to be same man.

In addition to the general avoidances for pregnant Baganda women, there were also clan-specific ones that were quite particular. A woman who had married into the Mpewo (Oribi) clan, for example, reported Mair, "might not lift up the leaves of the *ntula* – one of the forbidden fruits – to look underneath for the berries," and one who had married into the Musu (Edible Rat) clan "had to take a stick with her when walking along a narrow path, and push aside the grass so that it did not touch her." If a pregnant woman broke the avoidance of her husband's clan she risked miscarriage or a stillbirth.[54] Violating these taboos thus

[51] Gorju, *Entre le Victoria l'Albert et l'Edouard*, 327; Apolo Kagwa, *Ekitabo kye Mpisa za Baganda* [The Book of the Customs of the Baganda] (Kampala: Uganda Printing and Publishing, 1918), 180–1; Mair, *An African People in the Twentieth Century*, 39; Roscoe, *The Baganda*, 49. *Gonjâ* bananas are usually roasted or boiled.

[52] Gorju, *Entre le Victoria l'Albert et l'Edouard*, 326; Kagwa, *Ekitabo kye Mpisa za Baganda*, 181; Mair, *An African People in the Twentieth Century*, 40; Roscoe, *The Baganda*, 48–9. The dictionary compilers translate *amakiro* as 'nymphomania' but all other sources are clear that the noun refers to the disease, not the actions said to cause it. Le Veux, *Premier essai de vocabulaire luganda – français d'après l'ordre étymologique*, 379; Snoxall, *Luganda-English Dictionary*, 197.

[53] Mair, *An African People in the Twentieth Century*, 40; Roscoe, *The Baganda*, 102. GW-ETH-BUL-F-KJ, interview, 11 November 2004, Bugwere; GW-ETH-IKI-F-ZK, interview, 17 November 2004, Bugwere; SO-ETH-NAU-F-ME, interview, 21 January 2005, Busoga; SO-ETH-NAK-F-LK, interview, 8 March 2005, Busoga. For a study of *amakiro* from a modern psychiatric perspective, see John L. Cox, "Amakiro: A Ugandan Puerperal Psychosis?" *Social Psychiatry and Psychiatric Epidemiology* 14, no. 1 (1979): 49–52.

[54] Mair, *An African People in the Twentieth Century*, 40–1 (quote p. 40).

threatened not only a wife's place in her marital home, but also her ability to be a mother.

Despite these precautions, the anxiety felt by clan members with regards to marking a new child as a legitimate member continued after birth until the naming ceremony had been completed. This was the case in both societies descended from the North Nyanza speech community, but the increasingly exclusive emphasis in Buganda society on patrilineality at the expense of matrilateral ties gave the postpartum practices here a different texture than in South Kyoga to the east. These practices included the manner of disposal of the placenta and whether and how the umbilical cord stump was preserved. They also included three more performative elements: bringing the mother and baby out from the postpartum seclusion, testing the legitimacy of the baby, and naming the baby. Disposal of the placenta – under a banana plant or buried near the house – was determined by clan custom in both South Kyoga and Buganda.[55] Speakers of South Kyoga also kept or disposed of the dried umbilical cord stump according to clan preference, although all clans preserved the umbilical cord stumps of twins.[56] In Buganda the stumps of umbilical cords of all infants were kept, at least until they had been used to test the child's legitimacy. Clan members performed this test by dropping the umbilical cord stump into a container of water; if it floated the child was recognised as a member of the clan and if it sank the mother was accused of adultery.[57] This test had to be performed before the child was named because children were given the names of deceased clan members; if the child was not legitimately a member of it, she or he should not receive a clan name. Once the cord stumps had been used to test the child's legitimacy, clan custom determined whether they were preserved or disposed of.[58] It is difficult to date when Baganda created this ceremony of legitimacy, but the ceremony reflected the growing importance

[55] Cohen, ed., "Collected Texts of Busoga Traditional History," Texts 14, 41, 287, 380, 468, and 515; Roscoe, *The Baganda*, 54–7; Roscoe, *The Northern Bantu*, 214. GW-ETH-IKI-F-MN, interview, 16 November 2004, Bugwere; SO-ETH-KIT-F-NM, interview, 19 January 2005, Busoga; SO-ETH-NAU-F-ME, interview, 21 January 2005, Busoga; SO-ETH-BUG-F-YG, interview, 20 January 2005, Busoga.

[56] Roscoe, *The Northern Bantu*, 213–4, 215, 217–9. GW-ETH-IKI-F-KG, interview, 16 November 2004, Bugwere; GW-ETH-IKI-F-MN, interview, 16 November 2004, Bugwere; GW-ETH-BUL-F-KJ, interview, 11 November 2004, Bugwere; SO-ETH-NAU-F-ME, interview, 21 January 2005, Busoga; SO-15-BUG-F-KJ, interview, 20 January 2005, Busoga.

[57] Gorju, *Entre le Victoria l'Albert et l'Edouard*, 337; Mair, *An African People in the Twentieth Century*, 56–9; Roscoe, *The Baganda*, 61–2.

[58] Roscoe, *The Baganda*, 62–3.

that fathers should be biological parents, not just socially recognised as fathers through marriage. This was part of the move towards a more exclusive model of patrilineality that appears to have unfolded gradually as political power was increasingly centralised and struggled over.

Once the period of seclusion was complete, both Baganda and South Kyoga speakers marked the moment a mother emerged from the house in which she had given birth to her infant.[59] In Buganda, this was combined with another test of the child's legitimacy as a member of her or his patriclan. According to Mair's informants, this was called *kùkuzà eggwánga ly'ekikâ*, a phrase that Mair glosses as "to protect all the people of the clan," although a literal translation gives: 'to grow [increase] the people of the clan.'[60] This was another of the transitional moments of creation and danger (as with the marriage of a couple's daughter) that were marked by performing *kùkuzà*. Sometime after the mother and infant had emerged from seclusion, again in both South Kyoga and Ganda communities, a clan name was chosen for the child. This marked the final public recognition of the child as a legitimate member of her or his patriclan. In Buganda, this was performed immediately after the umbilical cord legitimacy test.[61] All the rituals around childbirth and naming children involved more complicated details if a Muganda or South Kyoga woman gave birth to twins, and it is most likely that these practices were inherited from the North Nyanza speech community. Twins represented bounteous creation and danger (to the mother and to themselves) and were both honoured and feared. And, again in a practice seemingly inherited from their North Nyanzan ancestors, the special respect accorded to parents of twins was marked through the bestowal of honorific titles.[62]

[59] Atkinson, ed., "Bugwere Historical Texts," Text 24; Cohen, ed., "Collected Texts of Busoga Traditional History," Texts 268, 380, 493, and 515; Gorju, *Entre le Victoria l'Albert et l'Edouard*, 338; Mair, *An African People in the Twentieth Century*, 42–3; Roscoe, *The Baganda*, 55; Roscoe, *The Northern Bantu*, 216.

[60] Mair, *An African People in the Twentieth Century*, 43. Literal translation from the Luganda my own.

[61] Atkinson, ed., "Bugwere Historical Texts," Text 24; Cohen, ed., "Collected Texts of Busoga Traditional History," Text 515; Roscoe, *The Baganda*, 61–4.

[62] Cohen, ed., "Collected Texts of Busoga Traditional History," Text 614; Gorju, *Entre le Victoria l'Albert et l'Edouard*, 348; Minah Nabirye, *Eiwanika ly'Olusoga: Eiwanika ly'Aboogezi b'Olusoga n'Abo Abenda Okwega Olusoga* [A Treasury of Lusoga: A Treasury for Speakers of Lusoga and Those Who Want to Learn Lusoga] (Kampala: Menha Publishers, 2009), 178; Roscoe, *The Baganda*, 65; GE-ETH-IKI-F-KG, interview, 16 November 2004, Bugwere; GW-ETH-IKI-F-MN, interview, 16 November 2004, Bugwere.

These various efforts at marking the legitimacy of children were important to both sets of lineages and clans because of the special relationship
that existed between a woman's children and her lineage and clan. Yet,
the roles mothers played in social organisation by creating interlineal networks through their marriages and their maternity took divergent paths
in the Luganda and South Kyoga speech communities. Speakers of North
Nyanza, while following patrilineal descent, had given a significant role
to matrilateral ties in their kin governance. This was centred on the relationship between *-ihwa (cl. 1/2) [20] and their mother's lineage and
clan members. While this was by no means exclusive to North Nyanza
society, there were some elements that were distinctive. In Chapter 2 we
saw that one of these was the innovation of a new – and unusual among
the Bantu languages – noun for 'maternal uncle': *koiza (cl. 1a/2) [27].
In South Kyoga, the children of female clan members or *-ihwa played
a similar role in kin governance as they had in North Nyanza. However,
the range of duties and rights that *-ihwa held expanded in the South
Kyoga communities, as they became ever more important to the healthy
social reproduction of their mothers' clans. They played essential roles in
preparing the bodies of the dead for burial and at funerals, in succession
rites, and in ceremonies to mark the birth of twins and appease their spirits.[63] While the special relationship between *-ihwa and their maternal
uncles continued in South Kyoga, it was not privileged to the exclusion of
other matrilateral ties, particularly that of the maternal grandfather.[64]

In Buganda àbajjwà remained at the centre of social organisation, but
the greater emphasis on more exclusive patrilineality was to the detriment
of the connections created by and through mothers.[65] Àbajjwà still played
important roles in various ritual ceremonies, especially those marking the
birth and naming of twins.[66] Maternal kin also benefited greatly should
their royal òmujjwà (born to a king's wife from their clan) succeed to the
throne on the king's death.[67] And at some point after Luganda began to
be spoken as a distinct language, the kòjjâ or maternal uncle became the
most important relative on the maternal side.[68] He had strong rights to

---

[63] Cohen, The Historical Tradition of Busoga, 9–10; Laight and Lubogo, "Basoga Death
and Burial Rites"; Atkinson, ed., "Bugwere Historical Texts," Texts 37, 45, 47, and 48.
[64] Long, "Notes of the Bugwere District," 459; Tantala, "Gonza Bato and the Consolidation
of Abaisengobi Rule in Southern Kigulu," 15; Tantala, "Community and Polity in
Southern Kigulu," 12; Cohen, Womunafu's Bunafu, 27–8.
[65] The Luganda reflexes of *-ihwa (cl. 1/2) are òmujjwà (s.) and àbajjwà (pl.).
[66] Mair, An African People in the Twentieth Century, 46–8.
[67] Schiller, "The Royal Women of Buganda," 460.
[68] The Luganda reflexes of *koiza (cl. 1a/2) are kòjjâ (s.) and bakòjjâ (pl.).

his sister's children – particularly her daughters – unless their father gave him compensatory payment; this was payment for the maternal uncle's *èndóbòló* or 'share' of his sister's children.[69] This relationship is highlighted in another proverb: *Omwana tiyeerabira bukojja bwe: ettooke lifaanana ng'omuyini gw'enkumbi* ('A child does not forget her/his maternal relations: bananas resemble the handle of the hoe'). Walser gives the following explanation for the proverb: "The child is the off-spring of their sister, as the banana is the result of the woman's labour."[70]

The relationship between Baganda *bàjjwa* and *bakòjjâ* was a complicated one. Writing about historical practices in Buganda, Mair recorded that a child for whom *èndóbòló* had been paid "was entitled to ask for anything he liked in his mother's brother's house and, if his request was refused, to help himself."[71] On the other hand, however, a *kòjjâ* could abuse his rights in his *bàjjwa*. Indeed any *bàjjwa* who lived with their *kòjjâ* because they had not been claimed and compensated for by their father were, according to ethnographic descriptions, treated with disdain in the household. Mair notes that there was "nothing to prevent [the maternal uncle] selling [his sister's child] into slavery, though of course this was disapproved."[72] The anthropologist Audrey Richards noted in 1953 that she was told by Maryamu, a woman who was older than seventy, that if a mother's brother was not compensated for his sister's children, "he could sell them into slavery to redeem a debt."[73] Although this was an extreme illustration of the rights of the maternal uncle, an example no doubt embedded in the economic and political events of the nineteenth century, the broader shifts in kin governance that made possible this abuse of the relationship between maternal uncles and sororal children occurred earlier. While patrilineal descent was followed by North Nyanza speakers and all their descendants, it was among the Baganda that it was applied

---

[69] *Èndobòlo* means 'sample, share, daughter of my sister, daughter of my slave' and is derived from the verb *-lobòla* 'to take a share' (Le Veux, *Premier essai de vocabulaire luganda – français d'après l'ordre étymologique*, 546). The extension of the meaning to name the child of a sister is an innovation in Luganda with Lusoga retaining only the meaning of 'fraction or share.' See also Mair, *An African People in the Twentieth Century*, 61–2.

[70] Walser, *Luganda Proverbs*, 398, no. 4446. My translation of the proverb, which differs from that offered by Walser.

[71] Mair, *An African People in the Twentieth Century*, 63.

[72] Mair, *An African People in the Twentieth Century*, 62 (quote). The Ganda situation has some parallels in the role of *baihwa* in Bunyoro where there was "a manifest ambivalence in the *bwihwa* relationship." See Beattie, "Nyoro Marriage and Affinity," 18.

[73] Audrey Richards, "MS. Marriage, Kinship (Powers of F & M's B), 6.4.53," file 6/2, 31, Audrey Isabel Richards Collection, London School of Economics Archives.

most rigidly. The rights of maternal kin – and of the *kòjjâ* in particular –
in the children of their *mùkô* or son-in-law sat uneasily with the increasingly exclusive patrilineality of Buganda society. Because a child's social
identity derived so heavily from her or his patrilineage, those children
not redeemed through payment to their *kòjjâ* had an indeterminate social
identity that made them vulnerable to abuse in their maternal uncle's
household.

This tension between the rights of maternal kin and the patrilineal
descent system in Buganda is enshrined in the foundation myth of the
Baganda, the story of Kintu and Nnambi, as discussed briefly earlier. In
this story, Nnambi lived in the sky with her father, Ggulu, and her brother,
Walumbe. Kintu married Nnambi and they went to live in Buganda,
but were followed by Walumbe. When they had children, Walumbe as
their *kòjjâ* asked Kintu for his *èndóbòló* from among the children. Kintu
refused him, so Walumbe threatened to kill all the children. When Kintu
and Nnambi had yet more children, Walumbe returned and asked again
for his *èndóbòló*. When Kintu refused once more, Walumbe carried out
his threat and so introduced death to Buganda.[74] By refusing to recognise his brother-in-law's right to his *èndóbòló* among Nnambi's children,
Kintu broke an ancient social more with dire consequences for his land
and descendants. But it was the maternal uncle Walumbe – whose name
literally means death – who embodied this destruction.

At the heart of its social charter, then, was the growing tension within
Ganda society between the recognition of patrilineal descent and the
rights of maternal kin. We have no sure means of knowing when the tale
of Kintu and Nnambi was composed. The multiple forms of the story

---

[74] This summary is based primarily on the version of the story given in Le Veux, *Manuel de
langue luganda comprenant la grammaire et un recueil de contes et de légendes*, 449–58.
Other versions can be found in: Harry Johnston, *The Uganda Protectorate: An Attempt
to Give Some Description of the Physical Geography, Botany, Zoology, Anthropology,
Languages and History of the Territories under British Protection in East Central Africa,
between the Congo Free State and the Rift Valley and between the First Degree of South
Latitude and the Fifth Degree of North Latitude*. Vol. 2. (London: Hutchinson, 1904),
700–5; Apolo Kagwa, *Engero za Baganda* [The Tales of the Baganda] (London: Sheldon
Press, 1927), 1–8; Roscoe, *The Baganda*, 460–4. Benjamin Ray notes that Kagwa "refers
to Walumbe incorrectly as Kintu's brother," in Apolo Kagwa, *Ekitabo kya Basekabaka
be Buganda na be Bunyoro, na be Koki, na be Toro, na be Nkole* [The Book of the
Kings of Buganda and of Bunyoro, and of Koki, and of Toro, and of Nkole] (1901, repr.
Kampala: Uganda Bookshop and East African Publishing House, 1971), 1. Benjamin C.
Ray, *Myth, Ritual, and Kingship in Buganda* (New York: Oxford University Press, 1991),
216, fn. 5. For a detailed discussion and interpretation of the story of Kintu and Nnambi,
see Kodesh, *Beyond the Royal Gaze*, 50–9.

suggest it was of some antiquity by the nineteenth century, but those multiple versions also underscore the pliability of such traditions in the face of political or ideological expediency. All the same, this particular aspect of the story was not the focus of disputes in the late nineteenth and early twentieth centuries, when the Kintu and Nnambi narrative came to be recomposed as a correlate of the fall of Adam and Eve in the Garden of Eden.[75] This suggests that it may have been one of the more enduring features of the Ganda foundation narrative. Furthermore, the centrality of an older social and political organisation that had motherhood as an ideology at its core in Buganda is highlighted by the fact that the *kòjjâ*'s rights continued to be enshrined in the story despite growing hostility to that very ideology.

THE ECONOMICS OF REPRODUCTION IN BUGANDA AND SOUTH KYOGA

This shift to a more exclusively patrilineal model in Buganda was not the inevitable conclusion of a gradual shift from the matrilineal descent practised by the proto-East Bantu ancestors of North Nyanza speakers.[76] Indeed, their nearest neighbours and relatives who spoke South Kyoga, and later Lusoga and Lugwere, did not follow the same trajectory. Why did Baganda make the decision to change the nature of their kin governance to minimise or distort the role of relationships and networks formed through mothers? One reason for this may lie in the growing importance of banana cultivation to the Ganda economy. As we have seen, North Nyanza speakers grew bananas and developed new varieties of the crop, indicating that they had some expertise in growing the fruit. But it was among Luganda speakers that banana farming really took off, with the development of tens of new varieties. Because banana plantations can survive for several generations, the growing importance of bananas to the economy changed the nature of wealth in Buganda. Wealth came to be centralised in immobile banana plantations with competition for the best banana-growing land. This strengthened the position of patriclans that controlled that land and may have contributed to a more exclusive model of patrilineality.

---

[75] Kodesh, *Beyond the Royal Gaze*, 52–3.

[76] Marck and Bostoen, "Proto-Oceanic Society (Austronesian) and Proto-East Bantu Society (Niger-Congo) Residence, Descent, and Kin Terms, ca. 1000 BC."

Bananas were only one of many crops grown by South Kyoga and Luganda speakers from around the thirteenth century. The other primary staple was millet, but several legumes also formed an important part of their diet, with fish and wild animals providing additional nutrition. The organisation of food procurement reflected the ways in which South Kyoga speakers and Baganda imbued it with cultural meaning, especially in connection to rituals associated with healthy social reproduction. There were continuities from North Nyanza times and parallels between the two communities, but significant differences also emerged that reflected not only the distinct ecological realities they faced but also the changing ideologies underpinning their social organisation.

In contrast to the innovation of terms for banana varieties and for a banana plantation by North Nyanza speakers and to the development of several new banana varieties by Baganda, South Kyogans innovated only one name for a banana variety – *sagasaga* (cl. 9) [40]. It may be that as South Kyogans moved into unfamiliar lands further to the east they did not have the security to develop extensive banana plantations that took time to establish and relied rather on annual grain crops. In addition, although the lands immediately to the north of Lake Victoria–Nyanza were ideally suited for banana cultivation, this was not necessarily the case further inland, where rainfall was less regular throughout the year. Indeed as Cohen notes, rain there would fall only occasionally and "in heavy squalls, unleashing as much as ten centimeters within a few hours. The water rushes down the hillslopes, cutting into the soil, forming rivulets and gullies, carrying the soil down toward the stream banks." This pattern of rainfall had helped shape the landscape. "The action of water on the hillslopes over tens of thousands of years has exposed the previously enclosed tips of the lateral sheets which, piled one on top of another, form the ridge."[77] Here then cereal crops, especially millet, were the safer choice.

Banana cultivation was an important part of the Ganda economy, and Baganda developed significant expertise in growing bananas and in propagating new varieties of the crop. Where their North Nyanza–speaking ancestors coined seven new names for banana varieties, Luganda speakers today have some sixty different terms.[78] The role of bananas in a number of rituals associated with social reproduction also underscores

---

[77] Cohen, *Womanafu's Bunafu*, 41.
[78] Schoenbrun, *A Green Place, A Good Place*, 80.

the way in which the crop came to be at the heart of Ganda social and economic life. And yet, Baganda did not live on bananas alone. The nineteenth century adventurer Henry Morton Stanley described a wealth of crops in a Muganda peasant's garden, in October 1875:

> It is laid out in several plats, with curving paths between. In it grow large sweet potatoes, yams, green peas, kidney beans, some crawling over the ground, others clinging to supporters, field beans, vetches, and tomatoes. The garden is bordered by castor-oil, manioc, coffee, and tobacco plants. On either side are small patches of millets, sesamum, and sugar-cane. Behind the house and courts, and enfolding them, are the more extensive banana and plantain plantations and grain crops, which furnish his principal food, and from one of which he manufactures his wine and from the other his potent pombé. Interspersed among the bananas are the umbrageous fig trees, from the bark of which he manufactures his cloth. Beyond the plantations is an extensive tract left for grazing, for the common use of his own and his neighbours' cattle and goats.[79]

The historian Richard Reid reminds us that this is an idealised vision and that many of the crops (tomatoes and sugarcane, for instance) were recent introductions in the nineteenth century, "but it does seem likely that most Ganda cultivated a wide variety of crops within their enclosures, and that such crops were carefully chosen."[80] Such crops served to provide Baganda with a nutritionally varied diet, but some of them also played a role in ceremonies to ensure the healthy social reproduction of Baganda communities.

Millet and *empîndi* (pigeon peas, *cajanus*) were two crops that were closely associated with the reproduction of the lineage. The prime minister of Buganda and ethnographer Apolo Kagwa reported that there was a special meal to mark the eating of the first millet of the new season for which "the husband had to kill a goat." After the meal, the husband performed the *kùkuzà* rite by jumping "over his wife."[81] As we have seen, this rite was intimately associated with reproduction and with the marking of moments of danger and creation. The 'new millet ceremony' was not, however, an innovation of the Baganda, having been practised by proto-North Nyanza speakers as well as their descendants. Among Luganda speakers, the harvesting of *empîndi* served to mark a woman's successful motherhood as she called her eldest son to eat the first cooked

[79] Henry M. Stanley, *Through the Dark Continent or The Sources of the Nile Around the Great Lakes of Equatorial Africa and Down the Livingstone River to the Atlantic Ocean*, vol. 1 (New York: Harper & Brothers, 1878), 383.

[80] Reid, *Political Power in Pre-Colonial Buganda*, 27.

[81] Kagwa, *The Customs of the Baganda*, 108.

peas of the season. According to Roscoe's informants, if she failed to call him, "she would (it was thought) incur the displeasure of the gods and fall ill." After the meal had been eaten, the harvester's husband again performed the *kùkuzà* rite in which he "jumped over her ... and the beans thereafter might be eaten by all." Roscoe reports that sweet potatoes also required special treatment at harvest and Kagwa notes the same for sesame.[82] Whereas sweet potatoes would have reached the Great Lakes region only after the seventeenth century, both *empîndi* or pigeon peas and sesame are of greater antiquity.[83]

The associations between food procurement and social reproduction and the tension between the creative and destructive potential of reproduction were reflected in Ganda taboos around hunting and fishing. A central part of this was the separation of women's work of reproduction and men's work of killing wild animals for meat through hunting. Baganda men should not cross paths with women as they set out on a hunt. To facilitate this avoidance, when Ganda hunters gathered in the morning, the leader of the hunt blew a horn, which called the hunters together and "warned women from the path." Roscoe notes that this was done "because it was believed that if a huntsman met a woman when he was setting out, the hunt would be a failure, and the animals would escape." If, on returning from hunting, a hunter found another man in his homestead, "he speared him slightly, just enough to draw blood." This was clearly a reference to the required sexual fidelity of hunters' wives during their (sometimes prolonged) absence. As with the avoidance of women at the outset of the hunt, if these practices were not followed the consequence would be the failure of the next hunt in which the hunter participated.[84]

Ideas about social reproduction lay at the heart of these restrictions. Eugenia Herbert has emphasised the importance of recognising not just the destructive aspect of hunting, but also its creativity.[85] A successful hunt would bring meat to the household and skins to give to the chief or even the king in prestation. Such prestations would put the householder in favour with his patron and bring prestige to the hunter and his family. Elsewhere in Africa, direct associations were historically drawn

---

[82] Roscoe, *The Baganda*, 428 (quote); Kagwa, *The Customs of the Baganda*, 108.

[83] J.-P. Chrétien, "Les années de l'éleusine, du sorgho et du haricot dans l'ancien Burundi: Écologie et idéologie," *African Economic History* 7 (1979): 80; Ehret, *An African Classical Age*, 7, 78.

[84] Roscoe, *The Baganda*, 448–50 (quotes p. 449, p. 450).

[85] Herbert, *Iron, Gender, and Power*, 170–1.

between hunting and human reproduction.[86] In Buganda, the avoidances observed by hunters and their wives suggest that Baganda viewed hunting and childbearing as sharing the same tension between destruction and creation. Both hunting and childbearing held the potential for social mobility: by becoming the mother of the heir in a household or by killing a prestigious animal, such as a leopard. Both activities held dangers too, for the hunter might not survive the hunt and a pregnant woman might well not survive childbirth. For Baganda it was, explicitly, social reproduction – not simply biological reproduction – that could affect and be affected by contact with hunting. If a man returned from a hunting trip and found another man in his home, this threatened both his position as the male head of the household and his position as the socially recognised father or *pater* to his children. In order to reinforce his position, he had to symbolically defeat his potential usurper through cutting him with his hunting spear.

Fishing on lakes, especially on Lake Victoria–Nyanza, could be as hazardous as hunting on land and these dangers (and its benefits) were similarly connected to social reproduction, in particular to sexual abstinence at moments of ritual danger. While making a drag-net, a Muganda fisherman lived apart from his wife "until the first catch of fish had been taken."[87] The catch was not divided among the fishing crew until the owner of the net "had cooked and eaten some of it" and had performed the *kùkuzà* rite with his wife, which we have seen performed in association with particular moments of social reproduction and the harvesting of certain crops. Similar practices were followed with regards to line fishing and the setting of fish traps. When the wife of a fisherman was pregnant, "he presented her with a basket of small fish" to eat or to share.[88] Just as with hunting, successful lake fishing could improve the social, political, and economic status of a fisherman, but the lake could not always be trusted and also held great dangers. The connections that Baganda perceived between specialised fishing activities and social reproduction were marked through avoidances and gift-giving at the household level. Ideologies around reproduction thus intersected with economic practices in complex ways, particularly with regard to highly specialised activities. The social institution of motherhood and ideologies of it also lay at the heart of centralised political authority.

[86] Among the Ndembu, for example. Herbert, *Iron, Gender, and Power*, 169–70.
[87] Roscoe, *The Baganda*, 393.
[88] Kagwa, *The Customs of the Baganda*, 150; Roscoe, *The Baganda*, 393–5 (quotes p. 393, p. 395).

LEGITIMACY AND POLITICAL POWER

In spite of an increasingly exclusive patrilineality combined with the stress on biological reproduction in Buganda, public motherhood was a prominent part of the political system. The relationships between a woman, her children (especially her sons), and her own kin group and clan were a central feature of political life in both South Kyoga and Buganda. This continuity occurred despite an important divide that emerged between the two communities in terms of the selection of the heir and the existence of a royal clan. In South Kyoga the king was preferentially the son of his father's *kaidu* or senior wife, whereas in Buganda – as we have seen – no such preference existed. This had the corollary that in the polities of South Kyoga, the queen mother was ideally the *kaidu* of the former king even if she was not a biological mother.[89] In Buganda, by contrast, the queen mother could be any of the deceased king's wives, but should ideally be the biological mother of the new king.

Buganda as a kingdom has attracted significant scholarly attention since Roscoe and Kagwa's early studies, and historians have pointed out the powerful offices reserved for women.[90] Many scholars, while noting, for example, that the queen mother wielded equal power as her son, have focused primarily on the person and office of the king and his ministers and chiefs.[91] Others have, however, examined the roles and lives of royal women in the kingdom.[92] The first scholar to address royal women in Buganda explicitly was Karen Sacks. Her analysis takes a theoretical approach that divides women into sisters and wives. She argues that sisters are equals in their kin group, but only after bearing and raising their own children to adulthood. Wives, by contrast, usually have young children

---

[89] Atkinson, ed., "Bugwere Historical Texts," Text 41; Cohen, ed., "Collected Texts of Busoga Traditional History," Text 917; Cohen, *Womunafu's Bunafu*, 25; Fallers, *Bantu Bureaucracy*, 135.

[90] Among others, see Hanson, *Landed Obligation*; Kagwa, *The Kings of Buganda*; Kiwanuka, *A History of Buganda*; Kodesh, *Beyond the Royal Gaze*; Médard, *Le royaume du Buganda au XIXᵉ siècle*; Musisi, "Transformations of Baganda Women"; Ray, *Myth, Ritual, and Kingship in Buganda*; Reid, *Political Power in Pre-Colonial Buganda*; Sacks, *Sisters and Wives*; Schiller, "The Royal Women of Buganda"; Wrigley, *Kingship and State*.

[91] Wrigley, *Kingship and State*, 67.

[92] Including Holly Hanson, "Queen Mothers and Good Government in Buganda: The Loss of Women's Political Power in Nineteenth-Century East Africa," in *Women in African Colonial Histories*, ed. Jean Allman, Susan Geiger, and Nakanyike Musisi (Bloomington: Indiana University Press, 2002), 219–36; Musisi, "Transformations of Baganda Women"; Sacks, *Sisters and Wives*; Schiller, "The Royal Women of Buganda."

and live and work for their husband's household.[93] Sacks notes that, while "the queen mother and the king's sister [*lubuga*] wielded political and economic authority. ... No royal sisters were allowed to rear children or marry." She thus concludes that within the Ganda royal family, it was not possible for a woman to be a sister and a wife: she could either have power or reproduction, but not both.[94] The historian Laurence Schiller argues that the queen mother held real political power because she was the king's mother and "the chief link to a kabaka's main support group, his matrilineal [sic] clan."[95] The queen sister's importance in his analysis, however, lay more "in the ritual areas of inheritance and tomb tending than formal or informal political power at court." Princesses "had special rank and status.... but they had no official position of power" and the influence a princess held "varied according to her personality and relationship with the kabaka."[96] The king's wives, meanwhile, represented "the physical links of political alliances between clans and king, and they used their influence to secure places for their relations."[97]

For us to understand the apparent contradiction between Baganda women's general lack of power and autonomy and the significant power some women wielded in the palace, Schiller argues that we need to recognise that there was a "hierarchy of political status [that] took precedence over the hierarchy of gender status."[98] The ethnomusicologist Sylvia Nannyonga-Tamusuza goes further and makes the case that the power of princesses "was related to the fact that they were men," not women, in terms of the Ganda gender system.[99] Gender relations and the emergence of the precolonial Ganda state are the primary interest of the historian Nakanyike Musisi. The most salient feature of life for women in the palace, in her analysis, was the level of "state control" over their lives, especially with regard to marriage and reproduction. In examining the 'how and why' of the political power of the queen mother, Musisi uses Sack's analytical framework of sisters and wives to explain the queen mother's position with reference to her status as a widow, rather than as a mother.[100] Drawing on the broader ideologies of motherhood that shaped

[93] Sacks, *Sisters and Wives*, 6.
[94] Sacks, *Sisters and Wives*, 214.
[95] Schiller, "The Royal Women of Buganda," 472.
[96] Schiller, "The Royal Women of Buganda," 466, 468.
[97] Schiller, "The Royal Women of Buganda," 470.
[98] Schiller, "The Royal Women of Buganda," 471.
[99] Sylvia A. Nannyonga-Tamusuza, *Baakisimba: Gender in the Music and Dance of the Baganda People of Uganda* (New York: Routledge, 2005), 83.
[100] Musisi, "Transformations of Baganda Women," 52, 70–86.

social organisation in Buganda and its ancestral North Nyanza–speaking community, an alternative explanation emerges: the *nnàmasòle*'s power derived from her maternity and was activated by her widowhood.

Baganda, as we have seen, most likely did not invent the political office of queen mother, but rather inherited it from the smaller polities of their North Nyanza–speaking ancestors. As such, it is not surprising that the historical traditions of Buganda portray the queen mother as part of the political hierarchies from its foundation. In these historical traditions, the first two kings were Kintu and Cwa, who are widely understood to be mythical figures.[101] The third king, Kimera, reigned following an interregnum.[102] Kimera, the traditions narrate, came from Bunyoro and was the illegitimate son of Wanyana, a wife of King Wunyi of Bunyoro. His father was Kalimera, son of Cwa. Kimera was raised in secret in Bunyoro and as an adult travelled with Wanyana to Buganda, where he took the throne. On his accession, Wanyana received her own palace at Lusaka.[103] Whether Kimera is a historical figure or a mythical one and what the tradition of his ascent to the Ganda throne tells us about the origins of the kingdom have been much debated in the literature.[104] What is generally agreed, however, is that his reign at the very least institutionalised the trappings of royal authority in Buganda. One of those trappings was the construction of a separate palace for the queen mother, marking her political authority alongside that of her son.[105]

Despite inheriting the office of queen mother from their North Nyanza–speaking ancestors, Baganda innovated a new noun to describe her and the office she held, *nnamásole* (cl. 1a) [33]. Père Gorju posited an etymology for this noun from the Luganda word *bùsòlê* (cl. 14), 'small puppies.'

---

[101] Ray, *Myth, Ritual, and Kingship in Buganda*; Wrigley, *Kingship and State*. But for an alternative interpretation, see Kodesh, *Beyond the Royal Gaze*.

[102] The following is based on Kagwa, *The Customs of the Baganda*, 19–20; Kagwa, *The Kings of Buganda*, 15–17; Roscoe, *The Baganda*, 215–16.

[103] Roscoe, *The Baganda*, 215. Kagwa notes only that Wanyana was buried at Lusaka after her death. Kagwa, *The Kings of Buganda*, 16.

[104] For a thorough overview of these debates, see Neil Kodesh, "Beyond the Royal Gaze: Clanship and Collective Well-Being in Buganda" (PhD diss., Northwestern University, 2004), 200–16.

[105] Musisi dates the origin of the office of *nnàmasòle* to the reign of Nakibinge in the sixteenth century and the honour he bestowed upon his wife, Nanzigu (Musisi, "Transformations of Baganda Women," 77). However, this seems to be based on a mis-reading of the tradition relating to King Nakibinge and his wife Nanzigu who could not become queen mother because she gave her child away. Nanzigu is recognised among all other authors as being one of the titled wives of the king. See Kagwa, *The Customs of the Baganda*, 23; Kagwa, *The Kings of Buganda*, 187; Roscoe, *The Baganda*, 84–5.

He was clearly uncomfortable with referring to the queen mother as the 'mother of little dogs' and developed an explanation that fit with his European sensibilities: "We would like to believe that 'Mother of the puppies' was an affectionate name which the mother of the king earned from her role as a 'persuasive power.'"[106] An alternative etymology proposed by N. B. Nsimbi derives *nnàmasòle* from name of the *kyegamansole* plant, the leaves of which Queen Mother Wanyana is said to have made use of during her first weeks in Buganda.[107] On a linguistic level, however, neither of these etymologies is entirely convincing, owing to the prosody of the first and phonology of the second. The proto-Great Lakes Bantu verbal root *-sola* (tr.) gives us an alternative etymology and intellectual history for *nnàmasòle*. The verb *-sola* is derived from the proto-Bantu verb *-còd-*, 'choose, pay tax.'[108] Schoenbrun's reconstruction of *-sola* gives a primary meaning of 'remove, gather, collect,' with a derived meaning of 'reveal, judge by ordeal' in proto-Great Lakes Bantu.[109] In proto-West Nyanza, *-sola* also had the meaning of 'uproot.' In Luganda, the verb *-sola* glosses as 'dig up ground nuts, clear, sift, peel, examine,' linking the *nnàmasòle* or queen mother to the collection of crops, the levying of taxes, and judging of crimes.[110] This etymology, which sees Luganda speakers as having derived *nnàmasòle* from *-sola*, is phonetically more convincing than the earlier etymologies and is semantically clearer in directly linking the queen mother to her political role and authority.

The office of *nnàmasòle* of Buganda was a powerful one. She shared with her son and his queen sister or *lùbugà* [6] the title of *kàbàkà* and was the most powerful commoner in the kingdom.[111] In his study of the Buganda dynasty, Wrigley notes that "the queen mother was a power in the land at least equal to her son."[112] John Hanning Speke, in his published

[106] "Nous aimons à croire que 'Mère des petits chiens' fut un nom de tendresse que valut à la mère du roi son rôle de 'puissance suppliante'" (Gorju, *Entre le Victoria, l'Albert et l'Edouard*, 139, fn. 1.) My translation.

[107] N. B. Nsimbi, "Baganda Traditional Personal Names," *Uganda Journal* 14, no. 2 (1950): 206.

[108] Bastin and Schadeberg, "Bantu Lexical Reconstructions 3," ID main 636, ID main 6982 (Accessed 9 January 2013). Please note that Bastin and Schadeberg indicate that the meaning 'pay tax' may be a neologism. This may be a problem of translation as 'pay tribute' would fit well with broader iterations of this verb in Bantu languages.

[109] Schoenbrun, *The Historical Reconstruction of Great Lakes Bantu Cultural Vocabulary*, 160, root 241, 156, root 235.

[110] Le Veux, *Premier essai de vocabulaire luganda – français d'après l'ordre étymologique*, 915; Snoxall, *Luganda-English Dictionary*, 291.

[111] Schiller, "The Royal Women of Buganda," 458–9.

[112] Wrigley, *Kingship and State*, 67.

account of his visit to Buganda in 1862, described the *nnàmasòle*'s position in the following terms:

> The mother of the king by this measure became queen-dowager, or N'yamasoré. She halved with her son all the wives of the deceased king not stationed at his grave, taking second choice; kept up a palace only little inferior to her son's with large estates, guided the prince elect in the government of the country, and remained until the end of his minority the virtual ruler of the land; at any rate, no radical political changes could take place without her sanction.[113]

On acceding to her office the *nnàmasòle* lived in a separate palace from that of her son; the physical and symbolic division between the two palaces was marked by a stream.[114] Though on a slightly smaller scale than the king's, her palace otherwise replicated his and by the nineteenth century, at the latest, included large retinues of women.[115] She had her own chiefs in "a hierarchy which mirrored the [king's] in structure and titles" and which ranged from *kàtikkiro* or prime minister at the top to estate managers at the bottom. She also governed parts of the kingdom directly. These estates were extensive and were "scattered around every province," extending her power into every part of the kingdom. She raised taxes on these estates to maintain herself and her retinue. The *nnàmasòle*'s people did not fall under the jurisdiction of the king or his chiefs; instead she held her own court in which she held the "power of life and death over her own people, who were directly responsible to her."[116]

Just as in wider society the son of any wife could become his father's heir, so in the palace could almost any prince succeed his father.[117] Because the position of queen mother was such a powerful one, royal wives and their families set out to create alliances with influential chiefs to ensure that their *mùjjwa* (female clan member's child) became king and his mother became *nnàmasòle*. In the traditions, histories of intrigues by royal wives go all the way back to the reigns of Kimera and his grandson, Ttembo, who – if we accept them as historical figures – reigned in the fourteenth or early fifteenth century. According to tradition, King Kimera sent his son, Lumansi, to raid for cattle at Kalagala's place in what would become Busoga. Lumansi fell sick and died on his way to Kalagala's, leaving

[113] John Hanning Speke, *Journal of the Discovery of the Source of the Nile* (New York: Harper and Brothers Publishers, 1864), 249.

[114] Roscoe, *The Baganda*, 203; Wrigley, *Kingship and State*, 150.

[115] Speke, *Journal of the Discovery of the Source of the Nile*, 249, 294–5.

[116] Kagwa, *The Customs of the Baganda*, 95; Roscoe, *The Baganda*, 244–6; Schiller, "The Royal Women of Buganda," 458–9 (quotes).

[117] With the exception of the first-born prince. Roscoe, *The Baganda*, 188.

two widows and four children. One of the widows was Nattembo, the
mother of Ttembo. When her son had matured, Nattembo told him that
Kimera had killed Lumansi and she persuaded him to avenge his father's
death. Ttembo did so during a hunting party, clubbing his grandfather on
the back of the head. He then succeeded his grandfather and Nattembo
became *nnàmasòle*. Nattembo's machinations meant that she gained her
own palace and that she moved from the somewhat precarious position
of the widow of a prince into the powerful position of queen mother.[118]

In the sixteenth century, another royal widow endeavoured to become
queen mother: Nannono, wife of King Nakibinge. Nannono was famous
for helping her husband in a war against Bunyoro by sharpening reeds
for him to fight with "when his supply of spears was exhausted."[119] When
Nakibinge was killed and the army retreated, Nannono reigned for some
time as regent. The traditions give two explanations for this unusual
event: none of Nakibinge's children from his other wives was old enough
to take the throne and Nannono herself was pregnant. Nannono hoped
to give birth to a son. She could thus become *nnàmasòle* and rule as
regent for her son until he came of age. Her child was a girl, however,
and Mulondo, son of another of Nakibinge's wives, was elected king by
the chiefs.[120] Although biology ultimately conspired against her, the fact
that Nannono was able to postpone the election of a successor for her
husband is an indication of the power and political influence that some
of the king's wives were able to wield in the kingdom. She could not have
done so, however, without the political support of her clan members and
at least some of the important chiefs.

Mulondo – the prince chosen to succeed Nakibinge when Nannono
gave birth to a girl – is remembered in the traditions for the influence
his maternal kin held during his reign. He was still very young when he
ascended the throne, and although the traditions do not directly state
that his mother, *Nnàmasòle* Namulondo, acted as regent until he reached
maturity, they do refer to her power and influence. The stool on which

[118] This narrative draws on Kagwa, *The Customs of the Baganda*, 20; Kagwa, *The Kings of Buganda*, 16–17; Roscoe, *The Baganda*, 215–16. Kagwa writes that it was Nakku, Lumansi's mother, who told this to Ttembo. Nakku would have been the more powerful of the two women, but being the wife of the king she had everything to lose and little to gain from Kimera's death; Nattembo had everything to gain.
[119] Kagwa, *The Kings of Buganda*, 28. Kagwa recorded that "the warriors all lost their spears" and so "Nanono cut reeds to sharp points and gave these to the soldiers to use as spears." Kagwa, *The Customs of the Baganda*, 24. See also, Musisi, "Transformations of Baganda Women," 110.
[120] Kagwa, *The Customs of the Baganda*, 24; Kagwa, *The Kings of Buganda*, 28–9.

he sat, "so that he could look big enough in the Councils," was named
after her, a physical symbol of the *nnàmasòle*'s influence especially over a
young king. The influence of Namulondo's brothers over the king is also
apparent. It was they who made his stool and when Namulondo died
during his reign they brought several of her female relatives to Mulondo
in order for the king to select an heir to the office of *nnàmasòle*.[121]

Not many aspiring queen mothers feature in the historical traditions of Buganda. That Nattembo and Nannono do so is no doubt due
to the exceptionality of their actions. Most queen mothers would have
gained their offices through a combination of their own political skill
and the influence of their lineages and clans. To succeed his father to
the throne, a prince almost certainly required the political support of
his mother and her relatives. The role his maternal kin played was recognised by the successful prince, and the relatives of a royal wife could
expect to receive significant benefits from the political transformation
of their kinswoman into the *nnàmasòle* and of their *mùjjwa* or nephew
into the king. According to Wrigley, "the *katikkiro* had regularly been
the king's mother's brother," but the sources are not in agreement on this
matter.[122] What is certain is that one of the *nnàmasòle*'s brothers would
be appointed to the powerful chiefship of *ssaàbaganzi*.[123] The political
relationship between the king and his *kòjjâ* continued into the following
generation: each of the king's sons was introduced to the *ssaàbaganzi*
on being weaned. The *ssaàbaganzi* then gave each of his great-nephews
"a well-dressed skin to wear."[124] Those great-nephews belonged to a different clan from their royal father, for the king's children were members
of their mother's clan. Through their relationship with the *ssaàbaganzi*,
however, they retained a public connection with the clan of their paternal
grandmother, the *nnàmasòle*.

Despite the struggles over its function as a social institution in Buganda
and the push to emphasise biological reproduction during this period,
motherhood continued to be a central feature of social organisation, food
procurement, and political life. There were growing tensions between the
ideology of motherhood in social organisation and efforts by patrilineages to control the most fertile lands in Buganda. Nonetheless the role of
women's children in the social reproduction of their maternal patriclans

[121] Kagwa, *Kings of Buganda*, 30–1 (quote p. 30).
[122] Wrigley, *Kingship and State*, 190.
[123] Kagwa, *The Kings of Buganda*, 104; Schiller, "The Royal Women of Buganda," 460.
[124] Roscoe, *The Baganda*, 73 (quote), see 104–10 for the role of the *ssaàbaganzi* in the
preparations and rites following the death of the king.

remained. Similarly, while the opportunities for wealth and prestige from successful hunting and fishing expeditions increased with the centralisation of political power and led to a clear exclusion of women from these important activities, taboos and rituals recognised the links between them and reproduction. At the heart of political power in the royal palaces, kings claimed their thrones only with the support of their mothers and their mothers' clan members and supporters. Queen mothers, meanwhile, held power that was at least nearly equal to that of their sons and used their political skills both to attain authority and hold onto it. The importance of the ideology of motherhood to political power in Buganda was manifested in the distribution of important chiefships and other political offices to the maternal kin of the king.

Across the Nile among the people speaking South Kyoga, the particular challenges they faced in expanding their communities in a less familiar landscape and with increasing engagement with Nilotic-speaking peoples meant that they evolved a particular ideology of motherhood that stressed its social aspects. Here social motherhood enabled the reconstitution of social networks through strong matrilateral ties and the preferential treatment of senior wives, something that followed through into the polities of the eastern region that again placed motherhood at the heart of political authority. This motherhood-focused political model would facilitate the incorporation of Nilotic-speaking elites over the course of the next two centuries.

4

Mothering the Kingdoms

Buganda, Busoga, and East Kyoga, Sixteenth through Eighteenth Centuries

From the sixteenth century, after the breakup of South Kyoga into Lusoga and East Kyoga, strong differences emerged in the ideologies of motherhood held by the then three major North Nyanzan speech communities: those of Luganda, Lusoga, and East Kyoga (or pre-Lugwere).[1] Buganda's move towards biological motherhood intensified, making it the dominant form there. Much of what we know about the Ganda ideology of motherhood for this period derives from the royal palaces, but it is likely that it was shaped by a dynamic relationship between the royal family and wider society. In Busoga, meanwhile, social motherhood was institutionalised in a manner that meant that many women were excluded from accessing it. As speakers of East Kyoga settled lands further to the east, motherhood appears to have remained a more fluid social institution most likely as a result of the particular social environment in which the speech community lived. By the eighteenth century, then, the role of motherhood in society and politics varied significantly across the speech communities descended from North Nyanza.

In the two centuries or so from the sixteenth century, Baganda women and men moved towards creating a single highly centralised kingdom that fostered cultural and linguistic coherence, even as the territory under its control expanded rapidly. While multiple Luganda dialects existed they remained mutually intelligible. Similarly while new clans came into being through fissions in existing ones as well as through immigration, political power was increasingly held by a single royal family – the Buganda

---

[1] I use East Kyoga to distinguish between the period before the emergence of Rushana, but the language can be seen as an early version of modern Lugwere.

dynasty – which, theoretically at least, belonged to no single clan, and therefore in a sense encompassed them all.[2] As the Ganda royal family grew in power and importance, internal struggles over the ideology that defined and legitimised political rule became more pronounced. Those struggles frequently involved efforts to sideline public motherhood in the political organisation of the kingdom, with profound consequences for Ganda society.

To the east of the Nile, in the lands between Lakes Victoria–Nyanza and Kyoga, people no longer spoke South Kyoga; they now spoke one of two different languages: Lusoga or East Kyoga. Those speaking Lusoga remained in the old South Kyoga heartland and consolidated the communities they had built since the twelfth century. From the start of the sixteenth century, however, the arrival of Southern Luo–speaking people who had migrated southwards from their original homeland in the Bahr-el-Ghazal initiated major transformations in Soga society and political life.[3] Although this represented a meeting of two very different linguistic and cultural groups, the mobilisation of the Soga ideology of social motherhood facilitated processes of integration. Marriage and motherhood lay at the interface of these two communities; as wives and mothers to husbands and children from the other community, women bridged the linguistic and cultural divide. And it was through the social motherhood of Lusoga-speaking women that Luo-descendant families legitimated their reign in a number of Soga states, especially in the northern part of the region.

East Kyoga speakers, who lived further east across the Mpologoma River (see Map 3), inhabited a region of even greater linguistic and cultural diversity. The lands they settled consisted of low hills separated by swampy shallow valleys, with only about sixty metres difference in elevation between them. While rainfall was sufficiently spaced throughout the year to make banana cultivation possible, it was less reliable than in areas closer to Lake Victoria–Nyanza and the area was prone to severe drought, all of which required a more flexible and varied economic system.[4] In this challenging terrain, East Kyogan communities encountered the western

---

[2] For a detailed exploration of processes of clan formation in Buganda, see Kodesh, *Beyond the Royal Gaze*. I follow Wrigley in using the term 'Buganda dynasty.' Wrigley, *Kingship and State*.

[3] The Bahr-el-Ghazal is a river system that forms the main western affluent of the Nile in the modern-day South Sudan and has for millennia formed a focus of settled life in the region.

[4] For further detail see, David N. McMaster, *A Subsistence Crop Geography of Uganda* (Bude, U.K.: Geographical Publications, 1962), 13–14.

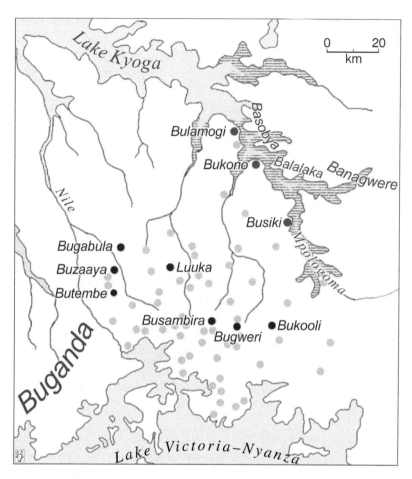

MAP 3. Soga kingdoms and Gwere Polities. Black dots denote kingdoms mentioned in text; grey dots denote some of the other early Soga kingdoms. Gwere polities are indicated to the east of the Mpologoma.

fringe of a region inhabited by speakers of Greater Luhyia languages and that served as a 'migration corridor' traversed by a variety of Nilotic speech communities.[5] This area can be seen in terms somewhat similar to, albeit in slightly different circumstances, what James Scott has described as "a zone of refuge or 'shatter zone,'" where the human shards

---

[5] David W. Cohen, "The River-Lake Nilotes from the Fifteenth to the Nineteenth Century," in *Zamani: A Survey of East African History*, ed. B. A. Ogot (1968; repr., Nairobi: Longman, 1974), 135–49.

of state formation and rivalry accumulated willy nilly, creating regions of bewildering ethnic and linguistic complexity."[6] The varying social organisation, domestic arrangements, and political practices of these diverse communities shaped East Kyoga thought and society. In particular, East Kyogans adopted more malleable ideas about motherhood as a social institution, especially as their language gave way to Lugwere. In a context where households were often composed of individuals from diverse cultural-linguistic backgrounds, flexibility was essential to social and political cohesion. This flexibility in constructions of motherhood meant that mothers served as links not only between lineages and clans, but also between East Kyogans and foreign groups. As such, motherhood was crucial in helping to ensure stability and peaceful relations in a complex and fluid environment. In all three societies – Buganda, Busoga, and East Kyoga – historically divergent ideologies of motherhood shaped power, legitimacy, and sustainability over these centuries.

BUSOGA

In Busoga, as in South Kyoga earlier, social motherhood was closely intertwined with the social category of senior wife, and it was here that this household position became most prominent. The heightened prominence of senior wives, however, foreclosed some of the opportunities for social advancement and security for wives outside this position. This was tied to the politics of social organisation and the way in which Basoga women and men mobilised their ideology of motherhood in it. As David William Cohen notes, "there were two principal institutions of social organization in pre-colonial Busoga: the clan, encompassing relationships of blood; and the state." At the end of the nineteenth century, there were about 220 clans and 68 states of significant size. Both kinds of institutions, however, were on a relatively small scale, with members or subjects most likely numbering in the low thousands.[7] The immigration of Southern Luo speakers into Busoga in the sixteenth and seventeenth centuries had important political consequences as Luo lineages came to rule several of

---

[6] James C. Scott, *The Art of Not Being Governed: An Anarchist History of Upland Southeast Asia* (New Haven, Conn.: Yale University Press, 2009), 7. Joan Vincent referred to the Serere peninsula just north of the East Kyoga–speaking area as "a shatter zone between the Nilotes of northern Uganda and the Bantu-speaking peoples to the south." Joan Vincent, *Teso in Transformation: The Political Economy of Peasant and Class in Eastern Africa* (Berkeley: University of California Press, 1982), 64.

[7] Cohen, *The Historical Tradition of Busoga*, 6–7, 12–16 (quote p. 6).

the northern Busoga kingdoms.[8] They did not, however, introduce the idea of political centralisation or monarchies. Indeed, their power was predicated on preexisting South Kyoga and Soga political ideologies that had motherhood at their core.

In the kingdom of Busiki, in eastern Busoga, people referred to the senior wife as *kaido*, and in southern and western Busoga she was called *kairu* or *kairulubaale*.[9] The importance of the senior wife as the mother of the heir was such that almost every clan history collected by Cohen names the clan of the *kairu* [19] or senior wife of the clan founder. The abaiseBabiro clan, for example, name their founder as Kagonda and note that his *kairu* was of the abaiseMubbala clan and the abaiseNkwanga clan's founder was Ibudi and his *kairu* was of the abaiseMukobe clan.[10] Clans fulfilled several functions for their members. They created a web of support by connecting clan members in different areas and significantly increasing the number of people an individual could turn to for assistance. Given the prominence of healers' shrines in the historical texts of Busoga, it is most likely that clans also served as networks of knowledge in a similar manner to what Neil Kodesh describes for Ganda clans.[11] Clans in Busoga thus mobilised a wide range of resources, not least of which was the prominent role their daughters could play as the senior wives of leaders of other clans.

Success through motherhood depended largely on achieving the status of senior wife. The ethnographic data emphasises the need for the senior wife to be the mother of a son, whether or not she had her own biological children. In several of the kingdoms, for example, the heir was ideally the son of the senior wife or *kairu*.[12] In the absence of a biological son, a senior wife could remedy the situation by bringing a woman from her clan as a junior wife in her husband's household. Any children born to the new wife would belong to the *kairu*.[13] Attaining the category of *kairu* in her husband's household almost certainly depended on the influence of

[8] Cohen, *The Historical Tradition of Busoga*, 1–2.
[9] Fallers, *Bantu Bureaucracy*, 83; SO-15-MAG-F-WR, interview, 20 March 2005, Busoga. The suffixing of *lúbáalé* 'deity' is the result of influence from Buganda.
[10] Cohen, ed., "Collected Texts of Busoga Traditional History," Texts 1 and 767. Please see idem, varia for a complete listing.
[11] Kodesh, *Beyond the Royal Gaze*.
[12] Cohen, ed., "Collected Texts of Busoga Traditional History," Text 917; Cohen, *Womunafu's Bunafu*, 25; Fallers, *Bantu Bureaucracy*, 135.
[13] Cohen, ed., "Collected Texts of Busoga Traditional History," Text 917; Roscoe, *The Northern Bantu*, 200. Fallers noted that the "Soga are extremely polygynous ... and sororal polygyny is the preferred form." See L. A. Fallers, "Some Determinants of Marriage Stability in Busoga: A Reformulation of Gluckman's Hypothesis," *Africa: Journal of the International African Institute* 27, no. 2 (1957): 112.

a woman's lineage and clan. Thus the category of senior wife would likely have been restricted to women already of relatively elevated social status. This would have been especially the case in the households of chiefs and kings. The benefits that ensued from achieving the position of senior wife are hinted at in the origin narrative for the kingdom of Bugweri in southeastern Busoga that describes a banana garden from which only the senior wife or *kairu* in the royal family could harvest fruit.[14] At the same time, the enduring influence of a version of social motherhood that enabled a senior wife to claim a junior wife's child as her own shows how an older, particular ideology of motherhood continued to shape the cultural construction of social reproduction in Busoga from the sixteenth century.

In both Buganda and Busoga being the senior wife of the king was a recognised position, but in many of the Busoga kingdoms the senior wife was the favoured one to become queen mother in contrast to the situation in Buganda. In the kingdoms of Busoga, the senior wife of the king wielded considerable authority. She had her own estates in the kingdom – like the queen mother – from which she collected taxes. She could demand corvée labour from the people living on her estates for works such as building and maintaining her palace and she could punish those who insulted her: "she was always armed with a very sharp knife which she could use to cut anybody that dared to insult her." And she could confiscate "any person's property." The Soga politician and local historian Y. K. Lubogo noted that for these reasons, "senior wives were often respected and much feared."[15] Furthermore, the office of *kairu* in the kingdoms was replicated in the households of chiefs across Busoga.[16]

The senior wife drew her power through two relationships: the one she had with the current king, her husband, and the one she had with the future king, her son. As *kairu* she would become queen mother on the death of her husband. Ideally, her son would succeed his father and when she did not have a (suitable) son of her own she adopted a sister's son (or the son of a female clan member) born to the king.[17] It is unlikely that succession would have always passed off without dispute, and a *kairu* undoubtedly formed alliances with important chiefs in the kingdom to

[14] Cohen, ed., "Collected Texts of Busoga Traditional History," Text 614.
[15] Lubogo, *A History of Busoga*, 152.
[16] Cunningham, *Uganda and Its Peoples*, 125.
[17] Certain sons could not succeed their fathers. For example, a prince suffering from leprosy or mental illness would not be eligible to inherit the throne. Cohen, ed., "Collected Texts of Busoga Traditional History," Text 917; Roscoe, *The Northern Bantu*, 200.

support her son's accession to the throne. She could also count on the support of her lineage and clan members, especially as princes tended to be raised in their mothers' natal homes and not in the king's palace.[18] This practice meant that princes had very strong connections to their maternal kin; they could draw on these connections when they sought to succeed to the throne. A senior wife drew on a range of strategies to ensure that her son became king. One of these was to be present in the immediate aftermath of the death of the old king and so prevent, or at least reduce the possibility of, other wives and their maternal kin scheming on behalf of their sons. In the kingdom of Bugabula, for example, the *kairu* had specific roles to perform during the funeral of her husband.[19] By being at the heart of funeral rites she gained a further opportunity to influence the succession in her own and her son's favour.

It appears that this narrowing of access to senior wifehood was paralleled by an increase in more informal marriage arrangements in wider Busoga society. By the first decade of the twentieth century, Catholic Mill Hill missionaries were describing Basoga marriages as "casual unions."[20] They were so casual that "when a man does not like any longer one of his women, he sells her or changes her for another one. And a woman having enough of her husband, goes for a walk and never comes back."[21] Even accounting for missionary zeal and for the social dislocation of the late nineteenth century, it does seem that less formal marriage arrangements became more common from the time that Lusoga was spoken. In the mid-twentieth century, Lloyd Fallers estimated that some 25 to 50 percent of all marriages in Busoga ended in separation and 90 percent of separations could be described as "formal divorce with repayment of bridewealth." Rather than this being a new development resulting from "a break-down in the traditional system," he concluded that such instability was in fact resistant to religious change or the acquisition of literacy.[22]

Lusoga-speakers coined a new verb to describe the act of eloping and, in contrast to their neighbours and to older verbs for this act, did not distinguish between women and men's actions in this regard. The etymology for this new verb, *-páála* (tr.) [34], 'elope' (of a women or a man), remains

[18] Cohen, *Womunafu's Bunafu*, 27.
[19] Cohen, ed., "Collected Texts of Busoga Traditional History," Text 719.
[20] Bishop Hanlon to Fr. Matthews, 6 March 1906, Mill Hill Fathers' Archive, UGA, Box 3, File 1906.
[21] Anthony van Term to Very Reverend Father Rector, 12 April 1901, Mill Hill Fathers' Archive, Personal Files, Box Per 1896, File 136.
[22] Fallers, "Some Determinants of Marriage Stability in Busoga," 106–23 (quote p. 114).

elusive. There is an Acholi verb *poorro* that also means 'elope,' but the sound change of the vowel is not plausible.[23] This shift away from gendering acts of elopement suggests a distinction between elite marriages with *kairu* or senior wife status and non-elite marriages (or marriages between an elite man and a non-elite woman), which were less secure but perhaps also enabled individuals to use different strategies to improve their economic situation. Such strategies may have included nullifying the marriage if it did not bring prosperity – or at least economic security – to one or both parties.

Fostering arrangements beyond those enabling the social motherhood of senior wives also existed in Busoga. Cohen has highlighted the strong preference both for men from royal Luo lineages to marry non-royal, non-Luo Basoga women and for the sons who issued from such marriages to be raised by their mothers' kin groups. This is well documented for the best-understood Luo group in Busoga, the Owiny Karuoth.[24] According to Cohen, this practice:

was the ideal for the royal families of the states located right across northern Busoga – that a son of a ruler should be raised at his mother's home. Born in the palace, yes; raised in the palace, no. Ibanda Ngobi, the father of the founders of the ruling houses of the Luuka and Kigulu kingdoms [in the early eighteenth century] was raised at Nhenda Hill in the fenced compound of the father of Tegula, the girl who was his mother.

As Cohen goes on to note, "the raising of these princes at the homes of their mothers served to bridge the prestigious bearing and exogenous culture of the northern ruling families in Busoga with the commoner homes of the Bantu-speaking local families."[25] These child-rearing preferences underscored the importance of marriages as alliances between important families or between an important local family and an ambitious immigrant family.

These alliances were sufficiently significant for them to be recorded in the oral traditions, such as the following example from the abaiseIgaga clan. In the early seventeenth century, a man called Nantamu migrated with his family to Bulamoogi in northeastern Busoga, where he came into contact with Kafamba, who was a mwiseMukose chief. "Nantamu is recalled as having given a woman to Kafamba and as having won

[23] Odonga, *Lwo-English Dictionary*, 219. Further systematic research on loan words borrowed by Lusoga-speakers from Luo languages will help to clarify this question.

[24] Cohen, 'The Face of Contact,' 352–3.

[25] Cohen, *Womunafu's Bunafu*, 27 (1st quote), 28 (2nd quote).

Kafamba's heart. When Kafamba died, Nantamu succeeded him as head-
man in the area. Later, the mwiseNgobi Lamogi [ruler] (Ngambani)
arrived from the eastern side of the Mpologoma and 'took over from
Nantamu without fighting.' Nantamu gave a woman, Nakuya, to Lamogi,
and Lamogi settled at Lubulo, near Gadumire." As a result of his influence in the area and his success at creating marital alliances, Nantamu's
lineage enjoyed "considerable autonomy" in the larger political unit.[26]
Because such marriages were intended to result in children, the alliances
that were thus created continued across generations.

   Basoga women and men – as is common among patrilineal societies in
sub-Saharan Africa – practised exogamous marriage, which meant that
marriage alliances linked different patriclans. In order to mark the children who ensued from these exogamous marriages as belonging to their
father's clan, there were a number of avoidances that pregnant women
had to follow. In the twentieth century, people remembered that a woman
married to a mwiseBandha man, for example, was not to eat salt during
her pregnancy, while one married to a mwiseKisige man should not step
over the exposed roots of a tree but instead walk around them.[27] If she
breached such taboos or avoidances the pregnant woman ran the risk
of miscarriage. Other rules prescribed where a woman should deliver
her baby: in the abaiseKaibaale clan, if a woman gave birth when visiting her natal home she would bring *ekítáló* on her family. The risk was
particularly grave if she gave birth to twins.[28] *Ekítáló*, in this context,
was the consequence of a serious breach of clan avoidances, such as com-
mitting incest, and purification rites had to be performed should it arise.
In Soga moral logics, childbirth occurred within marriage at the father's
homestead and children belonged to their father's clan. If a child was
born in the mother's natal home this complicated her or his social identity, which had consequences for both the maternal and paternal kin: the
rights of paternal kin to the child as a member of their lineage and clan
was challenged and the ability of the child to carry out ritually dangerous tasks for its maternal kin could be undermined by having been born

---

[26] Cohen, *The Historical Tradition of Busoga*, 179 (quote); Cohen, ed., "Collected Texts of
Busoga Traditional History," Text 71.
[27] Cohen, ed., "Collected Texts of Busoga Traditional History," Text 14; SO-ETH-BUG-F-YG,
interview, 20 January 2005, Busoga.
[28] SO-ETH-NAU-F-ME, interview, 21 January 2005, Busoga; SO-ETH-BUG-F-YG, interview, 20 January 2005, Busoga. *Ekítáló* glosses as "omen, taboo after incest, fabulous,
incestuous, marvel, forbidden, unmentionable, banned, prohibited, proscribed, out-
lawed, inviolable." *Dictionary: Lusoga-English English-Lusoga* (Jinja, Uganda: Cultural
Research Centre, 2000), part I, 69.

among them.[29] The potential danger posed to the clan and lineage of a pregnant woman was such that patriclans imposed another set of avoidances on their pregnant daughters.[30]

Once the risks of pregnancy and childbirth were over, Basoga women and their infants had a period of rest and seclusion. The end of seclusion was marked by a ceremony of 'bringing out' the new mother and her baby. This was called *okúfulumyá* (*omwâná*) and the specific details of the ceremony varied from clan to clan. The most salient difference was in the food used to test the faithfulness of the mother and hence the legitimacy of the child. Some clans used a mixture of roasted sesame and other seeds whereas those with strong fishing traditions used small fish called *enfúlú*.[31] Once *okúfulumyá* (*omwâná*) had been performed the child was welcomed as a new member of the paternal clan. The timing of this ceremony depended, in some clans at least, on the agricultural calendar. During the sowing season for millet, *okúfulumyá* (*omwâná*) had to be performed almost immediately because lineage members could not sow the new millet until the ritual had been completed.[32] Basoga closely associated millet with fertility, and sowing the crop while a member of the household remained in postnatal seclusion could affect both the fertility of the crop and of the women of the family. A few days after *okúfulumyá* (*omwâná*), clan members would give the name of an ancestor to the baby. In Busoga, the naming of a child was called either *okúgúlíká omwâná* or *okwálúlá omwâná*.[33] As elsewhere in eastern Africa and beyond, naming

[29] As Cohen notes, although Basoga princes were often raised in their mother's homes they should be born in their father's palace. Cohen, *Womunafu's Bunafu*, 27.

[30] For example, a mwiseIbaale woman should not allow a man who was not her clansman to touch her. Cohen, ed., "Collected Texts of Busoga Traditional History," Text 41.

[31] Cohen, ed., "Collected Texts of Busoga Traditional History," Texts 268, 287, 468, 493, and 515; Roscoe, *The Northern Bantu*, 216; SO-ETH-NAU-F-ME, interview, 21 January 2005, Busoga; SO-15-BUG-F-KJ, interview, 20 January 2005, Busoga; SO-ETH-BUG-F-YG, interview, 20 January 2005, Busoga. *Enfúlú* resemble whitebait.

[32] Cohen, ed., "Collected Texts of Busoga Traditional History," Texts 287 and 468.

[33] *-gúlíká* has the meaning 'name after the ancestor' (*Dictionary: Lusoga-English English-Lusoga*, part I, 41). Cohen translates *-álúlá* as 'differentiate' and connects it to distinguishing girls and boys. See Cohen, ed., "Collected Texts of Busoga Traditional History," Text 515, fn. 13. However, the Lusoga verb 'differentiate or separate' is *-âwulá* whereas *-álúlá* translates as 'hatch.' See *Dictionary: Lusoga-English English-Lusoga*, part I, 2, 3. Given the use of chickens in the naming process and the symbolism involved in giving a child a clan name, it is not difficult to see why this word would have been chosen. See SO-ETH-NAU-F-ME, interview, 20 January 2005, Busoga; SO-15-BUG-F-KJ, interview, 20 January 2005, Busoga; SO-ETH-KIT-F-NM, interview, 21 January 2005, Busoga. None of my informants and none of the preexisting ethnography suggested that the naming ceremony was particularly connected to publicly gendering infants.

a child after a clan ancestor was an integral part of the social reproduction of the clan, allowing the deceased to be remembered through
their descendants. However, should more than one child who was named
after the same ancestor die in infancy, the spirit of that ancestor was held
responsible and her or his name would no longer be passed on.[34]

The importance of a mother's children to her natal clan and lineage
was marked in Busoga by an unusual innovation: many of the patrilineal
clans (*ebíka* [22]) created specific names for their *abáiwa* (the children
of their female members). Many of these names, particularly those for
girls – again a noteworthy development – were coined from the name of
the eponymous founder of the clan. So, members of the abaiseIhemula
clan called a girl *omwîwa* Naihemula and those of the abaiseIruba clan
used the name Nairuba.[35] Dating the start of this practice is difficult,
but Cohen's work on the clans of Luo origin is suggestive. With reference to the Owiny Karuoth, he notes that although the sons of Karuoth
men were raised in the households of their Lusoga-speaking maternal
kin, daughters tended to remain in their fathers' households. As a result,
he argues, "the daughters may have been crucial in the cultural exchange
between Karuoth and non-Karuoth and may have been, more than any
other category of people, oriented toward a bilinguality and a cultural
education in two different worlds." This cultural straddling was intensified through their subsequent marriage to non-Karuoth men.[36] By giving
particular clan names to their daughters' children, Owiny Karuoth and
others living in Busoga emphasised the connection with their *abáiwa* and
reinforced their role as cultural intermediaries.

Basoga *abáiwa* performed essential roles in various ceremonies and
rites associated with the birth and naming of twins, as well as those
associated with funerals and successions, as had their South Kyoga– and
North Nyanza–speaking ancestors.[37] The relationship between maternal
kin and their *omwîwa* was strong, and a grievance committed against a
powerful *omwîwa* could lead to warfare as occurred between Busiki and
Nkono in the late eighteenth century, in an incident explored later.[38] For

---

[34] Roscoe, *The Northern Bantu*, 214.

[35] Cohen, ed., "Collected Texts of Busoga Traditional History," Texts 95 and 125.

[36] David W. Cohen, "The Political Transformation of Northern Busoga, 1600–1900,"
Cahiers d'Études Africaines 22, no. 87/88 (1982): 473.

[37] Cohen, *The Historical Tradition of Busoga*, 9–10; Laight and Lubogo, "Basoga Death
and Burial Rites."

[38] This contrasts with the relationship between *abaihwa* and their matrilateral kin in
Bunyoro where an *omwihwa* could be called to go to war for his mother's kin, but the
converse could not occur. Beattie, "Nyoro Marriage and Affinity," 20.

Basoga, *abáiwa*'s ritual connections with their mothers' kin groups were frequently supplemented by strong political ties. Powerful clan members would get involved in succession disputes because they stood to benefit greatly from the accession to the throne of an *omwîwa*.[39] Indeed, just as members of a mother's kin group benefitted from an *omwîwa*'s success, the *omwîwa* often depended on his maternal kin at achieve such success. This situation of mutual dependence served to reinforce the connections between *abáiwa* and their maternal kin.

Writing about the Busoga kingdoms from the seventeenth century, Cohen has shown how Southern Luo speakers and their (Lusoga-speaking) descendants formed new polities or took control of existing ones by creating networks of relationships with the indigenous Basoga population. As we have seen, they did this through exogamous marriage and by sending the sons born to these marriages to live with their maternal non-Luo kin. The pattern of exogamy that these Luo lineages followed required not only marrying outside of the clan, but also marrying outside the groups that claimed Luo origins.[40] For the ruling lineages, this meant that the heir to the throne was always the son of a Musoga woman raised in her natal household: by her parents or her brother. This practice placed the heir at the centre of a web of networks that connected his Luo-origin patrilineage and his Basoga maternal kin. "Not a single ruler," notes Cohen, "in Bugabula, Buzaaya, or Luuka (all of them descended from once Lwo-speaking people) to the end of the nineteenth century was born of a mother of a clan of Lwo origin."[41] The kingdom of Bugweri provides a good illustration of the centrality of Basoga women and the alliances formed by and through them to Luo authority. In the early seventeenth century, Kakaire arrived in Bugweri from Bunyoro after travelling across Busoga and seized power in the kingdom. As the Busoga historical texts relate, "Kakaire came with his wife Kawaga and the clan of his father-in-law [abaiseMbupi]... That was Kakaire's wife and he came with her. When he arrived in Busoga, he married again, to a woman who was a mwiseKaziba. She was the mother of Menha oweKibedi."[42] Kakaire's Musoga wife was called Nakaziba and it was *her* son who succeeded

[39] Cohen, *The Historical Tradition of Busoga*, 14–16.
[40] Cohen, "The Face of Contact," 352–3; Cohen, "The Political Transformation of Northern Busoga," 470.
[41] Cohen, *Womunafu's Bunafu*, 86.
[42] Cohen, ed., "Collected Texts of Busoga Traditional History," Text 333 (quote). For a detailed discussion of Kakaire's travels and establishment in Bugweri, see Cohen, *The Historical Tradition of Busoga*, 155–70.

his father to the throne, not any of his sons from his other, non-Musoga wives.[43] The requirement in the Luo-ruled Busoga kingdoms for the king's mother – and hence his queen mother – to be Musoga demonstrates that these polities derived much of their legitimacy through the motherhood of Basoga women. The Luo immigrants and their descendants introduced some of the ideological underpinnings of political power. But they also incorporated into their kingdoms the particular ideology of motherhood that underlay Soga social and political organisation, an ideology that had deep roots in South Kyogan and North Nyanzan history. Incorporating this preexisting ideology facilitated the maintenance, if not the seizure, of power by this 'outsider' elite.[44]

While Basoga wives and mothers were at the heart of Luo claims to political legitimacy, their natal kin also benefitted from their place at the centre of power. At the very end of the eighteenth century or perhaps at the start of the nineteenth century, a man called Mwondha of the abaise-Iruba clan settled in Namaganda in the kingdom of Bugabula.

At Namaganda he became very rich with many things. After Gabula [the king of Bugabula] had given him that village Namaganda, his herds used to go and trample the gardens of Gabula's wives at Naminage. The wives complained that this man's herds were spoiling the villages. Immediately, an order was despatched that he should be taken to a village where his cattle could be fed. That is why he was given Nakabiro. There he had a daughter named Kisasi.

Later, Kisasi must have married the king of Bugabula because, as the historical texts relate, she was "the mother of Kagoda. That is Kagoda the prince. Kagoda himself was a nephew of the abaiseIruba." It was because of their maternal connection, remembered the abaiseIruba, that "the royal family has given us Nakabira village as the estate of the Queen Mother [Nakazaire]."[45] The connection to power through having once been the clan of the queen mother of Bugabula was such that they were granted lands for the use of generations beyond Kisasi's reign.

Beyond material benefits, members of the queen mother's clan stood to gain significant political advantage through the accession to the throne

[43] Cohen, ed., "Collected Texts of Busoga Traditional History," Text 331.
[44] This contrasts with early and ongoing depictions of state formation in the wider Great Lakes region as resulting from the immigration of Luo (or pre-Luo) speakers. For an early, but influential overview of this argument, see Roland Oliver, "The Traditional Histories of Buganda, Bunyoro, and Nkole," *Journal of the Royal Anthropological Institute of Great Britain and Ireland* 85, no. 1/2 (1955): 111–7. For a more recent analysis along similar lines, see Wrigley, *Kingship and State*, 202–6.
[45] Cohen, ed., "Collected Texts of Busoga Traditional History," Text 125.

of their *omwîwa*, and a king could rely on their support for his reign. In some cases the king could also rely on his maternal kin for vengeance should he be wronged. Although the attempt at vengeance was posthumous, an example of the support for a king by his maternal kin can be found in the traditions of the kingdoms of Bukono and Busiki. In the late eighteenth century Wakauli, whose mother Nyanwa was from Busiki, succeeded his father King Kisozi to the throne of Bukono. Wakauli was a bloodthirsty tyrant who delighted "in shedding blood, and he accordingly killed many of his subjects." The people of Bukono rebelled against their ruler and killed him. "Somehow the secret of the murder was revealed to the deceased's mother's relatives in Busiki, who became furious." Wakauli's maternal kin gathered an army and attacked Bukono: "a bloody war commenced. The loss on both sides was shocking but the Basiki sustained a thorough defeat." King Wakauli was succeeded by his half-brother Ntumba, whose mother was not from Busiki.[46] Although ultimately unsuccessful, the attempted invasion of Bukono by Wakauli's maternal kin indicates the lengths to which clan members were prepared to go to defend their *omwîwa*, their connection to political power.

It is clear that the office of queen mother existed in Busoga and in at least some of the kingdoms she was a powerful political figure.[47] Despite this, historians have not paid much attention to this political office. Their failure to do so could be the result of a number of factors: efforts by elite Basoga men to shore up their own authority, the biases of colonial ethnographers who both underplayed the political evolution of Busoga in contrast to Buganda and sought to emphasise the degradation of women, and the gender biases of Western academics in the mid- to late-twentieth century.[48] Cohen, for example, refers to the existence of the institution, but he almost never explicitly discusses it.[49] Fallers, meanwhile, ignored the role of the queen mother entirely in his seminal work on the political structures of Busoga; in his analysis, Soga government consisted only of men.[50]

Despite the limitations of the sources, we know enough about the political institution of queen mother to know that the women who held this office had significant authority in the kingdoms that they ruled alongside

---

[46] Lubogo, *A History of Busoga*, 9–10.

[47] Cohen, *The Historical Tradition of Busoga*, 16; Cohen, *Womunafu's Bunafu*, 36.

[48] For a discussion of the Ganda-centrism of Europeans in late-nineteenth and early-twentieth century Uganda, see Vincent, *Teso in Transformation*.

[49] A rare exception is Cohen, *Womunafu's Bunafu*, 90, 107.

[50] Fallers, *Bantu Bureaucracy*.

their sons. Queen mothers had their own estates and so they held direct authority over certain parts of the kingdom.[51] This would have meant that chiefs in a queen mother's estates answered to her, rather than to her son, and prestations or taxes from those estates were paid to her and not to the king. Queen mothers also played crucial roles in the accession of their sons. Although the senior wife and her son would have been the primary candidates, political realities meant that much depended on the ability of a king's widow to mobilise her clan and other powerful clans behind her son.[52] By mobilising such support some queen mothers became very influential in their kingdoms. One such was Kabalu of Luuka, whose story is discussed in detail in Chapter 5.

Royal wives in Busoga, of course, gave birth to girls as well as boys. Just as did North Nyanza speakers, Basoga distinguished between the children of kings according to gender. Princesses or *abámbéédhá* [31] had a number of roles in the political life of the numerous Soga kingdoms. A tradition that relates the transfer of power in Bukooli from the abaiseNaminha clan to the abaiseWakooli clan, in the late seventeenth or early eighteenth century, records that the last mwiseNaminha ruler called the *abámbéédhá* of the kingdom together to witness his naming of the mwiseWakooli man he had chosen to be his successor.[53] Princesses were also frequently at the centre of marriage alliances either between royal families from different kingdoms or between a royal family and a commoner family to reward loyal service or to tie the family's loyalties to the state.[54] More directly powerful was the *omúmbéédhá*, who reigned as queen sister alongside her brother, the king. While the evidence is incomplete, this position existed in at least some of the Soga kingdoms.[55] Where the office of queen sister existed, she participated in the coronation ceremonies alongside the new king, as in the kingdom of Bunha. According to the historical traditions, the installation ceremony for the new ruler or *Menha* involved "two chairs made of stones. That is the chair for Menha, the one who was installed on the stone, and the other is for Lubuga, Queen Sister."[56]

---

[51] Cohen, ed., "Collected Texts of Busoga Traditional History," Text 125.
[52] Fallers, *Bantu Bureaucracy*, 135; Cohen, *The Historical Tradition of Busoga*, 14–6.
[53] Cohen, ed., "Collected Texts of Busoga Traditional History," Text 15. See also Cohen, *The Historical Tradition of Busoga*, 147–9, 202–3.
[54] See for example, Cohen, ed., "Collected Texts of Busoga Traditional History," Texts 41 and 202; Cohen, *The Historical Tradition of Busoga*, 149.
[55] Cohen, ed., "Collected Texts of Busoga Traditional History," Texts 330, 333, and 603.
[56] Cohen, ed., "Collected Texts of Busoga Traditional History," Text 333.

These possibilities for royal women took place against an economic backdrop in which banana cultivation was of increasing importance. Whereas the South Kyoga speech community practised a mixed agricultural economy that included bananas, their Lusoga-speaking descendants increasingly cultivated bananas in a more intensive manner. This emphasis on banana farming is reflected in the innovation of at least eight new Lusoga nouns for varieties of banana: *bikoyekoye, kalyankoko, malira, mpululu, naminwa, ntinti, ntúudhú* and *weete.*[57] These do not approach the numbers of varieties of bananas in Buganda, but it is worth noting, as did the geographer Brian Langlands, of Europeans travelling through south Busoga in the 1890s that "in some respects they provided a picture of a more complete cover under banana for this area than was given even for south Buganda."[58] Frederick Jackson, for example, wrote that on crossing into Busoga, "we at once left the glaring sunlight, and entered the pleasant shade of vast areas of bananas as abruptly as one enters a wood at home. Bananas at that time, except in marshy depressions and narrow strips of neutral ground between sultanships, were practically continuous, mile after mile, as far as the Nile." Having travelled in Buganda and Busoga, he concluded that in 1890 "with a few exceptions the care bestowed on the bananas in Busoga was, generally speaking, incomparably the greater. It was scarcely possible to find a drooping or dead leaf, or the stem with shreds of withered bark attached."[59] Busoga was, according to Captain Eric Smith, "a land of bananas and plenty."[60] Gerald Portal meanwhile wrote to his mother of his east to west journey through Busoga to the Nile: "We have been wandering through a country consisting entirely of banana groves, which took about five days to get through – miles and miles

---

[57] Stephens, "Field Notes, 2004–2005," in author's possession. Minah Nabirye lists *ntúudhú* as a beer banana: "Kika kya matooke ekisogolwamu omubisi ogukola mwengebigele," Nabirye, *Eiwanika ly'Olusoga*, 192. Further research may well uncover significantly more terms for varieties of bananas in Lusoga dialects.

[58] B.W. Langlands, "The Banana in Uganda – 1860–1920," *Uganda Journal* 30, no. 1 (1966): 43. The perception of Buganda must have been affected by the disruption of warfare and population dislocation in the late nineteenth century. "Agricultural production was deeply undermined from the late 1880s; large tracts of land both around the lake and further inland – notably in Singo and Bulemezi, which were badly affected by war – were laid waste of people and, thus, cultivation." Reid, *Political Power in Pre-colonial Buganda*, 37. Still, Busoga was not unaffected by the violence in Buganda and so this does not negate these observations.

[59] Frederick J. Jackson, *Early Days in East Africa* (London: Edward Arnold, 1930), 256.

[60] H. B. Thomas, "Captain Eric Smith's Expedition to Lake Victoria in 1892," *Uganda Journal* 23, no. 2 (1959): 142.

of bananas."[61] "The traveller at once knew when he entered Busoga owing to the endless banana plantations," noted the missionary J. F. Cunningham, while the Mill Hill Father L. V. Van Den Bergh described its "unlimited banana groves" in 1901.[62] Although southern Busoga along Lake Victoria–Nyanza was particularly suited to banana cultivation, even the northern area bordering Lake Kyoga was described in 1899 as being plentiful in "bananas, sheep, and fowls."[63] This depiction of Busoga at the dawn of the twentieth century suggests that bananas were more important there than the linguistic record indicates. Such a transformation of the agricultural landscape would have taken several generations to complete, and so Lusoga-speakers must have been increasingly moving to banana cultivation from much earlier times. These descriptions do not mention the varieties of banana that Basoga farmers grew with such success. It may well be that their flourishing plantations were successfully composed of a much narrower range of cultivars, or varieties of edible bananas, than those of their Baganda neighbours. Bananas were certainly of great significance to Basoga as a food crop. Cunningham argued that the reliance on bananas as the staple food was partially responsible for the severe hardship and suffering during years of drought. "The people at that time had no other food crop of importance to depend on," he noted, "and felt the pinch of hunger severely."[64]

The growing importance of bananas in the economic sphere was reflected in Soga rituals associated with new motherhood and other aspects of social reproduction. The placenta and dried umbilical cord of a newborn baby, for instance, were buried at the base of specific banana plants.[65] Some clans named a type of banana to be eaten by a new mother during her postnatal seclusion – the abaiseBandha prescribed the *ntinti* banana – and during that seclusion she slept on a bed of dried banana

---

[61] Gerald Portal, *The British Mission to Uganda in 1893* (London: Edward Arnold, 1894), 213.
[62] Cunningham, *Uganda and Its Peoples*, 107; "News from Our Missions: The Upper Nile – Uganda. Letter from L. V. Van Den Bergh to Father Henry, Nazigo, Uganda, 14th February, 1901," *St Joseph's Advocate: A Quarterly Illustrated Record of Foreign Missions and of Life and Suffering in Heathen Lands* 4, no. 3 (1901): 53.
[63] R.T. Kirkpatrick, "Lake Choga and Surrounding Country," *Uganda Journal* 10, no. 2 (1946): 161.
[64] Cunningham, *Uganda and Its Peoples*, 110.
[65] Cohen, ed., "Collected Texts of Busoga Traditional History," Texts 14, 41, 287, 380, 468, and 515; Roscoe, *The Northern Bantu*, 214; SO-ETH-KIT-F-NM, interview, 19 January 2005, Busoga; SO-ETH-NAU-F-ME, interview, 21 January 2005, Busoga; SO-15-BUG-F-KJ, interview, 20 January 2005, Busoga.

leaves.[66] At the far end of the life-cycle of an important chief, according to Lubogo, mourners wore strips of banana fibre "round their heads and necks and waists," while women would "girt themselves with split banana leaves, held in position by very broad belts of fibre," to mark their loss.[67] A few days after the burial of a lesser chief, beer would be brewed from "a bunch of very young beer bananas," and "a gourd of it was poured over the grave." Bananas and their products were also associated with the social position of the senior wife or *kairu*. During the 'Burning the Dead Banana Leaf' rite for a chief's funeral, for example, a dried piece of banana leaf was "taken from the pillow of the chief wife" and burned at a crossroads at dawn.[68] Such practices reflected the *kairu*'s centrality to the social reproduction of the household and of her husband's lineage.

Bananas were not, however, the only crop used as a staple food or in ceremonies of social reproduction in either Busoga or East Kyoga: millet was also central to economic life. Cunningham reported that as late as the turn of the twentieth century, Basoga grew millet, among other crops, although bananas formed the core of their diet.[69] John Roscoe meanwhile noted that millet (*"bulo"*) was grown for food and "large millet" (sorghum) was preferred for brewing beer.[70] Like their Baganda neighbours, Basoga retained the North Nyanza nouns for granary, millet, and sorghum. Millet, however, continued to hold particular cultural significance. At least two Soga clans insisted, as we have seen, that *okúfulumyá* (*omwâná*) (the 'bringing-out' ceremony) had to be performed before the new millet-sowing season could commence.[71] In addition, before the new millet could be sown, the field and the seed had to be 'activated' through words spoken by a healer and, according to Roscoe's informants, while she was sowing the seeds the farmer "might not speak to anyone until she had finished."[72] On harvesting their first millet crop, a newly married couple took a portion to the husband's father before consuming any of it themselves.[73] That this was an essential part of the process for establishing a new household highlights the ongoing importance of millet in social reproduction.

---

[66] Cohen, ed., "Collected Texts of Busoga Traditional History," Texts 14 and 287.
[67] Laight and Lubogo, "Basoga Death and Burial Rites," 121.
[68] Laight and Lubogo, "Basoga Death and Burial Rites," 125. Crossroads were ritually important in both Busoga and Bugwere.
[69] Cunningham, *Uganda and Its Peoples*, 110.
[70] Roscoe, *The Bagesu and Other Tribes of the Uganda Protectorate*, 111.
[71] Cohen, ed., "Collected Texts of Busoga Traditional History," Texts 287 and 468.
[72] Roscoe, *The Bagesu and Other Tribes of the Uganda Protectorate*, 111.
[73] Roscoe, *The Northern Bantu*, 235.

There were, then, essential ties between economic life – food procurement in particular – and social reproduction in Busoga that manifested themselves at moments of women's acts of biological reproduction and the establishment of new cross-lineal connections through marriage and, crucially, through motherhood. The cultural marking of these networks of interlineal and interclan connections through rites associated with the cultivation of both staple crops, bananas and millet, served to connect motherhood performatively as social institution to the sustainability and durability of the community.

EAST KYOGA

East of Busoga, people speaking proto-East Kyoga practised marriage and motherhood in a linguistically and culturally diverse terrain. The wider area was inhabited by long-established communities speaking Greater Luhyia languages, which would have sounded reasonably familiar to East Kyogans although not comprehensible, and newer and often more transitory communities speaking Nilotic languages. The area to the northeast of the Mpologoma consisted of somewhat flatter, drier lands more prone to periodic drought. While historical analysis that relies only on environmental causes underplays human agency, it is precisely that agency which enabled people to choose different crops and sustenance methods in the face of ecological change or new environments. Similarly, people were able to make decisions about how to structure their communities to make the best of their situation.[74] What is striking about East Kyoga society is the way in which people constructed a mutable ideology of motherhood that enabled them to do just that.

Many of the interactions between East Kyogans and their neighbours speaking Luhyia and Nilotic languages were peaceful, but outbreaks of violent conflict are recorded in the oral traditions. Intermarriage served as a means to end conflict and enhance peaceful relations between warring groups, as has been the case more widely in Africa.[75] Such marital alliances were later recorded in the oral traditions of the Bagwere, but

[74] James Scott makes similar arguments about the Zomia region of Southeast Asia. Scott, *The Art of Not Being Governed*, 179, 220–37.
[75] There are many examples of this across history. In southern Sudan, for example, a Dinka leader gave a young woman to the neighbouring Yibel people in the seventeenth century to end intermittent fighting after which there was much intermarriage in order to maintain the established peace. See Stephanie Beswick, *Sudan's Blood Memory: The Legacy of War, Ethnicity and Slavery in Early South Sudan* (Rochester, N.Y.: University of Rochester Press, 2004), 39.

the borrowing of a noun that described a core feature of the home lives of people speaking proto-East Kyoga underlines the fact that they were a quite regular feature of intergroup relations during this earlier period. This is the noun for granary, *-deero* (cl. 7/8) [9], borrowed by speakers of proto-East Kyoga from those speaking a Southern Luo language (or languages). It is today found in both Lugwere and Rushana, where it has the common meaning 'granary.' In Dholuo, spoken in western Kenya, *dero* has the closely related range of meanings: 'granary, store basket, grain crib, bin,' and in Acholi, *dero* glosses as 'granary for storing millet, groundnuts, etc., barn.'[76] In the case of this noun, we can see that there was a straightforward transfer of both the shape of the word and its meaning from the Southern Luo languages to proto-East Kyoga.[77] Although there are today no Dholuo speakers living in the areas bordering where East Kyoga was spoken, we know that several groups speaking Southern Luo languages lived in the region during the gradual migration of Nilotic-speaking communities from the Bahr-el-Ghazal to the northeastern shore of Lake Victoria–Nyanza.[78]

The borrowing of *-deero* (cl. 7/8) was a striking innovation, since speakers of East Kyoga would have inherited a word for granary from their South Kyoga–speaking ancestors and grain cultivation was an ancient practice in the region, dating back to pre-Bantu times.[79] Furthermore, as we saw in Chapter 2, their North Nyanza–speaking ancestors had coined a new noun to describe the very granary raised on stilts that East Kyogans renamed. That East Kyoga speakers adopted a new noun for granary from non-Bantu speakers suggests that there were close social relationships between proto-East Kyoga and Southern Luo–speaking communities. Indeed the most plausible explanation is that this noun was borrowed as a result of intermarriage: as Luo-speaking women married into East Kyoga–speaking households and vice versa. Such women would quickly have learnt the language of their new home, if they did not already know it. At the same time they would have brought their own language and culture with them, and because of the importance of networks formed through mothers to East Kyoga society,

---

[76] Carole J. Capen, *Bilingual Dholuo-English Dictionary* (Tucson, AZ: C. A. Capen, 1998), 30; Odonga, *Lwo-English Dictionary*, 54.

[77] The lengthening of the first vowel is a common feature of items borrowed into proto-South Kyoga and proto-East Kyoga from Nilotic languages.

[78] Cohen, "The River-Lake Nilotes from the Fifteenth to the Nineteenth Century," 135–49.

[79] Schoenbrun, "We Are What We Eat," 27–9.

women in all likelihood maintained close links with their natal homes and kin groups.[80] These links would have served to further facilitate cultural transfers between the two groups. In Bugwere, according to ethnographic descriptions, each wife in a polygynous household had her own granary, which was a focus of her economic contribution and her ability to feed her children.[81] The granary represented a wife and mother's agricultural contribution to the household. If intermarriage was a common occurrence, as seems likely, it is not surprising that the name Luo wives and mothers used for their granaries was adopted throughout the East Kyoga speech community.

That community had to contend with drier climatic conditions and higher insecurity than their Basoga neighbours, and certainly faced less consistent rainfall than their Baganda cousins. Despite this, East Kyoga speakers must have experienced some decades of calm in which to establish banana groves. Banana cultivation became sufficiently important for them to innovate a new noun that described both the banana plant itself and a banana grove: *-pandu (cl. 3/4) [35]. This term is also found in the Luhyia language Lunyole, which today borders Lugwere to the south. Because the noun was not inherited from their shared ancestor – Great Lakes Bantu – it must have been coined by either the Lunyole or East Kyoga speech community and then borrowed through contact between the two. If it originated in the Lunyole speech community, this could indicate a reintroduction of banana cultivation to East Kyoga speakers as they settled in the lands northwest of the Mpologoma River. Given the continued cultivation of bananas by the North Nyanza speech communities and its descendants, however, this seems unlikely. It may rather indicate the sharing of specialised knowledge about growing bananas in the particular conditions found in these plains that were slightly drier than the lush hills closer to Lake Victoria–Nyanza. When the Bashana went to live among the Sebei in the foothills of Mount Masaaba they took with them a ceremony to ensure the fertility of banana groves, according to people interviewed by Walter Goldschmidt.[82] For this to occur, the rite must have been practised before the breakup of proto-East Kyoga in the early nineteenth century.

---

[80] For a similar, though more tentative, argument, see Schoenbrun, "We Are What We Eat," 28.
[81] GW-ETH-BUL-F-KJ, interview, 27 October 2004, Bugwere; GW-ETH-IKI-F-MN, interview, 16 November 2004, Bugwere.
[82] Goldschmidt with Goldschmidt, *Culture and Behavior of the Sebei*, 160.

BUGANDA

In Buganda from the sixteenth century, the shift towards a more bio-logically oriented view of motherhood accelerated. This shift was likely accentuated by important demographic changes brought about by the influx of increasingly large numbers of enslaved girls and women taken during expansionary wars as the rulers of Buganda sought to extend their political power into neighbouring regions. Before the seventeenth century, Buganda was a small kingdom closely related to the Soga polities to the east and consisting mainly of Busiro and Kyaddondo on the northwestern tip of Lake Victoria–Nyanza's shoreline.[83] After the accession to power of King Kateregga and *Nnàmasòle* Nabuso Nabagereka in the early to mid-seventeenth century the political reach of the Buganda dynasty extended significantly. Kateregga expanded the land controlled by the Buganda royal family and cemented his hold over these new lands through marriage alliances. But the direction of expansion under the reigns of Kateregga and of his son, Mutebi, "was to the west, with the incorporation of Butambala, Gomba, Busujju and part of Singo." It was during the reign of King Mawanda and his *nnàmasòle* in the early eighteenth century that the Buganda kingdom expanded to the northeast and southwest until, as Wrigley notes, it "stretched from the Katonga to the Nile and far into the interior."[84] Mawanda and his successors embarked on repeated expansionary wars and punitive raids on neighbouring regions that resulted in the capture of large numbers of non-Baganda women and their incorporation into Ganda households as slaves.[85] In particular, Mawanda used Kyaggwe province as a base for organising raids across the Nile River into southern Busoga.[86] A significant proportion of the women brought into Buganda in this way would, therefore, have been Basoga.

The expansion of Buganda was accompanied by a rise in what Nakanyike Musisi has termed 'elite polygyny' from the reign of Mawanda onwards, which saw chiefly and royal households containing tens of women, and in some cases very many more.[87] These developments resulted

---

[83] Médard, *Le royaume du Buganda au XIXᵉ siècle*, 48, 57.

[84] Hanson, *Landed Obligation*, 78; Wrigley, *Kingship and State*, 207 (quotes).

[85] Médard, *Le royaume du Buganda au XIXᵉ siècle*, 59–61, 259; Richard Reid, "Human Booty in Buganda: Some Observations on the Seizure of People in War, c. 1700–1890," in *Slavery in the Great Lakes Region of East Africa*, ed. Henri Médard and Shane Doyle (Oxford: James Currey, 2007), 145–60.

[86] Wrigley, *Kingship and State*, 207.

[87] Nakanyike B. Musisi, "Women, 'Elite Polygyny,' and Buganda State Formation," *Signs* 16, no. 4 (1991): 757–86; Médard, *Le royaume du Buganda au XIXᵉ siècle*, 259.

over time in a lower social status for women in Buganda in general and reinforced the shift towards an ideology of motherhood grounded in biology. We saw in Chapter 3 that this shift narrowed the opportunity for a woman to maintain her social and economic status within her marital household and natal lineage, but it also enabled a lower status woman to aspire to be the mother of the heir in her widowhood. Just as in Bugwere and Busoga, the mother of the heir was assured of a secure position in her husband's household, even after his death. Indeed a proverb suggests that even a slave woman could achieve that status should she be reproductively successful: *Ddungu ayizze, ng'omuzaana azaalidde nnyinimu ddenzi* ('Ddungu [the god of hunting] has brought home his catch, says the slave woman on giving birth to her master's son'). Abasi Kiyimba describes such a status as the highest position to which an ordinary woman could aspire.[88]

The word used in this proverb is *òmùzaàna* rather than the alternative one for a female slave, *ènvùmâ*. This choice of noun highlights the existence of a hierarchy even among slaves in Buganda. Writing about slavery in the wider Great Lakes region, Schoenbrun notes that while *òmùzaàna* marked a slave girl or a slave woman as an outsider and a newcomer, *ènvùmâ* "was derived from a widespread verb, *kuvuma*, meaning 'to speak ill of, to scorn.'"[89] The difference in the status of women and girls so named is also evident in the prefixes of the nouns. *Òmùzaàna* has the 'human,' class one prefix, *omu-*, while *ènvùmâ* has the class nine prefix commonly used for animal names: *en-*.[90] The historian Michael Twaddle draws on work by Eridadi M. K. Mulira to note that these nouns named two distinct categories of female slave and that to be an *ènvùmâ* slave was significantly different and worse than to be an *òmùzaàna*.[91] As Schoenbrun comments, the former "had little prospect of bettering [her] circumstances."[92] We can surmise from this that an *òmùzaàna* could aspire to be the mother of her master's heir and thus dramatically improve her social standing, but that this opportunity was not open to an *ènvùmâ*, even if she bore her master's children. By the end of the nineteenth century, the focus of the next chapter but suggestive here nonetheless, the possibility of any enslaved woman achieving high

---

[88] Kiyimba, "Gender Stereotypes in the Folktales and Proverbs of the Baganda," 114.
[89] Schoenbrun, "Violence, Marginality, Scorn and Honour," 47.
[90] See also, Wrigley, *Kingship and State*, 240.
[91] Michael Twaddle, "Slaves and Peasants in Buganda," in *Slavery and Other Forms of Unfree Labour*, ed. Léonie J. Archer (London: Routledge, 1988), 121–2.
[92] Schoenbrun, "Violence, Marginality, Scorn and Honour," 47.

status in her master's household would seem to have been very remote. Analysing the records of fifty-five slave women interviewed by Mill Hill missionaries, the historian Michael Tuck noted that only eight had living children conceived with their masters. When most of those eight subsequently left the household of their master and returned to their families, they left their children behind.[93] In these admittedly few cases, motherhood did not serve to improve the social or economic standing of enslaved women.

Motherhood was, however, the route to the most powerful political office held by a woman in Buganda. The *nnàmasòle* [33] or queen mother, was understood to be able to influence her son's political judgment, in addition to wielding direct power over specific parts of the kingdom. For those queen mothers who acted as regents until their sons were of age to rule for themselves, this influence was significantly strengthened. In the 1930s, Ganda intellectuals depicted the *nnàmasòle* as a restraining influence. Ham Mukasa, for example, asserted that a motherless prince could not become king because "there would be no one to check him if he behaved too evilly."[94] (Here 'mother' must be viewed in a social perspective rather than a biological one for a prince's birth mother could be replaced by her sister or another kinswoman if she died. This was the case during the reign of King Kamaanya, at the end of the eighteenth century, whose *nnàmasòle* was Nnamisango, the "youngest sister of Kamaanya's real mother."[95]) Despite this view of them as advocating restraint, some queen mothers incited their sons to fight. Nanteza was *nnàmasòle* for both her sons, Jjunju and Ssemakookiro, in the mid- to late-eighteenth century. When he was king, Jjunju killed one of Ssemakookiro's wives who was pregnant. Nanteza was so angry with Jjunju for this fraternal betrayal that she encouraged Ssemakookiro to rebel against his brother. According to the traditions, she did this by sending Ssemakookiro "seventy fighting men [*àbàzira*] with the following challenge: 'If you are a woman, get married to these men.'" Suitably humiliated by his mother's questioning of his manhood, he rose to the challenge by gathering his followers

[93] Michael W. Tuck, "Women's Experiences of Enslavement and Slavery in late Nineteenth- and early Twentieth-Century Uganda," in *Slavery in the Great Lakes Region of East Africa*, ed. Henri Médard and Shane Doyle (Oxford: James Currey, 2007), 182.

[94] 'Tewali anamukomangako nga abade asukiride okukola obubi." Ham Mukasa, "Ebifa ku Mulembe gwa Kabaka Mutesa [The History of the Reign of Kabaka Mutesa]," trans. A. H. C., *Uganda Journal* 1, no. 2 (1934): 119, 128, cited in Hanson, "Queen Mothers and Good Government in Buganda," 224.

[95] Kagwa, *The Kings of Buganda*, 104.

and rebelling against King Jjunju.[96] The queen mother of Buganda can, therefore, be seen to have held considerable sway over her son, but it is not evident that her influence was necessarily a calming one. The ongoing political influence of the *nnàmasòle* over the king no doubt reflected to some extent the crucial role she played in his selection and, perhaps, her ability to help bring him down if he displeased her.

Although in the upheavals of the nineteenth century the authority of the *nnàmasòle* of Buganda was challenged by the king and his chiefs, as we see in Chapter 5, it is clear that prior to this she ruled her estates independently of her son and had absolute sovereignty over those estates and her palace. This is reflected in the actions of King Ssemakookiro's son, Kakungulu, who, at the turn of the nineteenth century, rebelled against his father and led an army supported by the neighbouring kingdom of Bunyoro to the west, in an effort to usurp the king from the Ganda throne. Defeated by Ssemakookiro's forces, Kakungulu fled to his grandmother *Nnàmasòle* Nanteza, who protected him before he moved back to Bunyoro. King Ssemakookiro did not follow his son to the *nnàmasòle*'s palace and, despite Ssemakookiro's fear that he would rise again in rebellion, Kakungulu was able to take refuge safely with Nanteza.[97] The king apparently feared the wrath of his queen mother and the consequences of violating her sovereignty more than a renewed attempt at rebellion by his son.

The ritual importance to the Buganda kingdom of the division of power between a king and his queen mother is clear in the earlier tradition of Mawanda and his *nnàmasòle*, Nakide Luiga. Sometime in the early eighteenth century, Mawanda's soldiers set fire to the shrine of the *lùbaalè* (deity) Nakibinge at Bbumbu in Kyaddondo and a "spark from the burning shrine flew up and burnt the queen mother's breast." The *nnàmasòle*'s wound healed only after the king's men rebuilt Nakibinge's shrine.[98] This incident invokes the tension between creative and instrumental power in Buganda. Kodesh notes that "Mawanda did not engage in spirit possession. His authority lay elsewhere, most significantly in his control over the means of violence."[99] As set out in Chapter 3, an important tension in Buganda was between the instrumental power wielded by the three *kabaka* – the king, the *nnàmasòle*, and the *lùbugà* [6] or queen

---

[96] Kagwa, *The Kings of Buganda*, 90–4 (quote p. 92). See also Wrigley, *Kingship and State*, 225.

[97] Kagwa, *The Kings of Buganda*, 98.

[98] Kagwa, *The Kings of Buganda*, 74 (quote). See also, Wrigley, *Kingship and State*, 211.

[99] Kodesh, *Beyond the Royal Gaze*, 143.

sister – and the creative power that coalesced in the shrines of mediums and healers. Whereas on other occasions it was the king himself who suffered after challenging the creative power of the *balùbaalè* and their mediums (such as Tebandeke, who ruled at the start of the eighteenth century and who became a medium after challenging the authority of the deity Mukasa), this time it was the *nnàmasòle* who suffered the consequences of her son's actions.[100] The powers of the king and the *nnàmasòle*, as this tradition demonstrates, were not divisible.

Just as in Busoga, there was a political symbiosis in Buganda between kings and their maternal relatives. The tradition that relates the reign of King Ndawula in the late seventeenth century, for example, records that "he gave the village of Kikaaya to his mother's relatives, where they could cultivate food for him."[101] The king could not, however, count on the loyalty of his maternal relatives regardless of his behaviour. The reign of Mwanga I, in the mid-eighteenth century, suggests that, while the connection between *àbakòjjâ* and royal *àbàjjwa* was an important one, it could be trumped by the loyalties between a king's maternal relatives and their patrilineal clan members. When he ascended the throne, King Mwanga was advised to kill the son of Nkunnumbi – his *kòjjâ* or maternal uncle – to ensure a long reign; he did as he was advised. Nkunnumbi was so distraught at his son's murder that he smuggled a knife into the palace and stabbed Mwanga to death. The historian Semakula Kiwanuka, in his commentary on Apolo Kagwa's transcription of the tradition, notes that Nkunnumbi's fellow Ndiga clan members did not protest Mwanga's assassination because King Namugala, who succeeded him, was his full brother and so their maternal connection to the kingship remained.[102]

The interdependence between Baganda kings and their maternal kin and the fact that an ideology of motherhood lay at the heart of the Buganda kingdom came into conflict with efforts by individual kings to expand their own authority. As a result, several kings sought to undermine the relationship between *àbakòjjâ*, royal *àbàjjwa*, and the institution of the queen mother. This reached its zenith towards the end of the nineteenth century, but the process began earlier. Ssemakookiro, who reigned in the second half of the eighteenth century, executed several of his son Kamaanya's maternal relatives, including Kamaanya's mother, Ndwadewaziba. He did so, according to Kagwa, "because he had wanted

[100] Kagwa, *The Kings of Buganda*, 56–7.
[101] Kagwa, *The Kings of Buganda*, 59.
[102] Kagwa, *The Kings of Buganda*, 77.

his son to ascend the throne without any relatives." Despite this effort by Ssemakookiro to break the role of motherhood in upholding political power, on his accession Kamaanya deliberately sought out his mother's remaining relatives and appointed them to several chiefships. He also asked his maternal kin to appoint a successor to Ndwadewaziba – his deceased mother – and so his mother's younger sister, Nnamisango, reigned as *nnàmasòle* alongside him.[103]

In addition to the king's mother and her kin, his sisters were a significant force in the kingdom's politics. The *àbàmbejja*, or princesses of Buganda, have received much more scholarly attention than those of Busoga and Bugwere.[104] Their roles were similar to their counterparts across the North Nyanzan region, but given the larger scope and growing strength of the Buganda kingdom, they had access to significantly greater power. Many princesses became spirit wives by 'marrying' the national deities or *balùbaalè* and were thus able to mobilise creative power to influence the king and the queen mother. The more influential of the princesses could also wield instrumental power, and this is remembered in the traditions of Buganda. In the early eighteenth century a particularly cruel king – Kagulu – ruled Buganda. He was remembered most infamously for having "made some spiked ring-chains, which he called mats, and when people came to him to have their cases tried, or to visit him, he ordered them to kneel upon the spiked rings; then if they did not go down on their faces, or if their greeting in any way displeased him, he had them speared to death." It was an *òmùmbejja* – Ndege Nassolo – who organised the successful rebellion of chiefs and princes against her brother. Although Kagulu managed to evade capture when his capital fell to the rebels, he was later "caught in the Kyagwe district by the princess Ndege, who had him drowned in the Lake Victoria-Nyanza."[105] When Mawanda succeeded his brother Kagulu as king, Ndege Nassolo translated her role in overthrowing Kagulu into official authority by becoming *lùbugà* or queen sister. In that role she is remembered for playing a central part in the key events of Mawanda's reign and, in particular, in an attempted séance with the spirit of Kintu, the mythical founder king of Buganda. Kintu's medium insisted that Ndege, as *lùbugà*, and no other

---

[103] Kagwa, *The Kings of Buganda*, 104.

[104] For example, Musisi, "Transformations of Baganda Women"; Nannyonga-Tamusuza, *Baakisimba*; Sacks, *Sisters and Wives*; Schiller, "The Royal Women of Buganda". *Òmùmbejja* and *àbàmbejja* are the singular and plural Luganda reflexes of **-mbeeza* (cl. 1/2) [31].

[105] Kagwa, *The Kings of Buganda*, 63; Roscoe, *The Baganda*, 221 (quotes).

person should accompany the king. This insistence on the part of the medium is indicative of the interdependence of the positions of king and queen sister in the eighteenth century.[106]

Thus, although many *àbàmbejja* held significant authority through their roles as wives to *balùbaalè* or deities, the most powerful of them was the one who was enthroned as *lùbugà* or queen sister alongside her brother the king, and who shared the title of *kabaka* with the king and the queen mother. She had her own palace and controlled her own estates with her own administration formed of chiefs who raised taxes for her. Furthermore, she heard court cases and held the power of life and death over the people in her jurisdiction.[107] On the death of the king, the *lùbugà* took the title *nnaalinnya* ('I will soon ascend') and became responsible for guarding the shrines in which the deceased king's jawbone and umbilical cord were kept. This shine was where the spirit or *òmuzimù* of the king resided and so the *lùbugà/nnaalinnya* held significant creative power even after leaving office. The *nnaalinnya* of the deceased king also played a prominent role in selecting the new *lùbugà*. The latter should not have the same mother as the new king nor should she have any brothers by her own mother.[108] This both ensured that there would be no competition for the kingship from a full sibling of the *lùbugà* and that two lineages and in all likelihood two clans – that of the queen mother and that of the mother of the queen sister – had vested interests in the success of the new rulers of the kingdom.

Although they described her as the 'wife' and 'queen' to the king, European missionary ethnographers and Christian Ganda ethnographers took great pains to point out that the king and his queen sister did not have sexual relations.[109] Wrigley believes that the 'marriage' of the king and the *lùbugà* was a relic of the "long-abandoned custom of royal incest" which "was embedded in the tradition but could survive there only in the guise of fantasy."[110] At the end of the eighteenth and in the early nineteenth century King Kamaanya and his son King Ssuuna 'married' some of their sisters, but whether this was in order to have sexual relations

---

[106] Kagwa, *The Kings of Buganda*, 72–3.

[107] Roscoe, *The Baganda*, 66, 84, 187, 236–7; Schiller, "The Royal Women of Buganda," 463; Martin Southwold, "Succession to the Throne in Buganda," in *Succession to High Office*, ed. Jack Goody (Cambridge: Cambridge University Press, 1966), 83; Snoxall, *Luganda-English Dictionary*, 182.

[108] Roscoe, *The Baganda*, 84, 114, 191, 283–4.

[109] For example, Roscoe, *The Baganda*, 84. But for a different view, see Gorju, *Entre le Victoria l'Albert et l'Edouard*, 95, fn. 1.

[110] Wrigley, *Kingship and State*, 157.

with them or simply an attempt at controlling their reproductive power is difficult to judge. The historical texts from Busoga clearly refer to royal incest between a king and his queen sister in the foundation myth of the Bugweri polity.[111] However, as Cohen remarks in his annotations on the texts, the incest is recorded as being between the Luo sibling immigrants who founded the state and there is little to suggest that incest was common, even in royal settings. Given the strong taboo placed on relationships defined as incest, including with any member of the mother's clan as well as any member of a person's own clan, we must assume that any socially sanctioned relationships between siblings were limited to royalty in North Nyanzan societies and even then not widely practiced.

The institution of the *lùbugà* existed in commoner Baganda households as well as in the royal palaces. Just as the heir to the throne could not become king without a queen sister, neither could an heir to his father inherit without a sister (real or classificatory) to be nominated as *lùbugà* and participate in the funeral and inheritance rites. Lucy Mair explained this by reference to blood-brotherhood ceremonies in which if a man was not married he "was provided with a fictitious wife" and posited that for both blood-brotherhood and inheritance "the relationships which the ceremony creates will affect not the man only, but his whole household." Because matters of inheritance were "purely clan affairs" the fictional wife had to be of the same clan and so could not be the heir's own wife.[112] But the explanation of this practice in terms of marriage fails to explain why even female heirs required a *lùbugà*. The marriage model also falls short because a man's sister would not be part of his household, just as the royal *lùbugà* had her own palace and estates away from those of her brother.

The intellectual history of the noun *lùbugà* [6] gives us an alternative analysis of the institutional role of royal queen sister and her commoner or *òmùkopi* counterpart. One possible etymology for *lùbugà* reflects her power over her subjects. In this etymology Luganda speakers derived the noun from an older verb, possibly of proto-Mashariki origin, *-bug-*, which had the meaning 'speak (with authority).' By using the prefix *lu-* from noun class eleven, the noun class used to denote languages, Baganda classified 'speaking with authority' as its own form of language. In so doing they emphasised the importance of 'powerful speech' to the

---

[111] Cohen, ed., "Collected Texts of Busoga Traditional History," Texts 330 and 603; Lubogo, *A History of Busoga*, 55–7.

[112] Mair, *An African People in the Twentieth Century*, 212–4 (quote p. 213); Schiller, "The Royal Women of Buganda," 465–6; Southwold, "Succession to the Throne in Buganda, 124, fn. 4.

standing of the queen sister. The second etymology traces its derivation from an ancient Bantu noun *-buga* with the meaning "free or clear land near home."[113] West Nyanza speakers innovated the noun **mbuga* from this older word to describe a chief's compound, and the same root is used in the Luganda *èkìbugà*, which refers to the royal capital. These two etymologies are not necessarily exclusive: acts of **-bug-* 'speaking (with authority)' would have been performed in the **mbuga* and in the *èkìbugà*. The term *lùbugà*, then, is intimately connected with the spatial configuration of power and with the 'civilisation' or domestication of the landscape. It seems likely that the innovation of this institution was connected to claims to specific plots of land by lineages and clans; by marking the land as inherited by a man and a woman of the clan – and not by a man of the clan and his wife from another clan – the patriclan's claim to the land was reinforced at each succession. Although this practice was unique to Buganda in the North Nyanza region, the institution of the *lùbugà* during the rites of succession and inheritance may have emerged first among commoners and then later been borrowed into the trappings of state. However, while the position of *lùbugà* in clans was limited to Buganda, the office of queen sister was widespread not only throughout North Nyanza but also West Nyanzan societies, suggesting that the political office may be the older of the two.

The queen sister could wield significant power within the kingdom of Buganda. While she often achieved that office through the influence of her maternal patriclan, she did not derive her authority through motherhood. Indeed, she was proscribed from being a mother. The queen mothers of Buganda and of the Busoga kingdoms reflected the importance of motherhood as ideology in political power, but reproduction was not an uncontested area of life for women in the royal palaces of Buganda. Attempts to control the reproductive lives of royal women divided between prohibitions on marriage and prohibitions on pregnancy. These prohibitions fell most heavily on the Baganda princesses or *àbàmbejja*, but were not limited to them. A crucial distinction between princesses in Buganda and those in the polities to the east was in relation to marriage. In South Kyoga and then in Busoga and, later, in Bugwere, princesses married important commoners or royals from other polities in order to create alliances.[114]

[113] Schoenbrun, *The Historical Reconstruction of Great Lakes Bantu Cultural Vocabulary*, 71–2, root 96; see also 34, root 4.
[114] Cohen, ed., "Collected Texts of Busoga Traditional History," Texts 41 and 202; Cohen, *The Historical Tradition of Busoga*, 147–9; Atkinson, ed., "Bugwere Historical Texts," Text 23. But see Text 1 for a different version of this story.

In Buganda princesses were forbidden to marry and, thus, prohibited from having legitimate children.[115] Scholars have debated the origins and the antiquity of this practice. One of the earliest outside commentators on Buganda, John Hanning Speke, who visited the kingdom in 1862, wrote that princesses could not marry because they became the wives of the king. He dated the practice to the reign of King Kimera and the foundation of the kingdom.[116] In the historical traditions, as they were transcribed by Apolo Kagwa, there is a suggestion that the prohibition was introduced as recently as the late eighteenth century by Kamaanya and continued into the nineteenth century by Ssuuna. Semakula Kiwanuka, in his translation and annotation of Kagwa's history of the kings of Buganda, ascribes the prohibition to Kamaanya's desire to marry some of his sisters.[117] Laurence Schiller draws on Kagwa's suggestion that the prohibition was introduced only in the eighteenth century to connect it to "the kabaka's increasing exclusion of all princesses and princes from power," while Nakanyike Musisi ascribes it to "the class interests of the royal family and male dominated social order."[118] Sylvia Nannyonga-Tamusuza argues, meanwhile, that the *àbàmbejja* could not marry because, in the gender system of Buganda, they were 'female-men.' Her argument is supported by nineteenth century reports that princesses were greeted as *ssebò* 'sir' rather than *nnyabò* 'madam,' and non-royal men were expected to kneel when greeting them, in contravention of the social norm.[119] By "assigning to Ganda princesses cultural characteristics usually reserved for men and, more importantly, for female spirit mediums and ritual specialists," argues Kodesh, "Ganda royal actors sought to imbue them with a type of authority that was widely associated with the practitioners of public healing." Together, the dedication of princesses as wives to *lubaale* or 'deities' and the prohibitions on their marrying men and having "socially recognized offspring" were part of the attempt by Baganda kings to control the particular kind of power that coalesced in shrines.[120]

In his analysis of patrilineality in Africa, Claude Meillassoux noted that women are exchanged between male elders in different communities

[115] Gorju, *Entre le Victoria l'Albert et l'Edouard*, 95, fn.1; Roscoe, *The Baganda*, 85, 187.
[116] Speke, *Journal of the Discovery of the Source of the Nile*, 249.
[117] Kagwa, *The Kings of Buganda*, 136–7.
[118] Schiller, "The Royal Women of Buganda," 467–8 (quote p. 467); Musisi, "Transformations of Baganda Women," 80.
[119] Nannyonga-Tamusuza, *Baakisimba*, 83.
[120] Kodesh, *Beyond the Royal Gaze*, 157.

in order to ensure the reproduction both of the community itself and of the power of male elders in the community.[121] The exchange of women between Baganda clans was essential for social reproduction because they practiced exogamous marriage and tabooed sexual relationships between clan members as incestuous. Not allowing princesses to marry broke the circle of exchange between clans, marking the royal family as distinct from the clans of commoners.[122] Furthermore, a woman's children and her fellow clan members retained strong ties. Indeed a Muganda child's position in her or his (father's) clan depended at least partially on recognition from the mother's clan, as noted in Chapter 3. The relationship between *àbàjjwa* and their maternal kin was an essential feature of social organisation and reproduction. Although they had strong relationships with their mother's clan, *àbàmbejja* did not belong to a clan because their father, the king, had no clan.[123] There was, thus, no one to refer to their children as *àbàjjwa*. Because of the essential role played by *àbàjjwa* in the social reproduction of their maternal patriclans and vice versa, it is plausible to argue that it was ideologically impossible in terms of Ganda social organisation for princesses to marry and bear the legitimate children that were the primary purpose of any marriage. If we accept this analysis, it suggests that the prohibition on *àbàmbejja* marrying dated to an early period in the kingdom's history.

It was not only princesses who faced limitations on their maternity. In the palace, only the king's wives could become mothers in the sense of bearing socially sanctioned children and restrictions existed even within this cohort. According to Roscoe, in most cases sons born to royal wives from a number of specified clans "were killed at birth, and only girls were allowed to live."[124] This was because those clans should not have an *òmùjjwa* on the throne. On acceding to office, the *nnàmasòle* or queen mother also faced limitations on her reproductive power. She was not allowed to remarry, as her husband would be in a position of authority over the king, nor was she allowed to have any more children, as they would be potential challengers to the throne. There were not, however,

[121] Meillassoux, *Maidens, Meal and Money*.
[122] Because there was no exchange of women involving the royal family, wife-givers had to be compensated by different means. As the predilection of kings for marrying a great number of wives became common, there was an increased need to find more resources to compensate the wife-givers. Wrigley, *Kingship and State*, 172.
[123] Southwold, "Succession to the Throne in Buganda," 85. For a thoughtful analysis of the history of relations between the royal family and the Ganda clans, see Kodesh, *Beyond the Royal Gaze*.
[124] Roscoe, *The Baganda*, 137, for the relevant clans, see 138–40.

limitations on her sexual life, but this may have had more to do with her political status than with her gender.[125]

The extension of the political reach of the Buganda kingdom and struggles to control and shape the ideological underpinnings of the polity, thus affected the sexual and reproductive lives of women in the royal palaces. Growing restrictions on wives and princesses, in particular, coincided with ever increasing numbers of women in the palaces, especially from the reign of King Mawanda and *Nnàmasòle* Nakide Luiga in the early eighteenth century onwards. More generally throughout Buganda this period saw an intensified emphasis on biological reproduction in the social construction of motherhood. This intensification held open the possibility, however remote, of enhanced social standing for marginal women in the household. But it also served to dramatically narrow the possibilities for those women who faced infertility or whose children did not survive. In Busoga, by contrast, the efforts by Luo elites to control the northern kingdoms placed social motherhood ever more firmly at the heart of political authority. The value of motherhood as a social institution that created cross-patrilineal and cross-patriclan ties in the broader society was similarly apparent in the multiple small kingdoms that proliferated over this period. This led to a reinforcement of a social form of motherhood that allowed women of the appropriate standing to adopt children in order to become mothers. Nonetheless, because this was predicated on preexisting social standing, it appears to have been limited to elite women and not a possibility for all. In East Kyoga communities, a more flexible institution of motherhood started to emerge in the face of high social and linguistic diversity, even within individual households, and more difficult ecological conditions that threatened the sustainability of the society. Intermarriage and a more diverse economic base meant that 'foreign' wives grew food for the household and were mothers to East Kyoga children. The dominant ideology of motherhood here was one that facilitated integration and adaptation.

---

[125] Roscoe, *The Baganda*, 237; Schiller, "The Royal Women of Buganda," 459. Musisi argues, by contrast, that the *nnàmasòle* was neither to remarry nor have sexual relations. She bases this interpretation on King Ssuuna II's execution of several chiefs that he suspected of having liaisons with his mother (Musisi, "Transformations of Baganda Women," 77–8).

5

Contesting the Authority of Mothers in the Nineteenth Century

The nineteenth century in East Africa has been described as a "century of ironies."[1] This was certainly true of the lands lying to the north and west of Lake Victoria–Nyanza. It was a period of accumulation of massive wealth and power for a few and of dislocation, warfare, famine, and disease for many. In Buganda, successful chiefs transformed their newfound trade wealth into political capital and challenged the royal family's hold on power. The rise in slave raiding by Baganda in order to sell ever more captives into the long-distance trade to plantations across East Africa and for export from the Swahili coast heightened instability both in neighbouring societies, including Busoga, and in Buganda itself.[2] At the same time, Buganda had by this period managed to exert its authority over the Soga polities to the extent that many of them paid tribute to their westerly neighbour.[3] Not all the disruption in North Nyanza societies was caused by expansionism and slave raiding from west of the Nile, however. The movement of new populations into Bugwere and neighbouring regions to the north and east also resulted in a number of wars and displacement as people competed for land and political authority. The

---

[1] Steven Feierman, "A Century of Ironies in East Africa (c. 1780–1890)," in *African History: From Earliest Times to Independence*, ed. Philip Curtin, et al. 2nd ed. (London: Longman, 1995), 352–76.

[2] Holly Hanson, "Stolen People and Autonomous Chiefs: The Social Consequences of Non-Free Followers," in *Slavery in the Great Lakes Region of East Africa*, ed. Henri Médard and Shane Doyle (Oxford: James Currey, 2007), 161–73; also Hanson, *Landed Obligation*.

[3] Cohen, *Womunafu's Bunafu*; Médard, *Le royaume du Buganda au XIXe siècle*; Reid, *Political Power in Pre-Colonial Buganda*.

social distortion caused by this confluence of crises undermined the place of motherhood in both politics and society, most acutely in Buganda and Busoga, but also in Bugwere. The arrival of European missionaries and colonisers exacerbated that distortion. By the early twentieth century elite men in Buganda and Busoga had negotiated a new political landscape with the British colonial authorities: one purged of powerful queen mothers and one in which women in general were presented as subservient. That particular landscape has been read back to earlier periods in Uganda's history to create a timeless vision of intense patriarchy, incorrectly shaping our understanding of gender relations in precolonial Uganda. But, it was new in the nineteenth century and needs to be understood as the outcome of bitter power struggles over political economy, not as an unchanging truth.

BUGWERE AND BUSHANA

The division of East Kyoga into the modern speech communities of Lugwere and Rushana was the abrupt product of warfare and famine, in marked contrast to the gradual dissolution of North Nyanza and South Kyoga. At the end of the eighteenth century, the people who were to become the Bashana lived with those who have come to call themselves Bagwere to the northeast of Busoga across the Mpologoma River and they spoke a common language, East Kyoga or early-Lugwere. This was a period of significant social and political disruption as a result of physical conflict and economic crisis. It was also a time of political innovation with the founding of new polities and of efforts to reestablish and sustain communities in the face of repeated episodes of instability. Through all of this, a flexible ideology of motherhood that facilitated the creation of intergroup networks and the incorporation of outsiders was of central importance. As these two peoples – Bagwere and Bashana – sought to rebuild their communities, they drew on their ideologies of reproduction in their social, economic, and political lives.

In the late seventeenth century, before the breakup of East Kyoga, the Banagwere chiefdom – seeking to avoid conflict – fled westwards across the Mpologoma River to northern Busoga.[4] Their chief, Nagwere, brought them back to southern Bugwere in the early to mid-eighteenth

---

[4] The following draws extensively on the Bugwere Historical Texts and on Ron Atkinson's working chronology of the events recorded in the Texts. I am indebted to him for sharing this material with me.

century.[5] Around the mid-1780s, a man called Laki Omugobera who was from southern Teso arrived in the Banagwere chiefdom, which was by then well reestablished in Bugwere. When he arrived he hid in the bush and hunted for food. "Two widows saw a fire in the forest. They tried to investigate and managed to see a man who looked like an animal – he had long hair, was naked, and very dirty." Laki Omugobera could not speak Lugwere, but he signalled to the widows that he had meat. This was a time of famine and the women "were starving and looking for food for their younger children who were left behind with their grandmother." Laki Omugobera gave the women meat to take "to their children and grandmother ... When the women took the meat to the old mother-in-law, she was surprised and very pleased." The next day the mother-in-law told the widows to return to Laki Omugobera and get more meat. "The women also brought that meat to the old woman who was the mother of their husband, and to her grandchildren. At that time the old woman suggested it would be better to move to the forest where the naked man was drying meat, to get help during the dangerous time of famine." Through his talent for hunting, Laki Omugobera was able to supply food to the family, including the widows' mother-in-law. The mother-in-law 'civilised' Laki Omugobera by asking the "widows to put a skin around the waist of the naked man, and also one across his chest." Having provided for the family and "because the widows were still young women, the man managed to stay with them and their four children ... He got married to the two widows and they produced more children."[6]

The tradition of Laki Omugobera has some aspects of myth to it, in particular the motif of the skilled hunter who overcomes his stranger status by providing food to the community. The historical evidence for Laki Omugobera's existence is strong, however. His son Yua, for example, is recorded as having founded the Balalaka chiefdom in c.1810. Equally strong is the evidence for famine around the time of Laki Omugobera's arrival in the Banagwere polity. The Bagwere called this famine *matyama* because many people fled to Bugwere from further north and east to avoid even worse shortages and then stayed. In Lugwere, people said of those immigrants that *baatyamíre*, 'they sat down,' from the verb *-tyamá*, 'sit down; dwell.'[7] Many of those who arrived at this time, like Laki Omugobera, were Ateso speakers. Drawing on oral traditions, the British

[5] Ron Atkinson suggests that this would almost certainly have been after the major drought and famine of the mid-1720s. Personal communication.
[6] Atkinson, ed., "Bugwere Historical Texts," Text 4.
[7] Atkinson, ed., "Bugwere Historical Texts," Text 13.

colonial official and ethnographer J. C. D. Lawrance argued that Iteso first started to settle in the area across the lake to the north of Bugwere during the eighteenth century and started to move into Bugwere only after 1800.[8] Later work by J. B. Webster suggested that these processes may have begun a little earlier.[9] Early Iteso migrants who moved into the Bugwere region integrated culturally and dropped the Ateso language in favour of Lugwere.

The prominent role women played in the tradition of Laki Omugobera's integration into Bugwere and his son's subsequent establishment of the Balalaka chiefdom suggests that women had essential roles in integrating Iteso and other immigrants. Intermarriage was a powerful tool of integration, and the linguistic and historical records for Bugwere indicate that this occurred at high levels. Yua's political control of the Balalaka chiefdom also underscores the place of public motherhood at the heart of political authority because his legitimacy as a ruler derived from his Mugwere mother, reflecting similar practices among the Luo immigrants in Busoga discussed in Chapter 4.

Interactions between those speaking East Kyoga or early Lugwere and immigrants speaking Nilotic languages were not always peaceful, however. Oral traditions report, for example, that warfare was the reason for the migration of the group that became the Bashana out of the area in the early nineteenth century.[10] Conflict was not borne out of primordial hatred of the 'other,' but rather from competition for diminishing resources, particularly at times of scarcity and famine. Towards the end of Yua's reign over the Balalaka chiefdom, around the mid-1830s, there was a famine that was called *bukwikwi* in reference to a type of wild grass similar to millet that people ate to survive during it.[11] This famine is remembered as having been much more deadly in Bugwere than the previous *matyama* famine and thus the cause of greater conflict within the area.[12] The *bukwikwi* famine appears to have been in part caused by conflict, which it in turn exacerbated. According to the historical traditions, Yua's establishment of the Balalaka chiefdom was not an entirely

[8] J. C. D. Lawrance, *The Iteso: Fifty Years of Change in a Nilo-Hamitic Tribe of Uganda* (London: Oxford University Press, 1957), 9–14.
[9] J. B. Webster, "Usuku: Homeland of the Iteso," in *The Iteso During the Asonya*, ed. J. B. Webster, et al. (Nairobi: East African Publishing House, 1973), 11.
[10] Atkinson, ed., "Bugwere Historical Texts," Texts 13 and 44; GW-ETH-KAA-M-YMW, interview, 2 December 2004, Bugwere.
[11] Samuel Mubbala, personal correspondence, 16 August 2010.
[12] Ron Atkinson, "Precolonial Bugwere Chronology – Working Version," personal communication; Atkinson, ed., "Bugwere Historical Texts," Text 13.

peaceful affair, with outbreaks of violence occurring as he sought to solidify and extend his political authority.

One consequence of the emergence of the Balalaka chiefdom on the political scene was the emigration of those who became Bashana. In one of the "Bugwere Historical Texts," Samwiri Kimuda narrated the events as follows:

> The people who first had *mitala* [land] in Kadoma were, remember, as I told you before, that the first Lugwere speaking people were the Baluba of the Bagwere. So most of the *abaami be'mitala* [chiefs of the land] in Kadoma were the people of Iruba. When Yuwa chased them out of those *mitala*, they separated. Some of them went to Bunyole and some of them went to Sebei. Those who went to Bunyole became the tribe Banyole; those who went to Sebei became of the tribe of Sebei. But the clan wasn't removed.[13]

In this version of the final dissolution of the North Nyanza languages, the Bashana are described as becoming Sebei. In an interview in Bugwere in 2004, Yokulamu Mutemere, a local historian also narrated the story of the Bashana's emigration from Bugwere as resulting from war. He referred to the Bashana by the name commonly used among the Bagwere for them – Balegenyi – and that derives from their post-emigration location in Bulegenyi in Sironko District. He made the point that they ran away from Bugwere, because there were many wars at the time, and went into the mountains to the east. But while the Balegenyi settled there and changed their group identity, they kept speaking a language similar to Lugwere.[14] While the Bashana did adopt several Sebei cultural practices, including male and female circumcision as part of initiation, and learned to speak Kupsabiny and Lumasaaba alongside Rushana, they maintained a distinct cultural-linguistic identity from the people among whom they settled.[15]

Perhaps their most striking cultural adoption was that of female and male circumcision. Walter Goldschmidt and Gale Goldschmidt, who briefly mentioned the Bashana in their work on the Sebei, noted that the former started to practice male circumcision at some point after their migration to the area as a way of establishing friendly relationships with the Sebei. According to Walter and Gale Goldschmidt, prior to the adoption of the

---

[13] Atkinson, ed., "Bugwere Historical Texts," Text 44.
[14] GW-ETH-KAA-M-YMW, interview, 2 December 2004, Bugwere. Other sources also largely correlate with a departure date of mid to late 1830s. See Roscoe, *The Bagesu and Other Tribes of the Uganda Protectorate*, 83; and SH-ETH-KLA-M-MH, interview, 18 June, 2005, Kampala.
[15] SH-ETH-BYI-M-MM, interview 15 October 2008, Bulegenyi.

practice of male circumcision by the Bashana, "the Sebei 'despised' them and refused to drink beer with them."[16] Personal relationships of another kind, intermarriage, appear to have been the major motivating factor for the Bashana to adopt the practice of female circumcision. "In an effort to please the Sebei who sought Bumatyek [Bashana] women as wives," noted Robert Edgerton, "the Bumatyek accepted the Sebei practice of female circumcision."[17] Rushana speakers changed the way that they talk about marriage, innovating a new verb to describe the act of marrying: *-bimbirra* [5] 'marry (of a man),' with the derived form *-bimbirrikana* [5] 'marry (of a woman).' This verb may be derived from the ancient verb **-bímb-*, 'to swell,' and thus refer to the pregnancies that should ideally follow marriage.[18] Although it must be of relatively recent origin – that is, less than two hundred years old – it does not seem to have been directly borrowed from the people among whom the Bashana settled. It may be that they innovated this new pair of verbs because the meaning of marriage in their community shifted as circumcision was adopted and a significant proportion of their daughters and sons married Sebei men and women.

While the Bashana adopted some Sebei cultural practices, they also maintained their own, including those around birth and the naming of infants. These practices closely resembled those of their Lugwere- and Lusoga-speaking relatives. For example, some weeks after a birth the clan would gather to give the newborn child the name of a grandparent of the clan. Neither a barren woman nor a person who had committed suicide would have her or his name given to a new member of the clan. Similarly, when twins were born, special ceremonies were performed. This ceremony was called *kyembwa kya kishana*, during which the mother and infant twins were first brought out from their seclusion. The parents of twins were given honorific titles: *makwana* for the mother of twins and *baaba w'obakwana* for their father.[19] These practices around reproduction reflect clear continuities from East Kyoga and earlier times, despite the new words used to talk about and name them.

---

[16] Goldschmidt with Goldschmidt, *Culture and Behavior of the Sebei*, 299.

[17] Robert B. Edgerton, *The Individual in Cultural Adaptation: A Study of Four East African Peoples* (Berkeley: University of California Press, 1971), 286. Note that the Sebei name for the Bashana is Bumatyek or Bumachek. During an interview in Bulegenyi in 2008, I was given an explanation that largely supported Edgerton's analysis. SH-ETH-BYI-M-MM, interview, 15 October 2008, Bulegenyi.

[18] **-bímb-* is a proto-Bantu verb. Bastin and Schadeberg, "Bantu Lexical Reconstructions 3," ID main 240 (Accessed 14 January 2013).

[19] SH-ETH-BYI-G-MN, interview, 20 October 2008, Bulegenyi. The etymologies for these names are unclear.

People speaking Lugwere in the lands to the northeast of the Mpologoma River also built on the practices of their ancestors to mark women's transition into motherhood through taboos, specific rituals, and ceremonies and through the use of particular plants associated with social reproduction. In so doing they were able to ground their community in continuities despite the frequently turbulent contexts in which they lived. Bagwere marked pregnancies with a series of clan-specific taboos. While different clans specified particular avoidances, there was also overlap between them. For example, in the Bakatikoko, Bakalijoko, and Balalaka clans pregnant wives were forbidden from eating intestines.[20] Not all the taboos centred on food avoidances. As in Busoga, there were also, in some clans, restrictions on pregnant women returning to their natal homes. Members of the Bakatikoko clan forbade their daughters-in-law from visiting their parents' home when they were pregnant, while the Bakalijoko clan forbade them from entering their parents' house although they could visit the compound.[21] Just as was the case for their neighbours across the Mpologoma, these restrictions on visiting the natal home while pregnant were designed to avoid the problematic and potentially ritually dangerous consequences of a woman giving birth there.

These pregnancy *émíziro* [52] tend to be explained in the ethnographic literature – and by members of the societies themselves – in terms of the physiological consequences of breaking them, the most likely consequence being miscarriage. But they also affected the nonbiological aspects of social reproduction. In Busoga, as we saw in Chapter 4, and in Bugwere, the concept of *ekítálo* was invoked, pointing to the broader social repercussions if a woman violated the cultural restrictions her husband's clan imposed on her. In part this was about maintaining clear lines of patrilineal descent. The multiple clan-specific avoidances suggest an anxiety within patrilineages and patriclans to lay claim to the children born to their sons' wives, women who married into the clan but who retained their natal clan identity. In the increasingly multiethnic, multilingual world inhabited by speakers of Lugwere and Lusoga, intermarriage was a common means of integrating newcomers and enabling those newcomers to establish themselves in society. Such exogamous marriages placed a premium on claiming the children born to the sons of the community. Through clan-specific pregnancy taboos, members of the patriclan

[20] Atkinson, ed., "Bugwere Historical Texts," Text 38; GW-ETH-IKI-F-KG, interview, 16 November 2004, Bugwere.
[21] GW-ETH-BUL-F-KJ, interview, 27 October 2004, Bugwere; GW-ETH-IKI-F-KG, interview, 16 November 2004, Bugwere.

marked the future child as theirs and reminded the anticipant mother of this. But these pregnancy taboos were also about ensuring that each clan had *ábaiwá* (children of its female members) to perform essential ceremonies associated with social reproduction, including carrying out actions that were taboo for clan members. This was particularly the case with regard to the restrictions on pregnant wives visiting their homes.

The economic, social, and biological aspects of reproduction came together in this cultural restriction that highlighted the importance of bananas to the sustenance of the community and the essential role that *ábaiwá* played in their mothers' clans. This can be seen, for example, in the way in which the placenta was disposed of. Bagwere people viewed the placenta (*ékitaní* [46]) as having features in common with infants, including having grown within the mother's womb. They thus treated the placenta with care, ensuring that it was buried appropriately. This perception of the placenta as slightly human is expressed in the Lugwere proverb: *Aminamina ekitani abyalisya eirongo* ('She who keeps turning over the placenta delivers twins'). Bagwere women and men interpret the proverb as meaning that if you persist in looking for a problem it will arise, but it derives from the belief that the placenta had some potential of becoming a baby.[22] Once delivered, the placenta was buried under a banana plant and Gwere custom dictated that an *ómwiwá* [20] (the child of a female lineage-member) should be the person to eat the first harvest of fruit from that plant; the parents of the baby whose placenta was buried beneath it should never eat its fruit.[23]

Despite the continued importance of connections created by and through mothers, Bagwere lineages followed patrilineal descent and took care to validate the legitimacy of children born to the wives of their lineage-member. While reminiscent of legitimacy ceremonies in Buganda, those held in Bugwere were less elaborate and conducted by the women of the lineage and clan. After the period of postnatal seclusion and rest, the *ókutooláku* or 'bringing out' of the new mother and her child coincided with the ceremony to test the legitimacy of the child and *ókwerúlá*, the giving of a clan name to the child. The new mother's parents were informed that she was to be brought out and they brought a cow and other food.[24] The *óísengá* [41] (paternal aunt) of the new father roasted groundnuts,

[22] Wabwezi Andrew, "The Bagwere Proverbs," (BA diss., Makerere University, Kampala, Uganda, 2004), 15–6.
[23] GW-ETH-IKI-F-KG, interview, 16 November 2004, Bugwere.
[24] Atkinson, ed., "Bugwere Historical Texts," Text 24.

sesame, white peas, and bambara nuts after which an *ómwiwá* of the new father gave them to the mother to eat as she emerged from seclusion. This was called *ókulyá embenenwa*, or eating 'embenenwa.'[25] It was believed that the baby of a woman who had committed adultery would fall sick and die if she ate the *embenenwa*.[26] Once the child had been shown to be a member of the paternal clan, an ancestor's name was chosen for her or him through a variety of methods. Usually the first name to be given was that of the father's maternal grandmother or his paternal grandfather. Among those whose names were not passed on to the next generation were lepers, people who had committed suicide, and barren women.[27]

As in other North Nyanzan, and indeed other Great Lakes Bantu, societies, all these ceremonies were elaborated on when a woman gave birth to twins in Bugwere. But, despite having inherited this practice of marking the birth of twins as of social and spiritual significance, Lugwere speakers borrowed *mabangi* – the honorific noun they gave to a mother of twins – from speakers of a Nilotic language, most likely Ateso. We can clearly see this when we look at the words for both mother of twins and twins in the Southern Nilotic languages. The noun for twin in Ateso is *ibaŋit*, while in Acholi the noun for the mother of twins is *min baŋŋi*.[28] As with the words connected to the fostering of children discussed in Chapter 4, that this noun was borrowed from Nilotic speakers strongly points to the role of mothers from both communities in introducing new terms to name shared social institutions within the family.

Not all women would have achieved motherhood through biological means and two linguistic innovations highlight the relevance of fostering and adoption in Bagwere households. The first is that Lugwere speakers restricted the meaning of the South Kyoga verb **piita* [38] to 'foster–in a child,' excluding its older reference to livestock. The second is that they borrowed and adapted a Nilo-Saharan verb for the act of fostering-out

[25] I have not been able to find an English translation for *embenenwa*. The only gloss I have come across is from the wordlist compiled by the Summer Institute of Languages Bible Translation Project for Lugwere. That list gives the meaning 'cartilage.' All the people I asked about this in interviews insisted that the only meaning of *embenenwa* was this particular dish given to a new mother on her emergence from postpartum seclusion.

[26] GW-ETH-BUL-F-KJ, interview, 11 November 2004, Bugwere; GW-ETH-IKI-F-KG, interview, 16 November 2004, Bugwere; GW-ETH-IKI-F-MN, interview, 16 November 2004, Bugwere.

[27] Atkinson, ed., "Bugwere Historical Texts," Text 24; GW-ETH-BUL-F-KJ, interview, 11 November 2004, Bugwere; GW-ETH-IKI-F-KG, interview, 16 November 2004, Bugwere; GW-ETH-IKI-F-MN, interview, 16 November 2004, Bugwere.

[28] Hilders and Lawrance, *An English-Ateso and Ateso-English Vocabulary*, 31; Odonga, *Lwo-English Dictionary*, 23.

or entrusting a child. In Lugwere this verb takes the form *-jooka* [21] and has a second and related meaning of 'entrust livestock,' mirroring the original South Kyoga meaning of **piita*. Ehret has reconstructed the form **nḍòk* in proto-Nilo-Saharan, with the gloss 'turn' (intr.).[29] This has modern reflexes in Acholi (*dwok* 'return, take back') and in Ik (i'jok-es 'lend').[30] Although the linguistic evidence for the relationship between these forms of the word is convincing, the route through which it reached people speaking Lugwere remains opaque. Despite this lack of clarity in the etymology, the fact that the Bagwere community used the same verb to describe the practice of fostering-out whether they were talking about children or livestock reflects their continuation of the tradition of drawing a close parallel between the fostering of children between households and entrusting livestock and the kinds of relationships of obligation created through such trusts.

Fostering of children and livestock may have become more common after the emergence of Lugwere, a development that is suggested by these two innovations. The context in which Bagwere women and men lived helps explain why this may have been so. In the economically less secure environment to the east of the Mpologoma River, with drier conditions and greater social conflict, Bagwere women – to avoid extreme poverty as they aged – needed adult children to provide for them. A mother with adult children could expect to rely on them when she was no longer able to grow food for herself. This is reflected in the Lugwere proverb: *Ompuwu owakula ayonka omwana*, 'when a pigeon grows old, it suckles its child.'[31] Just as the old pigeon feeds from its young in the proverb, so an aged mother would be provided for by her children. A woman without biological offspring could make use of the social structures of fostering to receive a child from a woman who had achieved greater reproductive success. Similarly, with regards to livestock, acts of lending and borrowing could serve as guarantees in uncertain times.[32]

Marriage shaped motherhood in Bugwere. Just as in Busoga and Buganda and their shared ancestral communities, motherhood was viewed as a social institution as much as an outcome of biological

---

[29] Ehret, *A Historical-Comparative Reconstruction of Nilo-Saharan*, 336, no. 354. Note that the International Phonetic Alphabet symbol 'ḍ' represents a voiced, retroflex stop.

[30] Odonga, *Lwo-English Dictionary*, 63; Bernd Heine, *Ik Dictionary* (Cologne: Rüdiger Köppe Verlag, 1999), 42. Note that the International Phonetic Alphabet symbol 'j' here represents a voiced palatal implosive.

[31] Andrew, "The Bagwere Proverbs," 25.

[32] Shipton, *The Nature of Entrustment*.

processes. Lugwere speakers used the noun they had inherited from their proto-North Nyanza–speaking ancestors to describe marriage, *eírya* [39], and they also used the proto-Great Lakes Bantu verb *-*kwa* to describe the transfer of bridewealth from the groom's family and lineage to the bride's. In addition to the transfer of the bridewealth, the groom's family gave a goat to his mother-in-law after the wedding night in recognition of her particular role. Lugwere speakers also innovated in this semantic field. One innovation is found in both Lugwere and Lulamoogi – the dialect of Lusoga that is geographically and linguistically closest to Lugwere – and is the verb to describe the act of marrying (in contrast to the noun describing the state of marriage). This new verb, *ókusúná mukalí*, 'marry a woman,' and *ókusúná musaizá*, 'marry a man,' is a simple derivation from the verb -*suná* 'get,' and may, therefore, suggest an easing of some of the formal processes of marriage. Strikingly, even in innovating a new verb for 'marry,' Bagwere retained its active meaning with reference to women's acts of marrying. What is more, they did not distinguish between women's and men's acts in this regard.

Bagwere also changed the word they used to describe the wedding companion and, again, they shared this innovation with speakers of Lulamoogi. Whereas all the other North Nyanza languages, including Rushana, retained the older noun *-*perekezi* (cl. 1a) [36] to name the female lineage-member who accompanied a bride to her marital home, Lugwere and Lulamoogi speakers used the term *mperya* (cl. 1a) [37]. This noun is also found in Lunyoro and was derived from the proto-Bantu verb *-*pá*, 'give.'[33] The distribution of this noun makes its history rather unclear. It does not seem likely that it is a shared retention from proto-West Nyanza, but rather that this is a case of independent innovation or borrowing, or perhaps both. Either speakers of both Runyoro and Lugwere (or Lulamoogi) coined the noun independently, or it was coined by one and borrowed into the other. If the latter, the most plausible direction of travel would be along the ancient trade routes that ran from Bunyoro across Lake Kyoga bringing salt from the manufacturing site at Kibiro.[34] The noun *mperya* would, therefore, have travelled from Lunyoro into Lulamoogi and then Lugwere. There were connections between northern Busoga and Bunyoro so this is not an improbable explanation, but it raises the question of why, of the northern Lusoga dialects, it was only

---

[33] Bastin and Schadeberg, "Bantu Lexical Reconstructions 3," ID main 2344 (Accessed 14 January 2013).

[34] For more on this see, Connah, *Kibiro*.

Lulamoogi speakers who borrowed this term that lay at the heart of the marriage process. Setting aside the complicated etymology, what is most salient about the noun *mperya* is that its derivation suggests she had an active role in the wedding. The *mperya* 'gave' the bride to her groom, rather than simply accompanying her as was the case with her *-perekezi* (cl. 1/2) counterparts in the other North Nyanzan societies.

Young people in Bugwere were just as likely to challenge the authority of their elders when it came to marriage as their North Nyanzan cousins. While the etymology of the verbs to describe elopement was similar to that of the verbs used by their North Nyanza–speaking ancestors in denoting violence, speakers of Lugwere did not use the same terms. Instead they innovated their own pair of verbs: *-bandúká* [2], 'elope (of a woman)' and *-bandúlá* [2], 'elope (of a man).' These verbs were derived from the verb *-banda*, 'force one's way through.' Despite the innovation, this verbal pair has two important continuities with the proto-West Nyanza verbal pair it replaced (*-hambuka/*-hambula*), which we saw in Chapter 2. The first is in their derivation which makes use of the *-ul-* and *-uk-* 'separative' suffixes that, in this case, again give an 'intensive' meaning to the verb. In addition, as with the older verb, while the female form *-banduka* is intransitive, it is not in the passive mood, suggesting that while Bagwere girls and women may not have 'forced their way through' men in order to elope, they did 'force' themselves into elopement. This reflects continuity in the long-standing view of women as active participants in elopement, rather than merely passive recipients of men's desires. The second continuity lies in the fact that the underlying verbs – *-banda*, 'force one's way through' in this case, and *-pamba*, 'seize' in the case of the older verbs – are ones of violence; indicating that elopement was a violent act. While the violence may have been in male acts of 'forcing their way through' to take women, the active – though intransitive – *-bandúká* again does not lend itself easily to this analysis. As in West Nyanzan and then North Nyanzan society, elopement was a socially violent act for members of the eloping couple's lineages in Bugwere. Such marriages did not serve to create the same networks of connections as did more formal marriage arrangements marked through the transfer of bridewealth. That Lugwere speakers felt the need to replace the older violent verb with a new one suggests some degree of social tension around elopement. It may be that as they lived in contexts of greater insecurity, so Bagwere elders placed greater emphasis on the role of socially sanctioned marriage in ensuring harmonious relations. The role of such marriages in smoothing tensions between groups may have contributed to the easing of the requirements of formal marriage as we have seen. Regardless, elopement undermined the possibility of using marital alliances in this way. At the same time, as in other societies, elopement must have served as a welcome possibility for some young women and men from poor families. This term for elopement is also found in the neighbouring Lusoga dialect, Lusiki, perhaps as a result of intermarriage, socially sanctioned or not, between the two communities.

For those women who married through the socially preferred process of bridewealth transfer and accompaniment to the marital home, attaining the position of senior wife helped secure her social and economic status. While Lugwere speakers continued to use the proto-North Nyanza noun **kaidu* (cl. 12) [19] to describe the senior wife in a household, they also innovated two new compound nouns for her: *omukali omukulu* and *omukali omuyoola ikoke*. The first of these is straightforward with a literal meaning of 'senior wife.' The second, however, is richer etymologically and suggests that the role of the senior wife in Bagwere households was shifting. The literal translation is 'a woman who is a collector of ashes.'[35] These multiple terms for senior wife and, in particular, the ambiguous attitude contained in the latter, suggest a de-institutionalisation of the position, in contrast to neighbouring Busoga, that was also manifest in the much more widely available right to foster children. But, the continued social importance of the senior wife in Bugwere is reflected in the proverb: *Owulya tiwende* ('Being the newly married wife does not mean being the most loved,'), which suggests that the position of the *kaidu* was not necessarily undermined by the arrival of new wives in the household.[36]

Lugwere speakers borrowed a new noun to describe a fundamental part of the social and physical structure of their communities: the homestead. They borrowed this noun, *-daala* (cl. 7/8) [8] from speakers of a Greater Luhyia language (or languages). It is particularly remarkable that Bagwere women and men chose to rename such a central focus of the community as the homestead itself. We can find an explanation for this innovation in the changing ideological place of mothers, and their work, in the community. In a patrilineal context such as this, women speaking Greater Luhyia languages – as mothers to Bagwere children – were central figures in the social reproduction of the society for reasons that extended beyond biological processes. They created essential connections

---

[35] Samuel Mubbala, personal correspondence, 16 August 2010.
[36] Andrew, "The Bagwere Proverbs," 36.

between distinct and at times conflicting groups, most basically those connections that took human form in their children. These wives and mothers also grew millet. Millet, physically and symbolically, was vital in this community that lived in a relatively dry area where bananas could not be relied upon in the same way as they could be to the west. The fact that Lugwere speakers adopted a Greater Luhyia noun for this central feature of their communities further emphasises the extent of the interactions that they had with people speaking different languages and a certain degree, at least, of bilingualism.

Millet was a key component of many of the ceremonies and rituals that marked the different stages of the life cycle.[37] Bagwere farmers placed significant emphasis on millet cultivation for food and sorghum cultivation for beer.[38] Just as they had for North Nyanzans, both products held cultural as well as nutritional importance. *Ámalwá* (cl. 6) [30] or millet beer was consumed and shared with the ancestors and other important spirits at ceremonies, weddings, and funerals.[39] One of the most important ceremonies in Bugwere was *okwakira obulo obwita obuyaka*, which marked the first eating of millet porridge, *óbwíta*, from the new crop.[40] This ceremony was performed by each lineage group that gathered together for that purpose. The head of the lineage made offerings of livestock and millet beer at the three household shrines: the *kibaali ky'oluwuuga* (the courtyard shrine), the *kibaali ky'oGasani* (the shrine to Gasani), and the *kibaali ky'oIseja* (the shrine to Iseja).[41] The women of the lineage would have threshed, dried, and ground the millet in preparation and on the day cooked the *óbwíta* or millet porridge. In addition to the lineage members, the *ábaiwá* (the children of female lineage members) also participated in this important ceremony; it was they who drank the *ámalwá* in the shrine to Iseja. Only after *okwakira obulo obwita obuyaka* had been performed could the newly harvested millet be eaten. As well as marking the completion of the harvest, Bagwere recognised the role of the spirits in

---

[37] Atkinson, ed., "Bugwere Historical Texts," Texts 25, 37, 41, 44, and 45; GW-ETH-IKI-F-MN, interview, 16 November 2004.

[38] Atkinson, ed., "Bugwere Historical Texts," Text 25.

[39] Atkinson, ed., "Bugwere Historical Texts," Texts 37, 41, and 45.

[40] The following is from Atkinson, ed., "Bugwere Historical Texts," Texts 44 and 45. GW-ETH-IKI-F-MN, interview, 16 November 2004, Bugwere.

[41] Gasani was the 'supreme being' in Bugwere and Iseja was the spirit responsible for congenital physical deformity. Each household had a shrine or *kibaali* (pl. *bibaali*) in the vicinity of the homestead to both Gasani and Iseja. Atkinson, ed., "Bugwere Historical Texts," Text 47; Long, "Notes of the Bugwere District," 470–1; GW-ETH-BUT-M-TH, interview, 1 December 2004, Bugwere.

the success of the crop when they sowed the millet grains. To sow the new crop, women would come together and sow the millet in each woman's field in turn in a process known as *ókuwulúkyá énsigó*, 'bringing out the seeds.' As they sowed the grains, they called aloud to the spirits to give them germination.[42]

That Bagwere marked both the start and end of the millet cycle indicates the cultural importance of the crop, which played a prominent role in social reproduction as well as feeding the community. It was women who sowed the seeds, who threshed the harvested stalks, who dried and ground the grains into flour and who prepared the millet porridge or *óbwíta*. Millet porridge was eaten in a homestead or *-daala* when a newborn baby was first brought out of the house in which she was born and a woman's children, though not lineage members, participated in her lineage's ceremony marking the successful completion of the millet harvest. In many ways, in Bugwere it was millet, not bananas, that was most closely connected to motherhood and to healthy social reproduction. Gwere motherhood both depended on a good harvest of millet in order for rituals surrounding the birth of children to be performed and helped ensure a good harvest through the participation of *ábaiwá* in the *okwakira obulo obwita obuyaka* ceremony.

Bashana, too, continued to grow millet and pigeon peas (*mpindi*) along with other legumes and bananas after they moved to Bulegenyi. Millet, in particular, held cultural importance with a ceremony to mark the harvest of the crop and the first consumption of the new millet grain. They called this ceremony *kukesa buro buyaka* and it involved sacrifices to their ancestors and to the nonancestral spirit, Kasani.[43] For both societies descended from East Kyoga, the ancient grain crop retained not only nutritional value in their diets but also a symbolic role in their social reproduction.

Although millet held crucial economic and symbolic value in both societies, bananas continued to be central to agricultural production and in ceremonies and rites marking moments of the lifecycle, particularly death. Despite living in lands quite different in nature to the fertile hills of Buganda that proved so suited to banana cultivation, both Bagwere and Bashana farmers continued growing the fruit. Bashana women and men, as they settled in the foothills of Mount Elgon with their steep slopes and cooler atmosphere, had to adapt their cultivation practices

---

[42] GW-ETH-IKI-F-MN, interview, 16 November 2004, Bugwere.
[43] SH-ETH-BYI-G-MN, interview, 20 October 2008, Bulegenyi.

from those used in the low hills and shallow valleys of Bugwere. Yet it is clear that bananas continued to form part of the agricultural economy of the Bashana after their migration. Goldschmidt noted that "there is a rite to increase the fertility of plantains, manifestly a recent introduction by the Bumachek [Bashana]."[44] Rushana speakers have at least nine nouns for specific types of banana, covering those for brewing, cooking and sweet bananas. Some of these nouns they inherited from their North Nyanza–speaking ancestors, such as the beer banana *manjaaya* (cl. 5/6) [32]. Others seem to be more recent borrowings from their Bamasaaba neighbours, such as the general term for beer bananas, *mamwa* (cl. 5/6).[45] Some banana names, however, appear to be innovations by Rushana speakers. Perhaps most likely of these is the cooking banana *ishana* (cl. 9/10), which may be connected to the ethnonym of its farmers, Bashana. While the Bashana may have introduced important rites associated with banana cultivation to their Sebei neighbours, their Bamasaaba neighbours have an older history of growing bananas. It is clear from the linguistic evidence that the Bashana adopted some of the cultivars grown by Bamasaaba farmers. The Bashana, however, have been more linguistically conservative with regards to other terminology associated with bananas and their cultivation. Whereas Lugwere speakers used a new noun for the banana grove and another for dry banana leaves, speakers of Rushana retained the words used by their North Nyanzan ancestors.

While bananas did not have the same economic and cultural value in Bugwere as they did in Buganda to the west, they were an important part of the agricultural landscape, seemingly to the detriment of the community. So much so that in 1902, the Mill Hill missionary Father Christopher Kirk wrote of Bugwere that "a great deal of the misery and appalling suffering sadly witnessed in famine time might be thus averted by the planting and sowing [of] other native foods to substitute the bananas [as] their sole staple diet."[46] Indeed, Bagwere farmers continued to expand their banana cultivation despite the disruption caused by warfare and drought during the nineteenth century. This expansion is reflected in the linguistic record as Lugwere speakers innovated several new terms in this semantic field. Lugwere has at least four unique terms for varieties of banana: *kabuluka, kasaaye, mawolu,* and *nalywanda*. It is likely that some of this

[44] Goldschmidt with Goldschmidt, *Culture and Behavior of the Sebei*, 160.
[45] Berthe Siertsema, *Masaba Word List: English-Masaba, Masaba-English* (Tervuren, Belgium: Musée Royal de l'Afrique Centrale, 1981), 173.
[46] "Christopher Kirk to Very Revd Father Rector, 21 July 1902," File 164, Box Per 1899, Mill Hill Mission Archives.

development in banana cultivation occurred during the time before the separation of Lugwere and Rushana but that Bashana farmers ultimately abandoned these new terms for banana varieties because they could not be productively cultivated in their new mountainous environment. This interest in naming banana varieties points to the importance of bananas to agriculture in Bugwere; another new term points to their importance in Gwere culture. This is the noun for a dry banana leaf, *kisoigi* (cl. 7/8) [44], which is also used to name a particular funeral ceremony that was performed twice: a small version performed approximately three weeks after the burial and a major version performed a year or so later.[47]

During the *kisoigi* ceremony, female mourners wore green banana leaf skirts called *bibenga* (cl. 7/8). As a sign of their bereavement and mourning, they did not replace the skirts with fresh ones each day, but rather wore the original skirts until the leaves had become *bisoigi* (plural of *kisoigi*).[48] In the Lulamoogi dialect of Lusoga to the west of Bugwere, the name Soigi is given to a daughter born to parents who have suffered the death of several children and is translated as 'condolence.'[49] The most likely etymology for the word is an original connection with funerals or specific clothing worn by the bereaved. As dry banana leaves began to feature prominently as symbols of mourning, the word was used to describe the dry leaves themselves. Banana leaf clothing appears to have been restricted to Bagwere women, with men preferring animal hides and barkcloth. Banana cultivation itself was not so strictly gendered.[50] The heavy work of clearing land for a new banana grove would have probably been the province of men, but both women and men were responsible for weeding and maintaining the grove once it was established.[51]

Although the staples of bananas and millet were central to social reproduction and cultural life in Bugwere, *mpindi* or pigeon peas also featured prominently. *Mpindi* was the only crop with a dedicated *ómusambwá* or 'territorial nature spirit.'[52] The *ómusambwá* for *mpindi* was Nakiriga,

[47] "Lugwere-English Wordlist," Lugwere Bible Translation Project, Summer Institute of Languages, Entebbe, Uganda.
[48] GW-ETH-BUT-M-TZ, interview, 1 December 2004, Bugwere.
[49] *Dictionary: Lusoga-English English-Lusoga*, part I, 131.
[50] Long, "Notes of the Bugwere District," 458; GW-ETH-BUT-M-TZ, interview, 1 December 2004, Bugwere.
[51] GW-ETH-BUL-F-KJ, interview, 27 October 2004, Bugwere; GW-ETH-IKI-F-MN, interview, 16 November 2004, Bugwere.
[52] Schoenbrun, *The Historical Reconstruction of Great Lakes Bantu Cultural Vocabulary*, 226–8, root 347; Schoenbrun, *A Green Place, A Good Place*, 197, see 197–203 for a discussion of the history of such spirits and their role in West Nyanza society.

and before the new crop could be sown, Nakiriga's medium made offerings to the *ómusambwá*. The women of the village gathered together and cooked millet and sesame seeds. Each woman took a portion of *óbwíta* (millet porridge) sprinkled with ground sesame seeds to her pea-field for that season. While singing 'Give me *mpindi*, I will give you *obwita* and sesame,' she threw small pieces of the food in each part of the field. It was at harvest time, however, that the *mpindi* crop was most important in terms of social reproduction. The *mpindi* were harvested by mature but unmarried girls who then used the peas to cook a dish called *magera* in a rite known as *ókwesumbírírá* or 'cooking for oneself.' The people of the village gathered to eat the *magera* with millet porridge and to see which girls were eligible for marriage.[53] The public display of such girls perhaps reflects a greater urgency in reproduction as Bagwere sought to reestablish their communities and polities in the face of periodic instability and competition between chiefdoms leading to warfare.

Hunting and fishing supplemented the diet of Bagwere families as it did elsewhere. But in an environment more prone to drought and famine than Busoga and Buganda to the west of the Mpologoma River, such supplements could be essential to survival. Hunting, as is depicted in the narrative of Laki Omugobera's arrival in Bugwere, was predominantly a male activity, just as in Busoga and Buganda. Fishing, which in Bugwere occurred most commonly in small waterways close to homesteads, was a different affair. In addition to inheriting a range of vocabulary items associated with fishing, Lugwere speakers coined a specific term to describe the form of fishing using a basket that was performed by women. They did this by changing the meaning of an older verb, *-toga* (tr.) [47]. This original meaning of this in proto-North Nyanza seems to have described actions in which people used their hands to mash food or to catch fish. The ethnographic material on Bugwere makes no reference to ritual precautions with regard to this form of fishing, but it was clearly marked as a female activity.[54] In Buganda and Busoga it was the dangerous, yet potentially rewarding, activity of lake fishing that was surrounded by ritual avoidances and performances. This more quotidian form of fishing, which was less prestigious but perhaps more effective at providing regular nutrition to the household and that was performed by women, did not require the same kind of precautions.

---

[53] Atkinson, ed., "Bugwere Historical Texts," Text 45; GW-ETH-BUL-F-KJ, interview, 27 October 2004, Bugwere.

[54] GW-15-KAI-M-MPM, interview, 17 November 2004, Bugwere.

The lower degree of specialised economic activity, particularly in terms of hunting and fishing, in Bugwere and Bushana reflected the political context in which there was less centralisation of power in relation to Busoga and to Buganda especially. That is not to say that these were decentralised or acephalous societies; all the historical evidence strongly suggests that there were chiefs, some of whom wielded significant power. But overall, there was less capacity to support economic specialisation through higher agricultural productivity and polities remained on a more local scale. In such a context, alliances and support networks created through marriage and maternity were all the more essential.

Little information remains about the political organisation of the Bashana after their migration to Bulegenyi, except that they have not had a chief of their own since the reign of the Muganda chief and warlord Semei Kakungulu in the early twentieth century when their last chief, Matui, was killed.[55] Although there is as yet nothing published on the precolonial history of Bugwere, the Bugwere Historical Texts collected in the early 1970s provide a substantial body of evidence about its political organisation. The Banagwere royal clan emerged in the early part of the seventeenth century, most likely soon after the people who came to speak East Kyoga settled to the east of the Mpologoma River from Busoga. The members of the Banagwere clan claim first-comer status in Bugwere and the historical texts record them as founding the first Gwere polity.

According to the texts, Nagwere founded the clan and the polity that it ruled.[56] Nagwere's claim to his position was, however, legitimated through his paternal grandmother. He is said to have been descended from Kintu, the notional father or grandfather of so many first kings and chiefs of the Lake Victoria–Nyanza littoral. According to tradition, Kintu travelled through Bugwere on his way to Buganda from Mount Masaaba (Mount Elgon) in the east. He broke his travels at Naboa, where he was the guest of a man named Luba and he stayed long enough to 'marry' Luba's daughter before continuing westwards. His 'wife' and their son, Mugoya, did not accompany him on his onward journey, but rather stayed with Luba. Mugoya, as with so many Basoga princes to the west, was therefore raised in his maternal grandfather's household. In his turn, Mugoya married. His son was Nagwere who founded the Banagwere clan and chiefdom and whose descendants ruled until Kakungulu's reign

55 GW-ETH-KLA-M-MH, interview, 18 June 2005, Kampala.
56 Atkinson, ed., "Bugwere Historical Texts," Text 4.

at the start of the twentieth century.[57] The claim of the Banagwere to be first-comers in Bugwere derived, thus, from the maternal and not paternal line. It may well be that the connection to Kintu was added as a means of bolstering a claim that was not fully patrilineal.

While we have less information on royal women in Bugwere than in Busoga and Buganda, there is evidence that shows that senior wives, queen mothers, and queen sisters, or their chiefly counterparts, were at the heart of political authority. The *kaidu* [19] or senior wife of the ruler wielded power through her influence over her husband and through her position as head of the royal household and her rank in court, as well as through her anticipated power as the future queen mother. The *kaidu* was also responsible for managing the wives in the royal household, including resolving any disputes that arose. The senior wife of the heir to the throne performed the ceremonies of succession with her husband, sitting on the royal leopard skin by his side. Tuluwa, who ruled the Banagwere polity in the mid-eighteenth century, is remembered as a skilled rainmaker, and his *kaidu* was responsible for looking after his rainmaking drums.[58] In this case, then, the royal *kaidu* was responsible for her husband's instruments of creative power over the people. The creative power of rainmaking was especially important when droughts threatened the well-being of the community. The Bugwere Historical Texts also highlight the influence of the *kaidu* over her husband, although not with positive results. In the mid-nineteenth century, most likely c. 1840, Kwiri Sika inherited the chiefship of the Banagwere from his father, Mulepo. Kwiri Sika's *kaidu* was Kalimo and she performed the rituals of succession with her husband. Kalimo's influence, however, was beneficial neither to the Banagwere chiefdom nor to Kwiri Sika's reign. She persuaded Sika to limit the redistribution of food from the royal household to the broader population, creating significant resentment towards the ruler and his wife. This meant that Kwiri Sika's support was already undermined when he was later defeated in battle by the neighbouring chief, Iwa. Kwiri Sika was soon thereafter overthrown in favour of his brother, Mukamba, having reigned for only a few months.[59]

Although there is not a great deal of evidence, it seems that Bagwere *abambeeza* [31] or princesses had roles similar to those of their Basoga

---

[57] Long, "Notes of the Bugwere District," 460.
[58] Atkinson, ed., "Bugwere Historical Texts," Texts 11, 42, and 46; GW-ETH-KAA-M-MY, interview, 2 December 2004, Bugwere.
[59] Atkinson, ed., "Bugwere Historical Texts," Text 11; Long, "Notes of the Bugwere District," 463.

counterparts, particularly in creating networks of alliances through marriage. One version of the traditions regarding how Lyada, a non-royal, came to rule a Gwere polity in the late nineteenth century refers to him marrying the daughter of an elder of the royal Banagwere clan.[60] Marital alliances were both a route to political power and a means of shoring up power once it had been achieved. An outsider would not have kin networks to draw upon for support, but by marrying into local families he created a series of *bukwe* or 'in-law' relationships that he could draw on for his own political ambitions. Furthermore, he could be sure that the maternal kin of his sons would support their future claims to power. *Abambeeza* also wielded creative power as the guardians of royal graves, including that of Nagwere, the founder of the Banagwere chiefdom. This was particularly important because the skulls of the deceased rulers were retained and, alongside the royal drums, formed a prominent feature of the installation ceremonies for a new ruler.[61] One of the *abambeeza* – the eldest sister of the *omulangira* or prince who was being installed – sat with him during his installation, as did the senior wife, or *kaidu*, of the deceased ruler who became queen mother.[62]

The limited data on Bugwere's precolonial political history tend to focus on the genealogy of the male chiefs, reflecting the primary interests of those who narrated the traditions and the dominant academic approach at the time that they were recorded. Despite this, the long history of maternal ideology at the heart of political power in the North Nyanzan communities continued into the Bugwere polities. The senior wives of deceased rulers were installed along with the heir and his sister in a practice that drew on maternal connections to give a number of clans and lineages a direct interest in the success and longevity of the new chief. Princesses, other than the new chief's eldest sister, helped cement the foundations of the polity through marital alliances and through their guardianship of the most important ritual objects of the chiefdom. Motherhood was also central to the political reproduction of the kingdom: male *ábaiwá*, the sons of female Banagwere clan members, took charge of interring the dead ruler and preserving his skull. They also assisted at the installation of the new ruler. During the installation ceremony, for example, the *ómwiwá omukulu*, or senior nephew, gave the heir to the chiefship "a spear in the

---

[60] Atkinson, ed., "Bugwere Historical Texts," Text 23. Another version asserts that although he was given Bagwere wives, they were *bakopi* (commoners) and not of the royal clan (Text 1).
[61] Atkinson, ed., "Bugwere Historical Texts," Texts 11, 41, 43, 44, and 46.
[62] Atkinson, ed., "Bugwere Historical Texts," Text 41.

right hand and a shield in the left hand." Furthermore it was only *ábaiwá* of the Banagwere clan who could assist in the rainmaking ceremonies conducted by the ruler of the chiefdom to ensure the two important rainy seasons of the year: *okwesengerera oikendi wa'mwiro* and *okwesengerera oikendi we'kisambya.*[63]

In the polities of Bugwere over the eighteenth and nineteenth centuries and in economic and social life in Bushana and Bugwere, a flexible ideology of motherhood emerged as people sought to reestablish and reproduce their communities. While they frequently had to do so under particularly complicated borderlands circumstances and, at times, under ecological pressures and the dislocation and disruption of warfare, they also emphasised continuities in their social organisation. Placing motherhood at the heart of networks of relationships between clans and between diverse peoples was one such continuity. Retaining the roles of senior wife and queen mother in political formations was another.

BUSOGA AND BUGANDA

The North Nyanzan social institution of motherhood thus continued – albeit in altered forms – in the polities of Bugwere, Busoga, and Buganda. The political authority that could be wielded by Basoga queen mothers is clearly shown in the history of the kingdom of Luuka in northern Busoga and in the person of Kabalu of the abaiseMunhana clan in particular. By the late eighteenth-century, the abaiseMunhana had lived just to the north of the kingdom of Luuka for some two generations.[64] At this time, Luuka was a fairly inconsequential kingdom governed by King Nhiro. Kabalu's family lived beyond the kingdom's reach, but sought an alliance with the palace through her marriage to Prince Inhensiko. Although she was not Inhensiko's first wife, Kabalu was his *kairu* or senior wife (underscoring that attaining the position of senior wife required the political support of one's kin group) and remained so throughout his reign after he succeeded his father to the throne. Kabalu and Inhensiko had a son named Wambuzi Munhana. When Inhensiko died in the early nineteenth century, he had many children from his several wives including sixteen sons who had "survived to maturity." But, "as the eldest surviving son of the senior wife, Wambuzi was in the best position to succeed to the

---

[63] Atkinson, ed., "Bugwere Historical Texts," Texts 11, 46, and 47 (quote Text 46).

[64] The following is from Cohen, ed., "Collected Texts of Busoga Traditional History," Text 717; Cohen, *Womunafu's Bunafu*, 21–5.

throne upon his father's death." Cohen notes that the peaceful transition
of power to Wambuzi suggests that Kabalu was able to create alliances
with powerful chiefs in the kingdom as well as mobilise her clan members
to support his claim. Kabalu thus moved from being the *kairu* of the king
to become queen mother of Luuka. At the end of the 1820s or the start
of the 1830s, the king of Buganda sent his army to sack King Wambuzi's
capital and occupy the kingdom. Wambuzi fled and sought shelter among
his maternal kin who still lived to the north of Luuka.[65] "Queen Mother
Kabalu... is said to have protected the king and to have held together the
families that had fled to the north. She is credited with having disciplined
the ambitious brothers of King Wambuzi during a time when they might
have forced their way to the throne through alliance with the Baganda."[66]
By abandoning his capital, Wambuzi risked losing his throne altogether
and it was his queen mother, Kabalu, who protected him and in so doing
also protected her own position of political authority.

Wambuzi died in the late 1830s or early 1840s and was succeeded by
his son Kakuku. When, some ten or fifteen years later, Kakuku and several
of his chiefs were executed in Buganda for having insulted King Ssuuna,
Kabalu sought to play kingmaker once more. This time she sought the
installation of Kakuku's son – Kabalu's great-grandson – Mudhungu.
Mudhungu was both too young and too far away, living as he was in
a palace of the king of Bugabula to the west, and Kabalu's attempt to
control the succession did not go smoothly. Kakuku's brother Kalogo
instead seized the throne of Luuka. His accession to power was disputed
and Kalogo survived only a year in power before being overthrown, after
which the kingdom entered a period of instability. Some of the historical texts record that Kabalu herself ruled Luuka while she was working to have Mudhungu installed as the heir and that she was driven off
the throne by Kalogo.[67] If the records are accurate, Kabalu would have
been quite old by this point, something that may also have reduced her
political power and thus her ability to intervene effectively in succession
disputes.

Kabalu is the only royal woman in Busoga to have been remembered
in such detail in the Busoga Historical Traditions and it is likely that both
she and the situation of the kingdom during her life were exceptional.
The kingdom of Luuka was small and weak when she married into the

---

[65] Cohen, *Womunafu's Bunafu*, 25, 78, 189, fn. 3 (quote p. 25).
[66] Cohen, *Womunafu's Bunafu*, 90.
[67] Cohen, ed., "Collected Texts of Busoga Traditional History," Texts 560 and 935; Cohen,
Womunafu's Bunafu, 106–7.

royal family and she and her clan were able to use their influence to their advantage. Her story is, however, illustrative of the ways in which senior royal wives and queen mothers could wield significant instrumental power. Kabalu was able to wield such influence in Luuka because she could rely on the support of her fellow clan members. Members of the queen mother's clan stood to gain significant political advantage through the accession to the throne of their *omwîwa* (nephew) and so he could rely on their support for his reign. Well into the nineteenth century, in the various kingdoms of Busoga, an ideology of motherhood remained at the heart of Soga political life and did so largely unchallenged.[68]

The situation was different in Buganda. As the kingdom extended its political and geographical reach starting with the reign of Mawanda in the eighteenth century, so ambitious kings increasingly sought to monopolise power, both creative and instrumental. One way they aimed to do so was by undermining the role motherhood played as ideology and practice at the heart of the kingdom, that is, to undermine the place of public motherhood in Buganda. On the one hand, kings sought to reduce the influence of maternal relatives, as in the case of Ssemakookiro, who assassinated his son's maternal relatives. On the other hand, they sought to reduce the power of the *nnàmasòle* [33] or queen mother. When King Ssuuna II Kalema ascended to the throne in the 1820s, he was still very young – perhaps as young as twelve. His mother, Nakazi Kaanyange of the Mmamba (Lungfish) clan, was also young, and notes Kiwanuka, she "was one of the most beautiful women in the country." Ssuuna, the traditions record, executed "countless numbers" of chiefs that he suspected of being his mother's lovers.[69] Queen mothers faced strict restrictions on their reproduction after acceding to office; they were neither to remarry nor to bear children. Both of these acts threatened the political relationship between the *nnàmasòle* and her son the king. When a rumour reached King Ssuuna that his mother was pregnant, therefore, he was so enraged that he sent a general in his army to uncover "the queen mother so as to look at her breasts and check whether she was really pregnant." In addition to this very serious public humiliation, the *nnàmasòle*'s estates were plundered and several of her chiefs arrested, despite the rumour having been shown to be false.[70] Ssuuna's actions not only violated a whole series of taboos regarding conduct between a mother and her son, and in

---

[68] These kingdoms included, Buzaaya, Bulamogi, Bukono, Butembe, Busiki, Bukoolo, Bugweri, and Busambira (see Map 3).

[69] Kagwa, *The Kings of Buganda*, 115.

[70] Kagwa, *The Kings of Buganda*, 127.

particular between a king and his *nnàmasòle*, they were also clearly an effort to undermine the queen mother's authority in the kingdom. This suggests that Ssuuna took advantage of the rumours to try to extend his political power over all branches of the governance of Buganda. Given Ssuuna's youthfulness when he became king and given that his first prime minister was quickly replaced by another, it seems likely that it was *Nnàmasòle* Nakazi Kaanyange who served as his regent in the early years of his reign. This is further supported by reports that he saw a good deal of his mother, in contravention of the general constitutional rule that the king and his queen mother should not meet following the completion of the installation ceremonies.[71] Ssuuna's actions can, thus, be interpreted as his attempt to exert his authority in the land once he had come of age.

Another story from fairly early in Ssuuna's reign, however, demonstrates the authority the queen mother held over the king in Buganda, even when the king was as tyrannical and violent as Ssuuna. The king ordered that, as part of the sanitary regulations for his *èkìbugà* or capital, no one was to excrete within the capital on pain of death. Reports of him having executed a number of people for violating the decree reached a powerful medium called Kigemuzi. When Ssuuna's men visited Kigemuzi's shrine in order to levy taxes, the traditions narrate that he gave them an oracle to ask the king on their return: "Why did you prevent people from excreting in the capital and why did you execute others for allegedly violating the so-called sanitary laws? Where do you yourself [the king] excrete?"[72] Ssuuna's ministers ordered that Kigemuzi be arrested and the medium was bound and brought before the king. King Ssuuna ordered Kigemuzi to repeat his oracle, but "he refused to do so while bound, because (he said) it was contrary to custom to bind a medicine-man or a medium."[73] The king ordered that if he would not speak, his lips should be stitched together. Kigemuzi responded: "Yours will also be stitched." In the face of such insolence towards the king, "a courtier called Kamuyi Kiyenje … struck the man. 'You will also be struck,' Kigemuzi threatened again." The soldier stitched his lips together and branded him with an iron and took him away to await execution the following day. That night, lightning struck the king's palace and Ssuuna was scorched on his face and along one side of his body. He sent for Kigemuzi, who said to him, "Did I not warn you that you would also be burnt?" In order to propitiate the god

[71] Kagwa, *The Kings of Buganda*, 119, 120.
[72] Kagwa, *The Kings of Buganda*, 118.
[73] Roscoe, *The Baganda*, 227.

of thunder, Ssuuna gave Kigemuzi "very many women, slaves, cattle and indeed everything he wanted." But it was *Nnàmasòle* Nakazi Kaanyange who gave Kigemuzi an estate to settle on "in order to propitiate the gods, and to save her son from further harm."[74] Despite his determination to change the balance of power in the kingdom in his favour, Ssuuna nonetheless relied on the queen mother's ability to intervene when he faced an opponent whose creative power challenged the legitimacy of the king's use of brute force.

Ssuuna's efforts to be the sole authority in the kingdom focused on his sisters as well as his mother and he ordered vicious raids on Princess Nanjobe, his *lùbùga* [6] or queen sister, and other powerful princesses. In his annotations on Apolo Kagwa's transcription of the traditions, Semakula Kiwanuka states that "this was an outburst of jealousy and fury on the part of Suuna," caused by his suspicion that the princesses were sexually involved with his chiefs. The *lùbùga* "bore most of the brunt of Suuna's anger because she was the (officially) senior princess, and perhaps she could be held responsible for the actions and behaviour of the other princesses."[75] While the king restrained from having Nanjobe executed, probably because she was the *lùbùga* (although this was no guarantee of safety), his army plundered her estates and "many [of her] men were arrested and executed." Ssuuna also ordered a violent raid on the estates of Princess Nakuyita, who clearly wielded significant instrumental power as she had organised "a very large army" to attack Busoga. "It had been prearranged," according to Kagwa, "that all the princesses' men, about four thousand, were to be massacred."[76] While the excessive violence of Ssuuna's reign may in part be explained by his "bloodthirsty" nature, the targets he chose to attack indicate that, just as the kingdom was weakening through the warfare and instability wrought by new trade and political opportunities that had lasted several decades, so the king sought to challenge the old tripartite headship of state and take sole control of Buganda.

Later in his reign these efforts focused on excessive violence towards his queen mother, queen sister, princesses and chiefs, but early instances of violence against his sisters, and against the *lùbùga* in particular, indicate

---

[74] Kagwa, *The Kings of Buganda*, 118–9 (first four quotes); Roscoe, *The Baganda*, 226–7 (last quote p. 227). See also Hanson, "Queen Mothers and Good Government in Buganda," 223.

[75] Kagwa, *The Kings of Buganda*, 121, fn. 13.

[76] Kagwa, *The Kings of Buganda*, 121.

that Ssuuna had long sought to constrain their political authority. According the Kagwa, the events unfolded in the following manner:

> Kamaanya forbade his sisters, the daughters of King Semakookiro, to get married. It so happened, however, that one of the princesses wanted to get married very badly, but Kamaanya beat her and even put her in custody. When Suuna came to the throne, his aunt Princess Nabinaka said: 'Because Kamaanya prevented us from getting married, I too shall do something nasty to his daughters.' So she went and challenged Suuna thus: 'Why have you neglected all your sisters and left them to commoners? There is nothing to prevent you from making them your wives. Take them to your palace and marry them.' Suuna fell an easy prey to this suggestion and took all his sisters to wife. But they resisted at first and refused to become his wives until he had executed Princess Nabanakulya, the *Lubuga*, and eight others. After nine of their sisters have been executed, the remainder agreed to become Suuna's wives.[77]

Whether or not the princesses became the king's wives in the conventional sense, this was a clear effort to control further the fertility and hence maternity of royal women in the palaces. In his ongoing efforts to police the sexual behaviour of his queen mother in addition to the queen sister and princesses, Ssuuna was attempting to co-opt and corral the ideological power that motherhood held in Buganda in order to shore up his own position, whilst undermining the alternative forms of authority motherhood created in the kingdom. As the kingdom continued to expand its reach over neighbouring areas through the eighteenth and early nineteenth centuries and the numbers of royal wives and female slaves in the capital grew almost exponentially a definite shift occurred.[78] Queen mothers saw their chiefs killed and their estates plundered, as did queen sisters and the more powerful princesses. Kings "took to wife" their sisters and attempted to bar them from taking lovers.[79] These actions were part of an attempt by Baganda kings to control political struggles through controlling royal women's reproductive power. And yet, even by the mid-nineteenth century when King Ssuuna died, the ideology of motherhood in the constitution of Buganda held sufficient sway for Mukaabya Mutesa to be chosen over his brother Kikulwe because of who their respective mothers were.

On the death of Ssuuna around 1854, Kayira – his *kàtikkiro* or prime minister – and another minister, Ndugga, who held the title of *mùkwenda*,

---

[77] Kagwa, *The Kings of Buganda*, 136–7.
[78] See Kagwa, *The Customs of the Baganda*, 18–67, for a listing of the numbers of wives and "concubines" in the households of the kings of Buganda.
[79] Kagwa, *The Kings of Buganda*, 137.

discussed the question of succession.[80] Ndugga favoured his own nephew, Kikulwe, the son of his sister Zawedde and the deceased king. The former Prime Minister Kayira agreed initially, but he was later reminded by Sebadduka, another chief, that Ssuuna had ordered the execution of Ndugga and Zawedde's father, and that Kayira himself had carried out the deed. If Kikulwe ascended to the throne, his mother and maternal uncle would no doubt seek to avenge their father's death. Sebadduka recommended that Mukaabya Mutesa be selected because he had been isolated from much of the palace intrigue during his father's reign. In order to ensure that Mukaabya succeeded his father, Kayira – who must have wielded great authority in the kingdom – arranged for his own son to make blood brotherhood with Muganzirwaza, Mukaabya's mother.[81] Kayira was able to bring the other chiefs and ministers round to his decision and Mukaabya Mutesa was duly enthroned king of Buganda alongside Muganzirwaza as *nnàmasòle*. When John Hanning Speke arrived in Buganda in 1862, he was struck by *Nnàmasòle* Muganzirwaza's authority in the kingdom and, in particular, her competition with the king. It is somewhat ironic, therefore, that her son had been chosen as king because "Kimera's mother's kinsmen," as Wrigley points out, "were over-powerful people."[82] While there had been struggles by kings to reduce the position of *nnàmasòle* and the role of motherhood as a legitimating ideology in Buganda over several generations, both of these remained resilient well into the nineteenth century.

Indeed, a power struggle in the kingdom some 25 years later centred on whether or not Muganzirwaza was Mukaabya Mutesa's birth mother. This was at a time of growing tension in Buganda. From around 1850 Muslim traders started visiting the capital and over the next two decades converted sufficient numbers of people in the capital to be able to withstand persecution. Protestant missionaries in the guise of the Church Missionary Society arrived in Buganda in 1877 and the Catholic *Société des missionaires d'Afrique* (*Pères blancs*) (White Fathers) followed in 1879. Both sects rapidly gained converts at court, most famously among the king's pages. As a result three powerful factions based on these new religions emerged to challenge the place of *lùbaalè* worship as the dominant creative power in Buganda. While Mutesa rejected conversion to

---

[80] The precise date is disputed among historians. Kiwanuka, in his translation of Kagwa's book, gives the date as 1854 (Kagwa, *The Kings of Buganda*, 195), while Médard gives 1856 (Médard, *Le royaume du Buganda au XIXe siècle*, 433).

[81] Kagwa, *The Kings of Buganda*, 141–5.

[82] Wrigley, *Kingship and State*, 227.

any of the religions of the book, his power was increasingly challenged by the converts in his court and by the continued power of *Nnàmasòle* Muganzirwaza. But his power was also waning as a result of having been on the throne since 1856 and his ill health. Furthermore, his army suffered a number of defeats in Bunyoro and Busoga and the general population was severely affected by outbreaks of a number of diseases, including smallpox, cholera, typhoid, and plague.[83]

It was in this context, and just three years before Mutesa died, that Father Lourdel of the Catholic missionaries at Rubaga, the White Fathers, wrote in the mission diary on 14 July 1881: "The Namasolé who came today to Roubaga is not the mother of Mtéca [Mutesa]. The real mother of the king was in the past sold to an Arab by Souna [Ssuuna]. On his father's death, Mtéca had her searched for everywhere, but in vain. He thus named to the title of Namasolé a trustworthy slave to whom his mother had entrusted him before leaving Ouganda."[84] When this story was printed in the *Uganda Journal* in 1934 by John Gray, two leading intellectual figures wrote to the journal insisting that Muganzirwaza was Mutesa's 'real' mother and that the story that Gwolyoka was his mother was fabricated to discredit the *nnàmasòle*.[85] Whatever the actual truth of the story – and Ham Mukasa's argument that "what would never be done, would be for a Kabaka to sell or give away any of his wives who had borne him a child. This was never done in Buganda," is surely an overstatement, given the many social violations committed by the kings of Buganda – what is clear is that claiming that the *nnàmasòle* was not the king's biological mother was a means to undermine her authority and by extension the authority of her son as well.[86] While the Luganda proverb, discussed in Chapter 4, suggested that slave women could aspire to be the mothers of their masters' heirs, the scornful accusation that not

[83] Jean Brierley and Thomas Spear, "Mutesa, the Missionaries, and Christian Conversion in Buganda," *International Journal of African Historical Studies* 21, no. 4 (1988): 601–2; Médard, *Le royaume du Buganda au XIXe siècle*, 367–84.

[84] "La Namasolé, qui est venue aujourd'hui à Roubaga n'est pas la mère de Mtéca. La vraie mère du roi a été autrefois vendue à un Arabe par Souna. À la mort de son père, Mteca la fit chercher partout, mais en vain. Il nomma alors au titre de Namasolé une ésclave de confiance à qui sa mère l'avait recommandé avant de quitter l'Ouganda" (Casier 148, Rubaga, Diaire or. du Nyanza-Rubaga 1879–1882, White Fathers Archives, Rome). My translation. Cited in John M. Gray, "Correspondence: Mutesa," *Uganda Journal* 2, no. 1 (1934): 84.

[85] J. M. Gray, "Mutesa of Buganda," *Uganda Journal* 1, no. 1 (1934): 23; Ham Mukasa refuted this in his version of Muteesa's biography. Mukasa, "Ebifa ku Mulembe gwa Kabaka Mutesa [The History of the Reign of Kabaka Mutesa]," 126–9.

[86] Mukasa, "Ebifa ku Mulembe gwa Kabaka Mutesa," 128.

only was Muganzirwaza not Mukaabya Mutesa's biological mother but that she was, furthermore, a slave underscores the reality that there were strict limits on social mobility for women in the Buganda. Given that previous kings had had queen mothers who were not their birth mothers, those seeking to undermine *Nnàmasòle* Muganzirwaza and her son, needed a second, more damning, element to their attack; the accusation of slavery served their purpose.

The nineteenth century was very much a period of contradictions with regard to the role played by motherhood as social institution and ideology in the North Nyanzan communities. On the one hand motherhood remained central to social cohesion, particularly in the east, as people moved to new areas and dealt with the realities of living in a culturally and linguistically diverse setting. The continued importance of the children of female clan members to the social reproduction of their mothers' clans strongly demonstrates the centrality of a particular ideology of motherhood in creating connections that cut across patrilineal divides. In political life, the most prominent queen mother whose life was documented in the Busoga Historical Texts and Lubogo's history of Busoga dates to the first half of the nineteenth century. Kabalu of Luuka was clearly a politically astute woman who wielded significant authority over several decades. And in Buganda, despite the predominance of biological over social motherhood, the political institution of the queen mother retained both its power and its central role in legitimating the kingship. On the other hand, however, the authority of the queen mother in Buganda came under repeated attack by the king as he and his male ministers and chiefs sought to undermine alternative centres of power in the kingdom. That the queen mother was weakened is demonstrated by the fact that successive kings in the nineteenth century raided the queen mother's estates and even publicly humiliated her person. As the economic and political revolutions of the nineteenth century unfolded, so the place of public motherhood at the heart of centralised political power was increasingly challenged. It survived throughout the reign of Mukaabya Mutesa, but it could not survive the civil wars of the 1880s or the fundamental political revolution codified by the 1900 Uganda Agreement.

Conclusion

Nnàmasòle Muganzirwaza of Buganda died in 1882. Despite his at times fierce struggles for power with his mother, King Mukaabya Mutesa is reported to have "mourned grievously for her." His grief, according to Apolo Kagwa, manifested itself in elaborate funerary rituals. It was said that "She was buried in four coffins, one of copper and three of wood. In addition to the coffins, her body was wrapped in three thousand sheets of the type of cloth called Doti and seven thousand bark-cloths. Then forty thousand cowrie shells, eighteen bundles, and ten loads of beads were put in her tomb. The funeral was really magnificent and dignified."[1] While the number of cloths and barkcloths that Kagwa listed demands scepticism, the sentiment holds true. The White Fathers at Rubaga noted in the mission diary entry for 5 May 1882 that "Father Livinhac goes to the Mbuga; a long and stupid visit; the king and his chiefs talked of the funeral of the Namasolé; the Arabs said that there is no man capable of knowing the total number of cloths and lubugo [barkcloth] that had been placed in the hole: only God." And seven days later, they recorded that the Church Missionary Society (CMS) missionary Alexander Mackay told them that, "the cloths and mbugo [barkcloths] spent for the Namasolé surpassed the sum of 40,000 francs."[2] Despite this ostentatious display for the deceased

---

[1] Kagwa, *The Kings of Buganda*, 179.
[2] Diaire or. du Nyanza-Rubaga, no. 2, 1881–82. 5/5/1882: "Le P. Livinhac va à Mbuga; séance longue et bête; le roi et ses grands parlent de l'enterrement de la Namasolé; les Arabes disent qu'il n'y a pas un homme capable de savoir toute l'étoffe et le lubugo qui ont été mis dans le trou: Dieu seul." 12 May 1882: "Il [Mackay] nous dit que les étoffes et le mbugo dépensées pour la Namasolé dépassent la somme de 40,000 francs." Casier 148. Rubaga. White Fathers' Archives, Rome. My translation from the French.

nnàmasòle, Mutesa did not appoint an heir to Muganzirwaza and thus effectively ended the political power of the queen mother in Buganda.

Mutesa, already sick at the time of *Nnàmasòle* Muganzirwaza's death, himself died in 1884. He was succeeded by his son Danyeri Mwanga, whose mother, Abisajji Bagalayaze of the Ngeye (black-and-white colobus monkey) clan, became the new *nnàmasòle*. Although she figures much less prominently in the sources than her predecessor, *Nnàmasòle* Abisajji Bagalayaze held significant property and attempted, at least, to assert her authority during her reign with King Mwanga II. In February 1886, for example, the White Fathers recorded in their diary that the *nnàmasòle* had lost twenty-four houses in a fire, highlighting the extensive scale of her palace. Four months later they wrote, "The *nnàmasòle* apparently is not happy that we have not been to visit her – we today made a visit to the king and asked him for an mbaka [messenger or representative] in order to go to see his mother."[3] Her son, Mwanga, was not well liked, particularly by the British Protestant missionaries. The CMS missionary and ethnographer John Roscoe, for example, described him as "a man of a weak nature, sensual, and lacking in character."[4] At a time when Catholic, Protestant, and Muslim factions in the capital were fiercely vying for political influence, *Nnàmasòle* Abisajji Bagalayaze's diplomatic gestures towards the Catholic missionaries announced that she had a role to play in the matrix of sectarian politics, even if the office of queen mother had lost much of its authority.

The place of the queen mother and of the old ideology of motherhood in the kingdom was further undermined as Buganda collapsed into a series of civil wars and political crises that lasted from 1888 until the capture of Mwanga by the British in 1899. When Mwanga left the royal capital in 1897 to take up arms against the British colonial authority, Major Trevor Ternan sent a message from Buganda to the British Prime Minister Robert Gascoyne-Cecil, the Marquess of Salisbury, in which he relayed the following: "It is, I think, clear that Mwanga can no long be considered King of Uganda, and I propose to take steps to proclaim his son, named Chua (a young child being baptized as a Protestant), as his successor, with a Regency during his minority ... The child in

---

[3] Diaire or. du Nyanza-Rubaga, no. 3, 1885–88. 15 February 1886: "Namasolé a 24 masons qui viennent de brûler." 21 June 1886: "Namasolé à ce qui paraît ne serait pas contente de ce que nous n'avons pas été la voir – ns rendons aujourd'hui visite du roi et ns lui demandons un mbaka pour aller voir sa mère." Casier 148. Rubaga. White Fathers' Archives, Rome. My translation from the French.

[4] Roscoe, *The Baganda*, 229.

question would appear to be the most suitable candidate, and his succession would be probably unopposed by any party."⁵ Daudi Cwa's can-
didacy was suitable to the British on two grounds: first, he was a very
young child and the British thought he would be easily manipulated
and groomed for their purposes; second, he was a Protestant. The conflict between the Protestant and Catholic factions in Buganda had in
large part been a proxy struggle for colonial control between the British
and French. The British won, but wanted to shore up their victory by
appointing a king with allegiance to the Anglican Church. What is most
interesting about this appointment, for our purposes, is that Cwa was
selected because of his mother. Mwanga II had played the religious sects
off against each other and did not convert to any of them, but his wives
did. Daudi Cwa's mother, Evailin Kulabako – who became *nnàmasòle* on
her son's accession to the throne – had converted to the Protestant faith
and had had the future king baptised at the Anglican mission. In a small
way and despite themselves, British colonial agents and the Baganda
chiefs with whom they worked to install King Daudi Cwa kept alive the
ideology of motherhood that had legitimised political authority in the
kingdom for so many generations.⁶ Indeed, Kagwa noted in his description of the enthronement of Daudi Cwa in *The Customs of Buganda* that
"His mother's relatives also offered gifts, and introduced themselves."⁷
While their role was much reduced, the lineage of the mother of the king
was involved in the succession of political power, as they had been for
centuries.

The long historical importance of public motherhood to the establishment and legitimacy of political power officially ended with the signing
of the Uganda Agreement of 1900, which stripped the authority of the
kingdom of Buganda by placing it and its people under the administration of the British Protectorate on a "permanent satisfactory footing."
As the historian of Uganda Samwiri Karugire notes, the 1900 Uganda
Agreement "tried at one and the same time to reconcile all imperial and
local interests."⁸ Some local interests, however, were recognised above

---

⁵ Major Ternan to the Marquess of Salisbury, 13 July 1897. Papers relating to Recent
Events in the Uganda Protectorate. Presented to both Houses of Parliament by command
of Her Majesty. February 1898. In Church Missionary Society Archive Section IV: Africa
Missions. Part 20: Uganda Mission 1898–1934, reel 406, G3A70 Original Papers 1898.
⁶ This period of Buganda's history has been the focus of a number of studies. For an overview see, among others, Samwiri Rubaraza Karugire, *A Political History of Uganda*
(Nairobi: Heinemann, 1980); Médard, *Le royaume du Buganda au XIXe siècle*.
⁷ Kagwa, *The Customs of the Baganda*, 65.
⁸ Karugire, *A Political History of Uganda*, 96 (1st quote), 102 (2nd quote).

others. The Uganda Agreement, Holly Hanson shows, enabled those chiefs who had succeeded in increasing their individual power over the course of the nineteenth century and at the expense of the Buganda dynasty to translate that power into vast wealth in the form of land. The Agreement privatised land holding in Buganda, turning estates that had been tied to political offices into the personal property of those holding office at the time. For example, Apolo Kagwa, who was one of Daudi Cwa's prime ministers and a highly influential member of the Ganda elite, infamously did very well out of the settlement.[9] *Nnàmasòle* Evailin Kulabako and her brother benefitted personally from this agreement because they received as private property the extensive estates that belonged to the offices of queen mother and *ssaabaganzi*. That the *nnàmasòle* and her brother could negotiate such a settlement offers a striking reminder of how important the queen mother and her kin remained, even after decades of conflict and upheaval had undermined the institution and the role of public motherhood at the heart of politics. On their deaths, however, the estates were to be inherited by their personal heirs, not by the successors to their political offices. By transferring the historic power of the queen mother into the private holdings of the current queen mother, the settlement with *Nnàmasòle* Evailin Kulabako destroyed the economic basis of the political office, and thus its main source of political influence. The office of the *ssaabaganzi*, Hanson notes, "ceased to have meaning in the new order of power and disappeared in all but name at the death of the person who had been holding the title in 1900." Of even greater significance was the fate of the office of the queen mother. Once stripped of economic and political authority, the *nnàmasòle* ceased to be "the king-maker, or the protector, defender, and regulator of the king's power."[10] No longer would she have the ability to create, legitimate, and wield royal power. From 1900, the *nnàmasòle* was merely the biological mother of the king of Buganda.

The Uganda Agreement brought Busoga directly under the purview of the British. As the anthropologist Lloyd Fallers noted, "In 1900, under the terms of an agreement between Buganda and the British Government, the Kabaka [of Buganda] relinquished all authority over Busoga and a separate District administration was established."[11] Just as happened repeatedly throughout colonial Africa, politics in Busoga was redefined

---

[9] See Hanson, *Landed Obligation.*
[10] Hanson, "Queen Mothers and Good Government in Buganda," 230.
[11] Fallers, *Bantu Bureaucracy*, 145.

as a purely male affair.[12] For the first decade and a half of the twentieth century, Busoga was ruled on behalf of the British by the infamous chief and warlord Semei Kakungulu. Kakungulu's dealings with the British authorities rarely ran smoothly, as the historian Michael Twaddle has extensively documented, and in 1914 he was relieved of his duties in Busoga. In his place, Governor Frederick Jackson constituted a "principal court of Busoga," composed of seven or more members of the *lukiiko* or 'council' but with no position of "President of the Lukiko of Busoga." All members of the *lukiiko* and of the 'principal court' were men. Among those men, who were mostly the rulers of the old Busoga polities or their mission-educated sons, there arose a demand for a paramount office. Their demands were met by the British in 1919 when Ezekieri Wako "was appointed chairman of the Busoga district council with the title *Isebantu Kyabazinga*."[13] Fallers translated *isebantu kyabazinga* as "The Father of the People Who Unites Them All."[14] There was no office of *inhebantu kyabazinga* ('Mother of the People Who Unites Them All') in 1919 and later when the title of *inhebantu* was awarded to a woman, it was to the wife of the *isebantu* and not his mother. Despite the long-standing and crucial importance of an ideology of motherhood in Soga polities, colonisation and the subsequent developments after 1900 ended the political role of public motherhood among the Basoga even more absolutely than in Buganda.

A similar story unfolded in Bugwere. Again, Semei Kakungulu was a principal actor. Kakungulu received the official backing of the British to "conquer Bukedi and incorporate it within the Uganda Protectorate." The problem was that 'Bukedi' was a rather vague term. In Buganda, it was the word used to describe the regions to the far east, beyond Busoga, where they believed the people to be uncivilised and naked. The British were little wiser.[15] Kakungulu, therefore, saw this as an opportunity to take control of a very significant area of land and levy taxes on its inhabitants. On hearing that there were banana groves in Bugwere, Kakungulu sent one of his followers, Isaka Nziga, to conquer the region with "150 guns, a sizeable quantity of powder and shot," and a flag that Governor

---

[12] As Semley notes, the examples of female political rulers under colonialism stand out for their exceptionalism. Semley, *Mother Is Gold, Father Is Glass*, 71, 184, fn. 1.

[13] Michael Twaddle, *Kakungulu and the Creation of Uganda, 1868–1928* (London: James Currey, 1993), 256.

[14] Fallers, *Bantu Bureaucracy*, 149.

[15] Joan Vincent shows this most effectively with her reproductions of late nineteenth century maps of the region which are largely blank space, (Vincent, *Teso in Transformation*, 19, 31).

Harry Johnston had given the chief. The Bagwere realised that they could not successfully fight against Kakungulu's guns and instead welcomed the soldiers with a feast.[16] As in Busoga, politics under this new dispensation involved only men and it involved men who claimed power first through guns and then through their preferential access to colonial education, which was less accessible for girls, at least initially.[17] The ideologies of motherhood that had helped legitimise and sustain political authority in the past were abandoned along with any real autonomy for the chiefdoms of the Balalaka, the Banagwere, and the Basobya. The forcible inclusion of the Bagwere into a political system based on the new colonial Ganda model violently ended the historical place of motherhood in chiefly power relations.

We might see this, then, as a narrative of decline in women's agency and in the place of public motherhood in society. Around 700 CE, people speaking North Nyanza and living on the northwestern shores of Lake Victoria–Nyanza used motherhood as a central means of creating durable communities. Recognising the role mothers played in linking families and lineages, as well as in biologically reproducing the community, North Nyanza speakers innovated a new verb to describe a woman's act of marrying a man, an innovation that shows that North Nyanzan women and men viewed their daughters as active participants in their marriages. Further evidence shows that the reason for this perception lay in the importance of mothers and motherhood to social organisation. North Nyanzans placed women's maternity at the centre of networks that cut across patrilineal clans. Because it was mothers who created the connections between lineages and clans, it was possible for women to achieve motherhood through social means if they could not do so biologically. While these interclan networks facilitated ordinary life through the creation of broad webs of obligation and support, these networks of ties of obligation underwrote the centralisation of political power in royal families. As a form of governance that embodied social reproduction, the ideologies and realities of motherhood lay at the heart of emergent kingdoms. In those kingdoms, public motherhood took on a central political as well as ideological role through the office and person of the queen mother.

---

[16] Twaddle, *Kakungulu and the Creation of Uganda*, 138–9.

[17] The education available to girls at mission schools focused heavily on domestic skills. A useful summary of girls' education and of women's economic opportunities in early colonial Uganda is Grace Bantebya Kyomuhendo and Marjorie Keniston McIntosh, *Women, Work & Domestic Virtue in Uganda, 1900–2003* (Oxford: James Currey, 2006), 52–6.

As the Luganda speech community took shape, its members reconstituted the ways they defined and understood motherhood. As competition grew for the best land and as political centralisation intensified, Baganda emphasised biology in their ideologies of motherhood. On the one hand, this opened up a possibility for more marginal women in a household to improve their position should they give birth to a son. But overall, we can see this as degrading women's social position. They played less active roles in their marriages and had very limited options if they were unable to have children. The disparagement of childless Baganda women is evident in oral literature and in the language itself. Nonetheless, through the powerful roles played by mothers and their kin groups in Ganda political life, public motherhood remained important in creating networks of obligation and support across clan divides, even if it was increasingly contested. There was a clear tension between kings and queen mothers in Buganda, a tension that varied over time and according to the personalities and precise power relations of each reign. But as Buganda expanded its borders and its political authority over neighbouring states, the struggle for control of the kingdom intensified. Just as that struggle was intensifying at the start of the nineteenth century, Buganda entered directly into the long-distance trade in slaves and ivory (for cloth and guns) with the Swahili coast. This trade created opportunities for individual chiefs to enrich themselves on an unprecedented scale and to build up their own militias. These new factors served to undermine the role of public motherhood in legitimating political authority in the kingdom, replacing it more and more with legitimation through violence. By the time colonial powers moved into Buganda, then, the social institution of motherhood had been fundamentally marginalised. Colonisation enabled men outside the royal family to remove it from the political system entirely. The implication for both royal and commoner Baganda women was the further devaluation of their place in society.

However, the history of motherhood in the eastern societies of Bugwere and Bushana offer an alternative narrative, one of human agency and adaptation, not simply reaction to declension. James Scott has powerfully argued that we should "emphasize the element of historical and strategic choice" in social and political change among diverse communities of people on the fringes of powerful states. "Patterns that may appear static, even timeless, at first sight," Scott explains, "display remarkable plasticity if one steps back and widens the historical lens to a span of a few generations, let alone a few hundred years or a millennium." In his analysis, patterns of migration, agriculture, kinship relations, and political structure are all "social and historical choices."[18] The role of motherhood in the communities of East Kyoga and its descendants in the eighteenth and nineteenth centuries should be understood as such a choice. Bagwere and Bashana drew on an older ideology of motherhood inherited from their North Nyanzan and South Kyogan ancestors as a central means to construct and reconstruct communities in a complex and changing human landscape. Motherhood as a social institution thus took on a flexible form enabling women and men to adapt to their new circumstances and situations, whether those involved social reproduction in a less forgiving environment or diplomatic relations among foreign people. In a context where drought and political instability threatened sustainability on a fairly regular basis, the mobilisation of motherhood in this way was a very productive social strategy for survival and sustainability. Bagwere women and men developed and used a more flexible ideology of motherhood to incorporate newcomers and new ideas into their social formations and as a means of minimising conflict through the creation of seriated networks of obligation and commitment. For the Bashana, who chose to move out of the shatter zone of their ancestors and into the foothills of Mount Masaaba, itself a shatter zone, this flexible motherhood enabled them to integrate with their new neighbours while maintaining their own distinct identity. This alternative view of the history of the role of motherhood in the societies of east central Uganda, then, highlights the way in which people have used it to successfully adapt to unforeseen circumstances all the while maintaining a deep historical connection with their ancestors through this essential part of society.

---

[18] Scott, *The Art of Not Being Governed*, 179.

APPENDIX

Vocabulary List

1. *-ba nda* 'be pregnant' (lit. 'to be a womb/stomach')
Bantu compound verb formed from *-bá*, 'to be' and the proto-Bantu
noun *-dà*, 'stomach, womb.'[1]
Lugwere: *ókuba kida*
Lusoga: *okúlí ndá*
Rushana: *olina kida*, 'she is pregnant'

2. *-bandúká* (intr.)/*-bandúlá* (tr.) 'elope (of a woman/of a man)'
Lugwere verbal pair derived with a separative suffix from the possible
proto-Bantu verb *-bànd-*, 'force one's way through.'[2]
Lugwere: *ókubandúká/ókubandúlá*
Lusoga: (Lusiki) *kubanduka*, 'marry (of a woman)'

3. *-bayira* (intr.) 'marry (of a woman)'
Proto-North Nyanza verb, etymology unclear.
Luganda: *-wayira*
Lugwere: *ókubaílá*
Lusoga: *okúbáyírá*

---

[1] Bastin and Schadeberg, "Bantu Lexical Reconstructions 3," ID main 4 and ID main 773 (Accessed 15 January 2013).
[2] Bastin and Schadeberg, "Bantu Lexical Reconstructions 3," ID no label 8493 (Accessed 15 January 2013).

For fuller distributions of many of the items in this appendix, see Stephens, "A History of Motherhood, Food Procurement and Politics in East-Central Uganda to the Nineteenth Century," 256–94. The main sources consulted are listed in the bibliography.

4. *-bįád- (tr.) 'give birth'
Proto-Bantu verb, *-bíad-, 'give birth.'[3]
Luganda: kùzaàla
Lugwere: ókubyalá/ókubyaalá
Lusoga: okúzaalá/okúbyaala
Rushana: kubyaara

5. –bimbirra (tr.)/-bimbirrikana (intr.) 'marry (of a man/of a woman)'
Rushana verb derived from the proto-Bantu verb *-bímb-, 'swell.'[4] The
    first innovation is in proto-East Kyoga with a semantic narrowing of
    the older verb to 'swell' and the second innovation to 'marry' is in
    Rushana.
Lugwere: ókubbimbá, 'swell'
Rushana: kubimbirra, 'marry (of a man),' kubimbirrikana, 'marry (of a
    woman)'

6. -bugà (cl. 11) 'queen-sister'
Luganda noun derived from either the Bantu verb *-buga, 'clear/free land
    near home' or from a Mashariki verb *-bug-, 'speak with authority.'[5]
Luganda: lùbugà
Lusoga: lubuga (probable loan-word)

7. *-bwazirume (cl. 9) 'cooking banana'
Proto-North Nyanza innovation, with possible areal spread to Rutara.
Luganda: mbwazirume, 'kind of cooking banana'
Lugwere: mbwazirume, 'cooking banana'

8. -daala (cl. 7/8) 'homestead'
Lugwere noun derived through borrowing from Greater Luhyia. Regular
    sound change: lengthening of stem vowel.[6]
Lugwere: kidaala, 'one-family homestead'
Lusaamya: ɛdala, 'homestead'

---

[3] Bastin and Schadeberg, "Bantu Lexical Reconstructions 3," ID main 226 (Accessed 15
    January 2013).
[4] Bastin and Schadeberg, "Bantu Lexical Reconstructions 3," ID main 240 (Accessed 15
    January 2013).
[5] Schoenbrun, The Historical Reconstruction of Great Lakes Bantu Cultural Vocabulary,
    34, root 4, 71–2, root 96.
[6] Guthrie, Comparative Bantu, vol. 4, 85, ps. 424; Bastin and Schadeberg, "Bantu Lexical
    Reconstructions 3," ID no label 2721 (Accessed 15 January 2013).

9. *-deero* (cl. 7/8) 'granary'
Proto-East Kyoga noun derived through borrowing from Southern Luo *dero*. Regular sound change: lengthening of stem vowel.
Lugwere: *kideero*
Rushana: *kideero*

10. *-fiirwa* (cl. 1/2) 'impotent man'
Proto-North Nyanza noun derived from the verb *-fa*, 'die' with a nominalised passive construction, giving the literal meaning, 'bereaved person.'
Luganda: *òmùfiìrwa*
Lugwere: *mufiirwa*
Lusoga: *omúfíírwá*

11. *-fuba* (cl. 12 or cl. 7/8) 'cooking banana'
Proto-North Nyanza noun derived from the verb *-fuba*, 'exert oneself, work hard.'
Luganda: *kàfubà*, 'type of boiling banana'
Lugwere: *kifuba*, 'cooking banana'

12. *-fuura* (tr.) 'foster-in/adopt'
Proto-West Nyanza verb from *-fuura*, 'change, bend.'
Luganda: *kufuula omwana*
Lunyoro: *-foora omwana*

13. *-fuli* (cl. 9/10) 'labia minora (after elongation?)'
Proto-North Nyanza noun derived from the proto-Great Lake Bantu verb *-fulika*, 'hide, cover.'
Luganda: *ènfulì*, 'labia minora'
Lugwere: *éífulí*, '(pulled) labia' (cl. 5/6)
Lusoga: *énfulí*, 'labia minora'

14. *-gábá* (tr.) 'foster-out'
South Kyoga verb derived through semantic extension from the proto-Bantu verb *-gàb-*, 'divide, give away, make a present.'[7]
Lusoga: *ókugábá*, 'foster-out'
Lugwere: *kugaba*, 'distribute'

---

[7] Bastin and Schadeberg, "Bantu Lexical Reconstructions 3," ID main 1274 (Accessed 15 January 2013).

15. *-gasa* (tr.) 'marry (of a man)'
Proto-North Nyanza verb derived from the proto-West Nyanza verb *-gasa*, 'mate, copulate.'
Luganda: *kùwasa*
Lusoga: *kuhasira* (Lulamoogi)

16. *-gólé* (cl. 1/2) 'bride with maternal potential'
Proto-North Nyanza noun derived through semantic narrowing from proto-Kaskazi noun *-gole*, 'maternal power.'
Luganda: *òmùgolè*, 'bride, mistress of the house' (*òbùgolè*, 'wedding')
Lugwere: *ómugóle*, 'bride, bridegroom' (*ékigóle*, 'wedding')
Lusoga: *omúgole*, 'bride, bridegroom' (*obúgóle*, 'wedding')
Rushana: *mugore*, 'bride, bridegroom' (*bugore*, 'wedding')

17. *-gumbà* (cl. 1/2) 'barren woman'
Proto-Bantu noun, *-gùmbà*, 'barren woman.'[8]
Luganda: *-gumba*, 'barren'
Lugwere: *ómúgúmba*
Lusoga: *omúgúmbá*
Rushana: *mugumba*

18. *-hambuka* (intr.)/*-hambula* (tr.) 'elope (of a woman/of a man)'
Proto-West Nyanza verbal pair derived from the proto-Bantu verb *-kamb-*, 'seize, capture.'[9]
Luganda: *kùwâmbuka/kuwâmbula*
Lunyoro: *-hambuka*

19. *-idu* (cl. 12) 'senior wife'
Proto-North Nyanza noun from same origin as *mwiru*, 'peasant' or 'farmer.'
Luganda: *kaddulubaalè*, 'chief wife of king, and of chief'
Lusoga: *kaidu* or *kairu*, 'senior wife'; *kaido*, 'senior wife' (Lusiki)
Lugwere: *kaidu*, 'first wife among many'

[8] Bastin and Schadeberg, "Bantu Lexical Reconstructions 3," ID main 1505 (Accessed 15 January 2013).
[9] Bastin and Schadeberg, "Bantu Lexical Reconstructions 3," ID main 8471 (Accessed 15 January 2013).

20. *-ihwa* (cl. 1/2) 'child of female clan member'
Noun of proto-Bantu origin, but with some semantic shift in proto-Great
Lakes Bantu.[10]
Luganda: òmujjwà, 'nephew or niece, sister's child only'
Lusoga: omwiwa
Lugwere: ómwiwá
Rushana: mwiwa

21. *-jooka* (tr.) 'foster-out'
Lugwere verb derived through borrowing from Nilotic.
Lugwere: kujooka, 'foster-out (children and animals)'

22. *-ka* (cl. 7/8) 'patriclan'
Proto-North Nyanza noun derived from proto-Great Lakes Bantu *-ka*
(cl. 5/6), 'household' with a noun class change to cl. 7/8 for augmenta-
tion from immediate family to clan.[11]
Luganda: èkìkâ
Lusoga: ekíka
Lugwere: ékiká
Rushana: kika

23. *-kádí* (cl. 1/2) 'woman, wife'
Proto-Bantu noun, *-kádí*, 'wife.'[12]
Luganda: òmùkazì
Lugwere: ómukalí
Lusoga: omúkazí
Rushana: omukare

24. *-kago* (cl. 9) 'cooking banana' (generic)
Proto-North Nyanza innovation (with Greater Luhyia areal spread).
Luganda: ènkagò, 'female plantain'
Lusoga: nkago, 'cooking banana' (Lugabula)
Lugwere: nkago, 'cooking banana'

[10] Schoenbrun, *The Historical Reconstruction of Great Lakes Bantu Cultural Vocabulary*, 86–7, root 120.
[11] Schoenbrun, *The Historical Reconstruction of Great Lakes Bantu Cultural Vocabulary*, 89–90, root 123.
[12] Bastin and Schadeberg, "Bantu Lexical Reconstructions 3," ID main 1674 (Accessed 15 January 2013); Schoenbrun, *The Historical Reconstruction of Great Lakes Bantu Cultural Vocabulary*, 90, root 124.

25. *-kíro* (cl. 6) a disease of pregnancy associated with adultery, which causes mother to eat infant if left untreated
Proto-North Nyanza noun, possibly derived from the proto-Bantu noun *-pi*, 'darkness, blackness.'[13]
Luganda: *àmàkirò*
Lugwere: *makiro*
Lusoga: *amákiró*

26. *-ko* (cl. 1/2) 'in-law'
Proto-Savannah Bantu noun derived from the proto-Bantu verb *-kó*, 'give bridewealth.'[14]
Luganda: *mùkô*, 'brother-in-law, son-in-law; in pl. 'in-laws' in general
Lugwere: *ómukó*
Lusoga: *ómúko*

27. *koiza* (cl. 1a/2) 'maternal uncle'
Proto-North Nyanza noun with areal spread to Greater Luhyia.
Luganda: *kòjjâ*
Lugwere: *ókóíza*
Lusoga: *koiza* (Lusiki)

28. *-kopí* (cl. 1/2) 'commoner/non-royal'
North Nyanza areal form?
Luganda: *òmùkopi*, 'peasant'
Lusoga: *omúkopí*, 'commoner, non-royal'
Lugwere: *mukopi*, 'commoner'

29. *-kwa* (tr.) 'pay bridewealth'
Likely proto-Great Lakes Bantu innovation derived from the proto-Bantu verb *-kó-*, 'give bridewealth.'[15]
Luganda: *kùkwanga*, 'give as present to'
Lugwere: *okukwa*, 'pay bridewealth'
Lusoga: *okúkwa*, 'pay, pay bridewealth'
Rushana: *kumukwa*, 'pay bridewealth for'

---

[13] Bastin and Schadeberg, "Bantu Lexical Reconstructions 3," ID main 6406 (Accessed 16 January 2013).
[14] Bastin and Schadeberg, "Bantu Lexical Reconstructions 3," ID main 7240 (Accessed 15 January 2013); Schoenbrun, *The Historical Reconstruction of Great Lakes Bantu Cultural Vocabulary*, 91–3, root 128.
[15] Bastin and Schadeberg, "Bantu Lexical Reconstructions 3," ID main 7240 (Accessed 15 January 2013).

30. *-lwa* (cl. 6) 'millet beer'
Derived from the proto-Bantu noun *-jàdúá* (cl. 14), 'beer;' semantic narrowing in proto-Great Lakes Bantu to 'millet beer.'[16]
Luganda: *àmàlwâ*
Lugwere: *ámalwá*
Lusoga: *amálwa*
Rushana: *marwa*, 'beer'

31. *-mbeeza* (cl. 1/2) 'princess/female hereditary royal'
North Nyanza innovation.
Luganda: *òmùmbejja*
Lugwere: *mumbeiza*
Lusoga: *omúmbéédhá*

32. *-njaaya* (cl. 5/6) 'type of cooking banana'
North Nyanza noun.
Luganda: *manjaayâ*, 'biggest kind of roasting banana'
Lugwere: *ómánjáya*, 'cooking banana'
Rushana: *manjaaya*, 'beer banana'

33. *nnàmasòle* (cl. 1a) 'queen mother'
Luganda innovation from the proto-Great Lakes Bantu verb *-sola*, 'remove, gather, collect.'[17]
Luganda: *nnàmasòle*

34. *-páála* (tr.) 'elope (of a woman or a man)'
Lusoga innovation. Etymology unclear. Possibly derived through borrowing from Nilotic languages or from the proto-Great Lakes Bantu verb, *-pád-*, 'vex, persecute,' but the sound changes are not regular.
Lusoga: *okúpáálá*

35. *-pandu* (cl. 3/4) 'banana grove'
Proto-East Kyoga noun, possibly borrowed from Greater Luhyia.
Lugwere: *ómpandú*, 'banana grove'
Rushana: *ompandu*, 'banana tree'

---

[16] Bastin and Schadeberg, "Bantu Lexical Reconstructions 3," ID main 3165 (Accessed 15 January 2013).
[17] Schoenbrun, *The Historical Reconstruction of Great Lakes Bantu Cultural Vocabulary*, 160, root 241.

36. *-perekezi* (cl. 1a) 'female escort of bride'
Proto-Mashariki noun derived from the proto-Bantu verb *-pédik-*, 'hand over.'[18]
Luganda: *èmperekezê, empélekezê,* 'bridesmaid'
Lusoga: *empélékéze, émperekézi, omúgherekézi,* 'escort of bride, companion'
Rushana: *emperekesa,* 'escort of bride'

37. *-perya* (cl. 1a) 'female escort of bride'
Lugwere noun, also found in the Lulamoogi dialect of Lusoga, innovation possibly through borrowing from Lunyoro. Derived from proto-Bantu verb *-pá*, 'give' with nominal prefix and causative suffix.[19]
Lugwere: *mperya,* 'escort of bride'
Lusoga: *mperya,* 'escort of bride' (Lulamoogi only)
Lunyoro: *empedya,* 'bridesmaid'

38. *-píítá* (tr.) 'foster-in/adopt (children and animals)'
Proto-South Kyoga verb innovated through borrowing from Southern Luo from the proto-Nilo-Saharan verb *-pīt*, 'rise'.[20]
Lusoga: *okúpíítá,* 'breed, look after with a lot of care (animals)'; 'foster-in' (Lusiki)
Lugwere: *kupiita,* 'foster in/adopt (child), rear animal'

39. *-rya* (cl. 5/6) 'marriage' (applied to a woman)
Proto-North Nyanza noun derived from the proto-Bantu verb *-dí-*, 'eat.'[21]
Luganda: *èddya,* 'married state' (as applied to a woman)
Lugwere: *éílya,* 'marriage' (generally refers to a woman)
Lusoga: *eílyá,* 'marriage, home of a married woman'

40. *sagasaga* (cl. 9) 'cooking banana'
Proto-South Kyoga noun.
Lusoga: *sagasaga*
Lugwere: *sagasaga*

---

[18] Bastin and Schadeberg, "Bantu Lexical Reconstructions 3," ID main 2427 (Accessed 15 January 2013).
[19] Bastin and Schadeberg, "Bantu Lexical Reconstructions 3," ID main 2344 (Accessed 15 January 2013).
[20] Ehret, *A Historical-Comparative Reconstruction of Nilo-Saharan,* 384–5, no. 581.
[21] Bastin and Schadeberg, "Bantu Lexical Reconstructions 3," ID main 944 (Accessed 15 January 2013).

41. **isenga* (cl. 1a/2) 'paternal aunt'
Proto-Mashariki noun with this meaning derived through semantic narrowing from possible proto-Bantu noun.[22]
Luganda: `ssèngâ
Lugwere: óísenga
Lusoga: séngâ/sónga
Rushana: isenga

42. **-síímá* (tr.) 'thank, appreciate'
Proto-Bantu verb **-cìim-*, 'admire, love, delight.'[23]
Luganda: kùsiima, 'be pleased with, appreciate'
Lugwere: ókusiimá, 'to thank'
Lusoga: okúsíímá, 'to thank, appreciate, approve, like'

43. **-síímo* (cl. 12/14) 'appreciation gift given as part of marriage arrangements'
North Nyanza noun through semantic narrowing, derived from the proto-Bantu verb **-cìim-*; see No. 42.
Luganda: àkàsiimo, 'gift given by suitor to parents of his intended bride'
Lugwere: ákásíímò, 'gift given in association with wedding'
Lusoga: akásíímó, 'gift of appreciation, thanks'

44. *-soigi* (cl. 7/8) 'dried banana leaf'
Lugwere noun, perhaps derived from the verb *-soiga*, 'kill wounded animal, person'?
Lugwere: kisoigi, ékisweigí, 'dried banana leaf; funeral ceremony performed after 3 weeks and a year.
Lusoga: Sóigí (Lulamoogi), 'consolation' (name given to girl whose mother lost many children)

45. **-subi* (cl. 7/8) 'beer banana'
North Nyanza noun with possible areal spread to Rutara.
Luganda: kìsùbî
Lugwere: ókisúbi
Lusoga: kísúbi

---

[22] See, Schoenbrun, *The Historical Reconstruction of Great Lakes Bantu Cultural Vocabulary*, 99–100, root 141.
[23] Bastin and Schadeberg, "Bantu Lexical Reconstructions 3," ID main 609 (Accessed 15 January 2013).

46. *-tani* (cl. 7/8) 'placenta'
Proto-North Nyanza noun derived from the proto-Bantu verb *-tá,
'throw away, throw, lose, put, trap, play game, do.'[24]
Luganda: *èkìtanyì*
Lugwere: *ékitaní*
Lusoga: *ekítaní*

47. *-toga* (tr.) 'feel in mud for fish; mash food with hands'
Proto-North Nyanza noun.
Luganda: *toga*, 'crush in hands; handle; mess about;' *–togereza*, 'feel
about in mud to catch'
Lugwere: *toga*, 'catch fish with basket' (done by women)
Lusoga: *toga*, 'fish in mud; mash something'

48. *-wâ* (tr.) 'give for adoption/fostering'
Proto-South Kyoga innovation through semantic change from pro-
to-Bantu verb *-pá, 'give.'[25]
Lugwere: *kuwa mwana*
Lusoga: *kuwa mwana*

49. *-wereka* (tr.) 'foster-out'
Proto-North Nyanza verb derived through semantic narrowing from
Proto-Great Lakes Bantu verb meaning 'entrust person/animal'
which was in turn derived from the Proto-Bantu verb *-pédik-, 'hand
over.'[26]
Luganda: *kùwerèka*, 'place (child) in care of somebody else to be
brought up'

50. *-(y)agi* (cl. 7/8) 'granary'
Proto-North Nyanza innovation, with possible areal spread to Greater
Luhyia, perhaps derived from the verb *-waga*, 'prop.'[27]
Luganda: *èkyagì*, 'small granary raised from ground on posts'
Lusoga: *ekyâgí*, 'raised granary'

[24] Bastin and Schadeberg, "Bantu Lexical Reconstructions 3," ID main 2708 (Accessed 15
January 2013).
[25] Bastin and Schadeberg, "Bantu Lexical Reconstructions 3," ID main 2344 (Accessed 15
January 2013).
[26] Bastin and Schadeberg, "Bantu Lexical Reconstructions 3," ID main 2427 (Accessed 15
January 2013).
[27] See also Bastin and Schadeberg, "Bantu Lexical Reconstructions 3," ID no label 9328,
jaga 'wicker work' (Accessed 16 January 2013).

51. **-yámbá* (tr.) 'foster-in/adopt'
Proto-South Kyoga innovation through semantic extension of the proto-West Nyanza verb, 'help.'
Lusoga: *kuyamba*, 'to adopt, foster'
Rushana: *kuyamba*, 'adopt'

52. **-ziro* (cl. 3/4) 'taboo'
Proto-Bantu noun **-gìdò* (cl. 3/4), 'taboo, abstinence.'[28]
Luganda: *òmùziro*, 'totem'
Lugwere: *ómúzílo*, 'totem, taboo'
Lusoga: *omúzíró*, 'totem, taboo, forbidden'
Rushana: *muzira*, 'taboo'

[28] Bastin and Schadeberg, "Bantu Lexical Reconstructions 3," ID der. 1400; derived from ID main 1394 **-gìd-*, 'abstain from, avoid, refuse, be taboo, be punished' (Accessed 15 January 2013). See also, Schoenbrun, *The Historical Reconstruction of Great Lakes Bantu Cultural Vocabulary*, 189–90, root 288.

Bibliography

I. Unpublished Sources and Archival Collections

Uganda

Entebbe

Summer Institute of Languages:
Logose, Gertrude. "Eirya lye Kigwere." ["Gwere Marriage"]. Lugwere Bible Translation Project.
"Lugwere-English Wordlist." Lugwere Bible Translation Project.

Kampala

Africana Library, Makerere University:
Andrew, Wabwezi. "The Bagwere Proverbs." BA diss., Makerere University, Kampala, 2004.
Kiyimba, Abasi. "Gender Stereotypes in the Folktales and Proverbs of the Baganda." PhD diss., University of Dar es Salaam, 2001.
Archives of the Kampala Archdiocese, Rubaga:
Le Veux, Henri. "Au temps jadis: Le mariage des Baganda (au Victoria Nyanza)."

United Kingdom

London

British Library:
Church Missionary Society Archive Section IV: African Missions. Part 20: Uganda Mission 1898–1934. Microfilm.
London School of Economics Archives:
Audrey Isabel Richards (1899–1984) Collection.

Liverpool

Mill Hill Missionaries' Archives:
Personal Files.
Kirk, Christopher.
Term, van, Anthony.
St. Joseph's Advocate.
Uganda Collection.

Italy

Rome

Archives de la Société des Missionaries d'Afrique (Pères Blancs) [White Fathers]:
Diaires originaux, Rubaga.

United States

Ronald R. Atkinson Private Collection:
Atkinson, Ronald R. ed. "Bugwere Historical Texts."
Long, W. H. "Notes of the Bugwere District," c. 1933. J. R. McD. Elliot Papers,
    Rhodes House Library.
David William Cohen Private Collection:
Cohen, David W. ed. "Collected Texts of Busoga Traditional History."
Tantala, Renée. "Community and Polity in Southern Kigulu."
    "Gonza Bato and the Consolidation of Abaisengobi Rule in Southern Kigulu."
David L. Schoenbrun Private Collection:
Birusha, Aramazani. "Description de la langue Havu (bantou J52): Grammaire et
    lexique." PhD diss., Université Libre de Bruxelles, 1984–1985.
Ehret, Christopher, Gary Okihiro, Terry Stamps, Barbara Turner, and Sherilyn
    Young. "Lacustrine History and Linguistic Evidence: Preliminary
    Conclusions." University of California, Los Angeles, 1973.
Schoenbrun, David. "Field Notes." Evanston, Ill.
Chicago, Center for Research Libraries:
Cohen, David W. ed. "Selected Texts of Busoga Traditional History." Baltimore,
    1969. Microfilm.
Other Dissertations:
de Luna, Kathryn. M. "Collecting Food, Cultivating Persons: Wild Resource Use
    in Central African Political Culture, c. 1000 B.C.E. to c. 1900 C.E." PhD
    diss., Northwestern University, 2008.
Kodesh, Neil. "Beyond the Royal Gaze: Clanship and Collective Well-Being in
    Buganda." PhD diss., Northwestern University, 2004.
Mould, Martin Joel. "Comparative Grammar Reconstruction and Language
    Subclassification: The North Victorian Bantu Languages." PhD diss.,
    University of California, Los Angeles, 1976.
Musisi, Nakanyike Beatrice. "Transformations of Baganda Women: From the
    Earliest Times to the Demise of the Kingdom in 1966." PhD diss., University
    of Toronto, 1992.

Schoenbrun, David Lee. "Early History in Eastern Africa's Great Lakes Region: Linguistic, Ecological, and Archaeological Approaches, ca. 500 B.C. to ca. A.D. 1000." PhD diss., University of California, Los Angeles, 1990.

Stephens, Rhiannon. "A History of Motherhood, Food Procurement and Politics in East-Central Uganda to the Nineteenth Century." PhD diss., Northwestern University, 2007.

Tantala, Renée Louise. "The Early History of Kitara in Western Uganda: Process Models of Religious and Political Change." PhD diss., University of Wisconsin-Madison, 1989.

Tappan, Jennifer. "'A Healthy Children Comes From A Healthy Mother': Mwanamugimu and Nutritional Science in Uganda, 1935–1973." PhD diss., Columbia University, 2010.

II. Published Sources

Allman, Jean. "Rounding Up Spinsters: Gender Chaos and Unmarried Women in Colonial Asante." In *"Wicked" Women and the Reconfiguration of Gender in Africa*, edited by Dorothy L. Hodgson and Sheryl A. McCurdy, 130–48. Portsmouth, N.H.: Heinemann, 2001.

Allman, Jean, Susan Geiger, and Nakanyike Musisi, eds., *Women in African Colonial Histories*. Bloomington: Indiana University Press, 2002.

Alpers, Edward A. *Ivory and Slaves: Changing Pattern of International Trade in East Central Africa to the Later Nineteenth Century*. Berkeley: University of California Press, 1975.

Anthony, David W. *The Horse, The Wheel, and Language: How Bronze-Age Riders from the Eurasian Steppes Shaped the Modern World*. Princeton: Princeton University Press, 2007.

Ashley, Ceri Z. "Towards a Socialised Archaeology of Ceramics in Great Lakes Africa." *African Archaeological Review* 27, no. 2 (2010): 135–63.

Atkinson, Clarissa W. *The Oldest Vocation: Christian Motherhood in the Middle Ages*. Ithaca: Cornell University Press, 1991.

Atkinson, Quentin D., and Russell D. Gray. "How Old Is the Indo-European Language Family? Illumination or More Moths to the Flame?" In *Phylogenetic Methods and the Prehistory of Languages*, edited by Peter Forster and Colin Renfrew, 91–109. Cambridge: McDonald Institute for Archaeological Research, 2006.

Barnes, Sandra T. "Gender and the Politics of Support and Protection in Precolonial West Africa." In *Queens, Queen Mothers, Priestesses, and Power: Case Studies in African Gender*, edited by Flora Edouwaye S. Kaplan, 1–18. New York: New York Academy of Sciences, 1997.

Bastin, Yvonne. *Les relations sémantiques dans les langues bantoues*, Classe des Sciences Morales et Politiques. Memoire in-8, N.S. 48, no. 4. Brussels: Académie Royale des Sciences d'Outre-Mer, 1985.

Bastin, Yvonne, André Coupez, and Michael Mann. *Continuity and Divergence in the Bantu Languages: Perspectives from a Lexicostatistic Study*, Annales Sciences Humaines 162. Tervuren, Belgium: Musée Royal de l'Afrique Centrale, 1999.

Bastin, Yvonne, and Thilo C. Schadeberg, eds. "Bantu Lexical Reconstructions 3." Tervuren, Belgium: Musée Royale de l'Afrique Centrale. http://www.metafro.be/blr/ (Accessed 16 January 2013).

Bay, Edna G. "Belief, Legitimacy and the *Kpojito*: An Institutional History of the 'Queen Mother' in Precolonial Dahomey." *Journal of African History* 36, no. 1 (1995): 1–27.

Beattie, J. M. "Nyoro Marriage and Affinity." *Africa: Journal of the International African Institute* 28, no. 1 (1958): 1–22.

Bellwood, Peter, James J. Fox, and Darrell Tryon, eds. *The Austronesians: Historical and Comparative Perspectives*. Canberra: Australian National University Press, 1995.

Berger, Iris. "Fertility as Power: Spirit Mediums, Priestesses and the Precolonial State in the Interlacustrine East Africa." In *Revealing Prophets: Prophecy in Eastern African History*, edited by David M. Anderson and Douglas H. Johnson, 65–82. London: James Currey, 1995.

Beswick, Stephanie. *Sudan's Blood Memory: The Legacy of War, Ethnicity, and Slavery in Early South Sudan*. Rochester, N.Y.: University of Rochester Press, 2004.

Blier, Suzanne Preston. "The Path of the Leopard: Motherhood and Majesty in Early Danhomè." *Journal of African History* 36, no. 3 (1995): 391–417.

Bongaarts, John. "Does Family Planning Reduce Infant Mortality Rates?" *Population and Development Review* 13, no. 2 (1987): 323–34.

Bourgeois, R. *Banyarwanda et Barundi: Tome I, éthnographie*. Classe des sciences morales et politiques. Mémoires In.8°, N.S. 15. Brussels: Académie Royale des Sciences Coloniales, 1958.

Bowers, Toni. *The Politics of Motherhood: British Writing and Culture, 1680–1760*. Cambridge: Cambridge University Press, 1996.

Brierley, Jean, and Thomas Spear, "Mutesa, the Missionaries, and Christian Conversion in Buganda." *International Journal of African Historical Studies* 21, no. 4 (1988): 601–18.

Bukenya, A., and L. Kamoga. *Standard Luganda–English Dictionary*. Kampala: Fountain Publishers, 2009.

Capen, Carole J. *Bilingual Dholuo-English Dictionary*. Tucson, A.Z.: C.A. Capen, 1998.

Chrétien, Jean-Pierre. "Les années de l'éleusine, du sorgho et du haricot dans l'ancien Burundi: Écologie et idéologie." *African Economic History* 7 (1979): 75–92.

The Great Lakes of Africa: Two Thousand Years of History. Translated by Scott Strauss. New York: Zone Books, 2003.

Cohen, David William "The Cultural Topography of a 'Bantu Borderland': Busoga, 1500–1850." *Journal of African History* 29, no. 1 (1988): 57–79.

"The Face of Contact: A Model of a Cultural and Linguistic Frontier in Early Eastern Uganda." In *Nilotic Studies: Proceedings of the International Symposium on Languages and History of the Nilotic Peoples, Cologne, January 4–6, 1982*, part II, edited by Rainer Vossen and Marianne Bechhaus-Gerst, 339–55. Berlin: Dietrich Reimer Verlag, 1983.

The Historical Tradition of Busoga: Mukama and Kintu. Oxford: Clarendon Press, 1972.

"The Political Transformation of Northern Busoga, 1600–1900." *Cahiers d'Études Africaines* 22, no. 87/88 (1982): 465–88.

"The River-Lake Nilotes from the Fifteenth to the Nineteenth Century." In *Zamani: A Survey of East African History,* edited by B. A. Ogot, 135–49. Nairobi: East African Publishing House, 1968; 2nd edition, 1974.

Towards a Reconstructed Past: Historical Texts from Busoga, Uganda. Oxford: Oxford University Press for the British Academy, 1986.

Womunafu's Bunafu: A Study of Authority in a Nineteenth-Century African Community. Princeton: Princeton University Press, 1977.

Connah, Graham. *Kibiro: The Salt of Bunyoro, Past and Present.* London: British Institute in Eastern Africa, 1996.

Coupez, A., Th. Kamanzi, S. Bizimana, G. Sematama, G. Rwabukumba, C. Ntazinda, and collaborators. *Inkoranya y'íkinyarwanda: Dictionnaire rwanda–rwanda et rwanda–français mu kinyanrwanda nó mu gifaraansá.* Tervuren, Belgium: Musée Royale de l'Afrique Centrale, 2005.

Cox, John L. "Amakiro: A Ugandan Puerperal Psychosis." *Social Psychiatry and Psychiatric Epidemiology* 14, no. 1 (1979): 49–52.

Cunningham, J. F. *Uganda and Its Peoples: Notes on the Protectorate of Uganda Especially the Anthropology of Its Indigenous Races.* London: Hutchinson, 1905.

Dammamm, E. "Inversiva und Repetitiva in Bantusprachen," *Afrika und Übersee* 43 (1959): 116–27.

Davis, Margaret. *A Lunyoro–Lunyankole–English and English–Lunyoro–Lunyankole Dictionary.* Kampala: Uganda Book Shop, 1952.

De Langhe, E., R. Swenne, and D. Vuylsteke. "Plantain in the Early Bantu World." *Azania* 29–30 (1994–1995): 147–60.

Demand, Nancy. *Birth, Death, and Motherhood in Classical Greece.* Baltimore: Johns Hopkins University Press, 1994.

Dictionary: Lusoga-English English-Lusoga. Jinja, Uganda: Cultural Research Centre, 2000.

Dike, K. Onwuka. *Trade and Politics in the Niger Delta, 1830–1885: An Introduction to the Economic and Political History of Nigeria.* Oxford: Clarendon Press, 1956.

Diop, Cheikh Anta. *L'unité culturelle de l'Afrique noire: Domaines du patriarcat et du matriarcat dans l'antiquité classique.* Paris: Présence Africaine, 1959.

Doyle, Shane. "Sexual Behavioural Change in Ankole, Western Uganda, c. 1880–1980." *Journal of Eastern African Studies,* 6, no.3 (2012): 490–506.

Edgerton, Robert B. *The Individual in Cultural Adaptation: A Study of Four East African Peoples.* Berkeley: University of California Press, 1971.

Ehret, Christopher. *An African Classical Age: Eastern and Southern Africa in World History, 1000 B.C. to A.D. 400.* Charlottesville: University of Virginia Press, 1998.

"Bantu Expansions: Re-Envisioning a Central Problem of Early African History." *International Journal of African Historical Studies* 34, no. 1 (2001): 5–41.

A Historical-Comparative Reconstruction of Nilo-Saharan. Cologne: Rüdiger Köppe Verlag, 2001.

History and the Testimony of Language. Berkeley: University of California Press, 2011.

"Language Change and the Material Correlates of Language and Ethnic Shift." *Antiquity* 62, no. 238 (1988): 564–74.

Southern Nilotic History: Linguistic Approaches to the Study of the Past. Evanston, Ill.: Northwestern University Press, 1971.

"Writing African History From Linguistic Evidence." In *Writing African History*, edited by John Edward Philips, 86–111. Rochester, N.Y.: University of Rochester Press, 2005.

Engels, Frederick. *The Origin of the Family, Private Property and the State: In the Light of the Researches of Lewis H. Morgan*, edited by Eleanor Burke Leacock, translated by Alec West. New York: International Publishers, 1972.

Fadlalla, Amal Hassan. *Embodying Honor: Fertility, Foreignness, and Regeneration in Eastern Sudan.* Madison: University of Wisconsin Press, 2007.

Fallers, Lloyd A. *Bantu Bureaucracy: A Century of Political Evolution among the Basoga of Uganda.* 2nd ed. Chicago: University of Chicago Press, 1965.

"Some Determinants of Marriage Stability in Busoga: A Reformulation of Gluck's Hypothesis." *Africa: Journal of the International African Institute* 27, no. 2 (1957): 106–23.

Feierman, Steven. "A Century of Ironies in East Africa (c. 1780–1890)." In *African History: From Earliest Times to Independence*, edited by Philip Curtin, Steven Feierman, Leonard Thompson, and Jan Vansina, 352–76. 2nd ed. London: Longman, 1995.

Peasant Intellectuals: Anthropology and History in Tanzania. Madison: University of Wisconsin Press, 1990.

The Shambaa Kingdom: A History. Madison: University of Wisconsin Press, 1974.

"Struggles for Control: The Social Roots of Health and Healing in Modern Africa." *African Studies Review* 28, no. 2–3 (1985): 73–147.

Fields-Black, Edda L. *Deep Roots: Rice Farmers in West Africa and the African Diaspora.* Bloomington: Indiana University Press, 2008.

Forster, Peter, and Colin Renfrew, eds. *Phylogenetic Methods and the Prehistory of Languages.* Cambridge: McDonald Institute for Archaeological Research, 2006.

Fraas, Pauline. *A Nande–English and English–Nande Dictionary.* Washington, D.C.: Laubach Literacy Fund, 1961.

Gailey, Christine Ward. *Kinship to Kingship: Gender Hierarchy and State Formation in the Tongan Islands.* Austin: University of Texas Press, 1987.

Garrett, Andrew. "Convergence in the Formation of Indo-European Subgroups: Phylogeny and Chronology." In *Phylogenetic Methods and the Prehistory of Languages*, edited by Peter Forster and Colin Renfrew, 139–51. Cambridge: McDonald Institute for Archaeological Research, 2006.

Gerring, John. "Ideology: A Definitional Analysis." *Political Research Quarterly* 50, no. 4 (1997): 957–94.

Goldschmidt, Walter. *The Sebei: A Study in Adaptation.* New York: Holt, Rinehart and Winston, 1986.

Goldschmidt, Walter, with Gale Goldschmidt. *Culture and Behavior of the Sebei: A Study in Continuity and Adaptation.* Berkeley: University of California Press, 1976.

Gonzales, Rhonda M. *Societies, Religion, and History: Central East Tanzanians and the World They Created, c. 200 B.C.E. to 1800 C.E.* New York: Columbia University Press, Gutenberg e-book, 2008. http://www.gutenberg-e.org/gonzales/ (Accessed 2 January 2013).

Goody, Jack. "The Mother's Brother and the Sister's Son in West Africa." *Journal of the Royal Anthropological Institute of Great Britain and Ireland* 89, no. 1 (1959): 61–88.

Gorju, Julien L. *Entre le Victoria l'Albert et l'Edouard: Ethnographie de la partie Anglaise du Vicariat de l'Uganda, Origines, histoire, religion, coutumes.* Rennes: Oberthür, 1920.

Gray, J. M. "Correspondence: Mutesa." *Uganda Journal* 2, no. 1 (1934): 83–5.

"Mutesa of Buganda, *Uganda Journal* 1, no. 1 (1934): 22–50.

Green, Toby. *The Rise of the Trans-Atlantic Slave Trade in Western Africa.* New York: Cambridge University Press, 2012.

Gulere, C. *Lusoga–English Dictionary Eibwanio.* Kampala: Fountain Publishers, 2009.

Guthrie, Malcolm. *Comparative Bantu: An Introduction to the Comparative Linguistics and Prehistory of the Bantu Languages,* vols. 1–4. Farnborough, U.K.: Gregg International, 1967–1970.

A Vocabulary of Icibemba, edited by M. Mann. London: School of Oriental and African Studies, 1995.

Guyer, Jane I., and Samuel M. Eno Belinga. "Wealth in People as Wealth in Knowledge: Accumulation and Composition in Equatorial Africa." *Journal of African History* 36, no. 1 (1995): 91–120.

Hage, Per, and Jeff Marck. "Proto-Bantu Descent Groups." In *Kinship, Language, and Prehistory: Per Hage and the Renaissance in Kinship Studies,* edited by Doug Jones and Bojka Milicic, 75–8. Salt Lake City: University of Utah Press, 2011.

Hall, Bruce S. *A History of Race in Muslim West Africa, 1600–1960.* New York: Cambridge University Press, 2011.

Hanson, Holly Elisabeth. "Queen Mothers and Good Government in Buganda: The Loss of Women's Political Power in Nineteenth-Century East Africa." In *Women in African Colonial Histories,* edited by Jean Allman, Susan Geiger, and Nakanyike Musisi, 219–36. Bloomington: Indiana University Press, 2002.

Landed Obligation: The Practice of Power in Buganda. Portsmouth, N.H.: Heinemann, 2003.

"Stolen People and Autonomous Chiefs in Nineteenth-Century Buganda: The Social Consequences of Non-Free Followers." In *Slavery in the Great Lakes Region of East Africa,* edited by Henri Médard and Shane Doyle, 161–73. Oxford: James Currey, 2007.

Heine, Bernd. *Ik Dictionary.* Cologne: Rüdiger Köppe Verlag, 1999.

Henige, David. "'The Disease of Writing': Ganda and Nyoro Kinglists in a Newly Literate World." In *The African Past Speaks: Essays on Oral Tradition and History*, edited by Joseph C. Miller, 240–61. Folkestone: Dawson, 1980.

Herbert, Eugenia W. *Iron, Gender, and Power: Rituals of Transformation in African Societies*. Bloomington: Indiana University Press, 1993.

Hilders, J. H., and J. C. D. Lawrance. *An English-Ateso and Ateso-English Vocabulary*. Nairobi: Eagle Press, 1958.

Hodgson, Dorothy L., and Sheryl A. McCurdy, eds. *"Wicked" Women and the Reconfiguration of Gender in Africa*. Portsmouth, N.H.: Heinemann, 2001.

Hunt, Nancy Rose. "'Le Bébé en Brousse': European Women, African Birth Spacing and Colonial Intervention in Breast Feeding in the Belgian Congo." *International Journal of African Historical Studies* 21, no. 3 (1988): 401–32.

Huntingford, G. W. B. "The Orusyan Language of Uganda." *Journal of African Languages* 4, no. 3 (1965): 145–69.

Hunwick, John O. *Sharī'a In Songhay: The Replies of al-Maghīlī to the Questions of Askia al-Hājj Muhammad*. Oxford: Oxford University Press for the British Academy, 1985.

Irstam, Tor V. H. *The King of Ganda: Studies in the Institutions of Sacral Kingship in Africa*, trans. Donald Burton. Lund: H. Ohlssons boktr., 1944.

Jackson, Frederick J. *Early Days in East Africa*. London: Edward Arnold, 1930.

Johnson, Frederick. *A Standard Swahili–English Dictionary (Founded on Madan's Swahili–English Dictionary)*. Nairobi: Oxford University Press, 1939. Reprint 1996.

Johnson-Hanks, Jennifer. *Uncertain Honor: Modern Motherhood in an African Crisis*. Chicago: University of Chicago Press, 2006.

Johnston, Harry. *The Uganda Protectorate: An Attempt to Give Some Description of the Physical Geography, Botany, Zoology, Anthropology, Languages and History of the Territories under British Protection in East Central Africa, between the Congo Free State and the Rift Valley and between the First Degree of South Latitude and the Fifth Degree of North Latitude*. Vol. 2. London: Hutchinson, 1904.

Joseph, Brian D., and Richard D. Janda, eds. *The Handbook of Historical Linguistics*. Oxford: Blackwell, 2003.

Kagaya, Ryohei. *A Gwere Vocabulary*. Asian and African Lexicon 48. Tokyo: Research Institute for Languages and Cultures of Asia and Africa, Tokyo University of Foreign Studies, 2006.

Kagwa, Apolo. *Ekitabo kye Mpisa za Baganda* [The Book of the Customs of the Baganda]. Kampala: Uganda Printing and Publishing, 1918.

Ekitabo kya Basekabaka be Buganda na be Bunyoro, na be Koki, na be Toro, na be Nkole [The Book of the Kings of Buganda and of Bunyoro, and of Koki, and of Toro, and of Nkole]. Kampala: Uganda Bookshop and Publishing House, 1927.

The Customs of the Baganda, translated by Ernest B. Kalibala, edited by May Mandelbaum (Edel). New York: Columbia University Press, 1934. Reprint, New York: AMS Press, 1969.

Engero za Baganda [The Tales of the Baganda]. London: Sheldon Press, 1927.

The Kings of Buganda, translated by M. S. M. Kiwanuka. Nairobi: East African Publishing House, 1971.

Kaji, Shigeki. *A Haya Vocabulary.* Asian and African Lexicon 37. Tokyo: Research Institute for Languages and Cultures of Asia and Africa, Tokyo University of Foreign Studies, 2000.

Lexique tembo I: Tembo–swahili du Zaïre–japonais– français. Asian and African Lexicon 16. Tokyo: Research Institute for Languages and Cultures of Asia and Africa, Tokyo University of Foreign Studies, 1986.

A Runyankore Vocabulary. Asian and African Lexicon 44. Tokyo: Research Institute for Languages and Cultures of Asia and Africa, Tokyo University of Foreign Studies, 2004.

Vocabulaire hunde. Asian and African Lexicon 24. Tokyo: Research Institute for Languages and Cultures of Asia and Africa, Tokyo University of Foreign Studies, 1992.

Kamusi ya Kiswahili Sanifu. Dar-es-Salaam: Oxford University Press for Taasisi ya Uchunguzi wa Kiswahili, 1981.

Kaplan, Flora Edouwaye S., ed. *Queens, Queen Mothers, Priestesses, and Power: Case Studies in African Gender.* New York: New York Academy of Sciences, 1997.

Karugire, Samwiri Rubaraza. *A History of the Kingdom of Nkore in Western Uganda to 1896.* Oxford: Clarendon Press, 1971.

A Political History of Uganda. Nairobi: Heinemann, 1980.

Kiingi, K. B. *Enkuluze y'Oluganda ey'e Makerere* [The Makerere Treasury of Luganda]. Kampala: Fountain Publishers, 2007.

Kimambo, Isaria N. *A Political History of the Pare of Tanzania c. 1500–1900.* Nairobi: East African Publishing House, 1969.

Kirkpatrick, R. T. "Lake Choga and Surrounding Country." *Uganda Journal* 10, no. 2 (1946): 160–2.

Kiwanuka, M. S. M. Semakula. *A History of Buganda: From the Foundation of the Kingdom to 1900.* London: Longman, 1971.

Klieman, Kairn A. *"The Pygmies Were Our Compass": Bantu and Batwa in the History of West Central Africa, Early Times to c. 1900 C.E.* Portsmouth, N.H.: Heinemann, 2003.

Knight, Kathleen. "Transformations in the Concept of Ideology in the Twentieth Century." *American Political Science Review* 100, no. 4 (2006): 619–26.

Kodesh, Neil. "History from the Healer's Shrine: Genre, Historical Imagination, and Early Ganda History." *Comparative Studies in Society and History* **49**, no. 3 (2007): 527–52.

Beyond the Royal Gaze: Clanship and Public Healing in Buganda. Charlottesville: University of Virginia Press, 2010.

Kottak, Conrad P. "Ecological Variables in the Origin and Evolution of African States: The Buganda Example." *Comparative Studies in Society and History* 14, no. 3 (1972): 351–80.

Kuhanen, Jan. *Poverty, Health and Reproduction in Early Colonial Uganda.* University of Joensuu Publications in the Humanities 37. Joensuu, Finland: University of Eastern Finland Electronic Publications, 2005. http://urn.fi/URN:ISBN:952-458-898-6/ (Accessed 9 January 2013).

Kyomuhendo, Grace Bantebya, and Marjorie Keniston McIntosh. *Women, Work & Domestic Virtue in Uganda, 1900–2003*. Oxford: James Currey, 2006.

Laight, Miss., and Y. K. Lubogo. "Basoga Death and Burial Rites." *Uganda Journal* 2, no. 2 (1934/1935): 120–32. (Note that this was initially erroneously published under the name of Ezekeri Zibondo. A letter rectifying the error was published in *Uganda Journal* 2, no. 3 (1935): 255.)

Lamphear, John. *The Traditional History of the Jie of Uganda*. Oxford: Clarendon Press, 1976.

Langlands, B. W. "The Banana in Uganda – 1860–1920." *Uganda Journal* 30, no. 1 (1966): 39–63.

Lawrance, J. C. D. *The Iteso: Fifty Years of Change in a Nilo-Hamitic Tribe of Uganda*. London: Oxford University Press, 1957.

Leacock, Eleanor. "Interpreting the Origins of Gender Inequality: Conceptual and Historical Problems." *Dialectical Anthropology* 7, no. 4 (1983): 263–84.

Lejju, B. Julius, Peter Robertshaw, and David Taylor. "Africa's Earliest Bananas?" *Journal of Archaeological Science* 33, no. 1 (2006): 102–13.

Le Veux, Père. *Manuel de langue luganda comprenant la grammaire et un recueil de contes et de légendes*. Maison-Carrée, Algeria: Imprimerie des Missionaires d'Afriques (Pères Blancs), 1914.

Premier essai de vocabulaire luganda – français d'après l'ordre étymologique. Maison-Carrée, Algeria: Imprimerie des Missionaires d'Afrique (Pères Blancs), 1917.

Lindsay, Lisa A., and Stephan F. Miescher, eds. *Men and Masculinities in Modern Africa*. Portsmouth, N.H.: Heinemann, 2003.

Lubogo, Y. K. *A History of Busoga*, translated by Eastern Province (Bantu Language) Literature Committee. Jinja: East African Literature Bureau, 1960.

MacGaffey, Wyatt. "Changing Representations in Central African History." *Journal of African History* 46, no. 2 (2005): 189–207.

Mair, L. P. *Native Marriage in Buganda*. London: Oxford University Press for the International Institute of African Languages and Cultures, 1940.

An African People in the Twentieth Century. London: Routledge and Kegan Paul, 1934. Reprint, New York: Russell and Russell, 1966.

Marck, Jeff. *Topics in Polynesian Language and Culture History*. Canberra: Pacifica Linguistics, Australian National University, 2000.

Marck, Jeff, and Koen Bostoen, "Proto-Oceanic Society (Austronesian) and Proto-East Bantu Society (Niger-Congo) Residence, Descent, and Kin Terms, ca. 1000 BC." In *Kinship, Language, and Prehistory: Per Hage and the Renaissance in Kinship Studies*, edited by Doug Jones and Bojka Milicic, 83–94. Salt Lake City: University of Utah Press, 2011.

Mark, Peter. *"Portuguese" Style and Luso-African Identity: Precolonial Senegambia, Sixteenth-Nineteenth Centuries*. Bloomington: Indiana University Press, 2002.

Maroney, Heather Jon. "Embracing Motherhood: New Feminist Theory." In *The Politics of Diversity: Feminism, Marxism and Nationalism*, edited by Roberta Hamilton and Michèle Barrett, 398–423. London: Verso, 1986.

McCaskie, T. C. "Denkyira in the Making of Asante, *c.* 1660–1720." *Journal of African History* 48, no. 1 (2007): 1–25.

McMahon, April, and Robert McMahon. *Language Classification by Numbers.* Oxford: Oxford University Press, 2005.

"Why Linguists Don't Do Dates: Evidence from Indo-European and Australian Languages." In *Phylogenetic Methods and the Prehistory of Languages,* edited by Peter Forster and Colin Renfrew, 153–60. Cambridge: McDonald Institute for Archaeological Research, 2006.

McMaster, David N. *A Subsistence Crop Geography of Uganda.* Bude, U.K.: Geographical Publications, 1962.

Médard, Henri. *Le royaume du Buganda au XIXe siècle: Mutations politiques et religieuses d'un ancien État d'Afrique de l'Est.* Paris: Karthala, 2007.

Médard, Henri, and Shane Doyle, eds. *Slavery in the Great Lakes Region of East Africa.* Oxford: James Currey, 2007.

Meillassoux, Claude. *Maidens, Meal, and Money: Capitalism and the Domestic Community,* translated by author. Cambridge: Cambridge University Press, 1981.

Merrett-Balkos, Leanne. "Just Add Water: Remaking Women through Childbirth, Anganen, Southern Highlands, Papua New Guinea." In *Maternities and Modernities: Colonial and Postcolonial Experiences in Asia and the Pacific,* edited by Kalpana Ram and Margaret Jolly, 213–38. Cambridge: Cambridge University Press, 1998.

Miers, Suzanne, and Igor Kopytoff, eds. *Slavery in Africa: Historical and Anthropological Perspectives.* Madison: University of Wisconsin Press, 1977.

de Moraes Farias, P. F. *Medieval Inscriptions from the Republic of Mali: Epigraphy, Chronicles and Songhay-Tuāreg History.* Oxford: Oxford University Press for the British Academy, 2003.

Morgan, Lewis H. *Ancient Society or Researches in the Lines of Human Progress from Savagery through Barbarism to Civilization.* Chicago: Charles H. Kerr, 1877.

Mukasa, Ham. "Ebifa ku Mulembe gwa Kabaka Mutesa [The History of the Reign of Kabaka Mutesa]," translated by A. H. C. *Uganda Journal* 1, no. 2 (1934): 116–33.

Muniko, S. M., B. Muita oMagige, and Malcolm Ruel. *Kuria–English Dictionary.* Hamburg: LIT, 1996.

Murdock, George Peter. *Africa: Its Peoples and Their Culture History.* New York: McGraw-Hill, 1959.

Muriuki, Godfrey. *A History of the Kikuyu, 1500–1900.* Nairobi: Oxford University Press, 1974.

Murphy, John D. *Luganda–English Dictionary,* Publications in the Languages of Africa 2. Washington, D.C.: Consortium Press for Catholic University of America, 1972.

Musisi, Nakanyike B. "Women, 'Elite Polygyny,' and Buganda State Formation." *Signs* 16, no. 4 (1991): 757–86.

Nabirye, Minah. *Eiwanika ly'Olusoga: Eiwanika ly'Aboogezi b'Olusoga n'Abo Abenda Okwega Olusoga* [A Treasury of Lusoga: A Treasury for Speakers of Lusoga and Those Who Want to Learn Lusoga]. Kampala: Menha Publishers, 2009.

Nannyonga-Tamusuza, Sylvia A. *Baakisimba: Gender in the Music and Dance of the Baganda People of Uganda*. New York: Routledge, 2005.

Neumann, Katharina, and Elisabeth Hildebrand. "Early Bananas in Africa: The State of the Art." *Ethnobotany Research and Applications* 7 (2009): 353–62.

Newbury, Catharine. *The Cohesion of Oppression: Clientship and Ethnicity in Rwanda, 1860–1960*. New York: Columbia University Press, 1988.

Newbury, David. *Kings and Clans: Ijwi Island and the Lake Kivu Rift, 1780–1840*. Madison: University of Wisconsin Press, 1991.

Nsimbi, N. B. "Baganda Traditional Personal Names." *Uganda Journal* 14, no. 2 (1950): 204–14.

Nurse, Derek, and Gérard Philippson. "The Bantu Languages of East Africa: A Lexicostatistical Survey." In *Language in Tanzania*, edited by Edgar C. Polomé and C. P. Hill, 26–67. Oxford: Oxford University Press for the International African Institute, 1980.

Nurse, Derek, and Thomas Spear. *The Swahili: Reconstructing the History and Language of an African Society, 800–1500*. Philadelphia: University of Pennsylvania Press, 1985.

Nwokeji, G. Ugo. *The Slave Trade and Culture in the Bight of Biafra: An African Society in the Atlantic World*. New York: Cambridge University Press, 2010.

Nyakoe O'Matenyo, F. *English-Ekegusii Companion*. Nairobi: Bookwise, 1981.

Ochieng', William Robert. *A Pre-colonial History of the Gusii of Western Kenya: From c. A.D. 1500 to 1914*. Kampala: East African Literature Bureau, 1974.

Odaga, Asenath Bole. *English-Dholuo Dictionary*. Kisumu, Kenya: Lake Publishers & Enterprises, 1997.

Odonga, Alexander. *Lwo-English Dictionary*. Kampala: Fountain Publishers, 2005.

Ogot, Bethwell A. *History of the Southern Luo. Volume One: Migration and Settlement 1500–1900*. Nairobi: East African Publishing House, 1967.

Ogunyemi, Chikwenye Okonjo. *Africa Wo/Man Palava: The Nigerian Novel by Women*. Chicago: Chicago University Press, 1996.

Oliver, Roland. "Ancient Capital Sites of Ankole." *Uganda Journal* 23, no. 1 (1959): 51–63.

"The Problem of the Bantu Expansion." *Journal of African History* 7, no. 3 (1966): 361–76.

"The Royal Tombs of Buganda." *Uganda Journal* 23, no. 2 (1959): 124–33.

"The Traditional Histories of Buganda, Bunyoro, and Nkole." *Journal of the Royal Anthropological Institute* 85, no. 1/2 (1955): 111–17.

O'Neil, Robert. *Mission to the Upper Nile: The Story of the St Joseph's Missionary Society of Mill Hill in Uganda*. London: Mission Book Service, 1999.

Ongodia, S. P., and A. Ejiet. *Ateso–English Dictionary*. Kampala: Fountain Publishers, 2008.

Oyěwùmí, Oyèrónké. "Family Bonds/Conceptual Binds: African Notes on Feminist Epistemologies." *Signs* 25, no. 4 (2000): 1093–8.

Pagel, Mark, and Andrew Meade. "Estimating Rates of Lexical Replacement on Phylogenetic Trees of Languages." In *Phylogenetic Methods and the*

Prehistory of Languages, edited by Peter Forster and Colin Renfrew, 173–82. Cambridge: McDonald Institute for Archaeological Research, 2006.

Pankhurst, Richard. *A Social History of Ethiopia: The Northern and Central Highlands from Early Medieval Times to the Rise of Emperor Téwodros II.* Trenton, N.J.: Red Sea Press, 1992.

Polak-Bynon, Louise. *Lexique shi–français suivi d'un index français–shi.* Tervuren, Belgium: Musée Royale de l'Afrique Central, 1978.

Portal, Gerald. *The British Mission to Uganda in 1893.* London: Edward Arnold, 1894.

Radcliffe-Brown, A. R. "Introduction." In *African Systems of Kinship and Marriage,* edited by A. R. Radcliffe-Brown and Daryll Forde, 1–85. London: Oxford University Press for the International African Institute, 1950.

Rapp, Reyna. "Gender and Class: An Archaeology of Knowledge Concerning the Origin of the State." *Dialectical Anthropology* 2, no. 4 (1977): 309–16.

Ray, Benjamin C. *Myth, Ritual, and Kingship in Buganda.* New York: Oxford University Press, 1991.

Reid, Andrew. "Bananas and the Archaeology of Buganda." *Antiquity* 75, no. 290 (2001): 811–12.

"Lake Victoria before Buganda." *African Heritage and Archaeology.* London: University College London, 2007. http://www.ucl.ac.uk/archaeology/aha/reid/buganda-lakev.htm/ (Accessed 4 January 2013).

"Ntusi and the Development of Social Complexity in Southern Uganda." In *Aspects of African Archaeology: Papers from the 10th Congress of the Panafrican Association for Prehistory and Related Studies,* edited by Gilbert Pwiti and Robert Soper, 621–7. Harare: University of Zimbabwe Publications, 1996.

Reid, Andrew, and Ceri Z. Ashley. "A Context for the Luzira Head." *Antiquity* 82, no. 315 (2008): 99–112.

Reid, Richard. *Political Power in Pre-Colonial Buganda: Economy, Society and Warfare in the Nineteenth Century.* Oxford: James Currey, 2002.

"Human Booty in Buganda: Some Observations on the Seizure of People in War, c. 1700–1890." In *Slavery in the Great Lakes Region of East Africa,* edited by Henri Médard and Shane Doyle, 145–60. Oxford: James Currey, 2007.

Robertshaw, Peter. "The Ancient Earthworks of Western Uganda: Capital Sites of a Cwezi Empire." *Uganda Journal* 48 (2002): 17–32.

"Beyond the Segmentary State: Creative and Instrumental Power in Western Uganda." *Journal of World Prehistory* 23, no. 4 (2010): 255–69.

"Women, Labor and State Formation in Western Uganda." *Archeological Papers of the American Anthropological Association* 9, no. 1 (1999): 51–65.

Robertshaw, Peter, and David Taylor. "Climate Change and the Rise of Political Complexity in Western Uganda." *Journal of African History* 41, no. 1 (2000): 1–28.

Robertshaw, Peter, David Taylor, Shane Doyle, and Rachel Marchant. "Famine, Climate and Crisis in Western Uganda." In *Past Climate Variability through Europe and Africa,* edited by Richard W. Batterbee, Françoise Gasse, and Catherine E. Stickley, vol. 6, 535–49. Dordrecht, Netherlands: Springer, 2004.

Rodegem, F. M. *Dictionnaire rundi–français*. Tervuren, Belgium: Musée Royal de l'Afrique Centrale, 1970.

Roscoe, John. *The Baganda: An Account of Their Native Customs and Beliefs*. London: Macmillan, 1911.

The Bagesu and Other Tribes of the Uganda Protectorate: The Third Part of the Report of the Mackie Ethnological Expedition to Central Africa. Cambridge: University Press, 1924.

The Northern Bantu: An Account of Some Central African Tribes of the Uganda Protectorate. Cambridge: University Press, 1915.

Rossel, Gerda. *Taxonomic-Linguistic Study of Plantain in Africa*. Leiden, Netherlands: CNWS Publications, 1998.

Rycroft, D. K. *Concise SiSwati Dictionary: SiSwati–English/English–SiSwati*. Pretoria: J. L. van Schaik, 1981.

Sacks, Karen. *Sisters and Wives: The Past and Future of Sexual Equality*. Westport, Conn.: Greenwood Press, 1979.

Saidi, Christine. *Women's Authority and Society in Early East-Central Africa*. Rochester, N.Y.: University of Rochester Press, 2010.

Sanchez-Mazas, Alicia, Roger Blench, Malcolm D. Ross, Ilia Peiros, and Marie Lin, eds. *Past Human Migrations in East Asia: Matching Archaeology, Linguistics and Genetics*. New York: Routledge, 2008.

Schadeberg, Thilo C. "Derivation." In *The Bantu Languages*, edited by Derek Nurse and Gérard Philippson, 71–89. London: Routledge, 2003.

Schiller, Laurence D. "The Royal Women of Buganda." *International Journal of African Historical Studies* 23, no. 3 (1990): 455–73.

Schoenbrun, David Lee. "Cattle Herds and Banana Gardens: The Historical Geography of the Western Great Lakes Region, ca. AD 800–1500." *African Archaeological Review* 11, no. 1 (1993): 39–72.

"Gendered Histories between the Great Lakes: Varities and Limits." *International Journal of African Historical Studies* 29, no. 3 (1996): 461–92.

"Great Lakes Bantu: Classification and Settlement Chronology." *Sprache und Geschichte in Afrika* 15 (1994): 91–152.

A Green Place, A Good Place: Agrarian Change, Gender, and Social Identity in the Great Lakes Region to the 15th Century. Portsmouth, N.H.: Heinemann, 1998.

The Historical Reconstruction of Great Lakes Bantu Cultural Vocabulary: Etymologies and Distributions. Cologne: Rüdiger Köppe Verlag, 1997.

"Treating an Interdisciplinary Allergy: Methodological Approaches to Pollen Studies for the Historian of Early Africa." *History in Africa* 18 (1991): 323–48.

"Violence, Marginality, Scorn and Honour: Language Evidence of Slavery to the Eighteenth Century." In *Slavery in the Great Lakes Region of East Africa*, edited by Henri Médard and Shane Doyle, 38–76. Oxford: James Currey, 2007.

"We Are What We Eat: Ancient Agriculture between the Great Lakes." *Journal of African History* 34, no. 1 (1993): 1–31.

Scott, James C. *The Art of Not Being Governed: An Anarchist History of Upland Southeast Asia*. New Haven, Conn.: Yale University Press, 2009.

Scott, Joan W. "Gender: A Useful Category of Historical Analysis." *American Historical Review* 91, no. 5 (1986): 1053–75.

Semley, Lorelle D. *Mother Is Gold, Father Is Glass: Gender and Colonialism in a Yoruba Town.* Bloomington: Indiana University Press, 2011.

Shipton, Parker. *The Nature of Entrustment: Intimacy, Exchange, and the Sacred in Africa.* New Haven, Conn.: Yale University Press, 2007.

Siertsema, Berthe. *Masaba Word List: English-Masaba, Masaba-English.* Tervuren, Belgium: Musée Royal de l'Afrique Centrale, 1981.

Snoxall, R.A. ed. *Luganda-English Dictionary.* Oxford: Clarendon Press, 1967.

Southwold, Martin. "Succession to the Throne in Buganda." In *Succession to High Office,* edited by Jack Goody, 82–126. Cambridge: Cambridge University Press, 1966.

Speke, John Hanning. *Journal of the Discovery of the Source of the Nile.* New York: Harper and Brothers, 1864.

Stanley, Henry M. *Through the Dark Continent or The Sources of the Nile Around the Great Lakes of Equatorial Africa and Down the Livingstone River to the Atlantic Ocean,* vol. I. New York: Harper and Brothers, 1878.

Starosin, Sergei. "Comparative-Historical Linguistics and Lexicostatistics," translated by N. Evans and I. Peiros. In *Time Depth in Historical Linguistics,* edited by Colin Renfrew, April McMahon, and R. Larry Trask, 223–65. Cambridge: McDonald Institute for Archaeological Research, 2000.

Stephens, Rhiannon. "Birthing Wealth? Motherhood and Poverty in East-Central Uganda, c. 700–1900." *Past and Present* 215 (2012): 235–68.

"Lineage and Society in Precolonial Uganda." *Journal of African History* 50, no. 2 (2009): 203–21.

Swadesh, Morris. "Lexico-Statistic Dating of Prehistoric Ethnic Contacts: With Special Reference to North American Indians and Eskimos." *Proceedings of the American Philosophical Society* 96, no. 4 (1952): 452–63.

"Towards Greater Accuracy in Lexicostatistic Dating." *International Journal of American Linguistics* 21, no. 2 (1955): 121–37.

Tantala, Renée L. "Verbal and Visual Imagery in Kitara (Western Uganda): Interpreting 'The Story of Isimbwa and Nyinamwiru.'" In *Paths Toward the Past: African Historical Essays in Honor of Jan Vansina,* edited by Robert W. Harms, Joseph C. Miller, David S. Newbury, and Michele D. Wagner, 223–43. Atlanta, Ga.: African Studies Association Press, 1994.

Taylor, Charles. *A Simplified Runyankore–Rukiga–English and English–Runyankore–Rukiga Dictionary in the 1955 Revised Orthography with Tone-Markings and Full Entries under Prefixes.* Kampala: Eagle Press for the East African Literature Bureau, 1959.

Thomas, H. B. "Captain Eric Smith's Expedition to Lake Victoria in 1891." *Uganda Journal* 23, no. 2 (1959): 134–52.

Thomas, Lynn M. *Politics of the Womb: Women, Reproduction, and the State in Kenya.* Berkeley: University of California Press, 2003.

Trussell, James and Anne R. Pebley, "The Potential Impact of Changes in Fertility on Infant, Child, and Maternal Mortality." *Studies in Family Planning* 15, no. 6 (1984): 267–80.

Tuck, Michael W. "Women's Experiences of Enslavement and Slavery in Late Nineteenth- and Early Twentieth-Century Uganda." In *Slavery in the Great Lakes*, edited by Henri Médard and Shane Doyle, 174–88. Oxford: James Currey, 2007.

Twaddle, Michael. "Slaves and Peasants in Buganda." In *Slavery and Other Forms of Unfree Labour*, edited by Léonie J. Archer, 118–29. London: Routledge, 1988.

    Kakungulu and the Creation of Uganda, 1868–1928. London: James Currey, 1993.

Vansina, Jan. *Antecedents to Modern Rwanda: The Nyiginya Kingdom*, translated by author. Madison: University of Wisconsin Press, 2004.

    How Societies Are Born: Governance in West Central Africa before 1600. Charlottesville: University of Virginia Press, 2004.

    Oral Tradition: A Study in Historical Methodology, translated by H. M. Wright. Chicago: Aldine Publishing, 1965.

    Paths in the Rainforests: Toward a History of Political Tradition in Equatorial Africa. Madison: University of Wisconsin Press, 1990.

    The Tio Kingdom of the Middle Congo: 1880–1892. London: Oxford University Press for the International African Institute, 1973.

    "The Use of Process-Models in African History." In *The Historian in Tropical Africa: Studies Presented and Discussed at the Fourth International African Seminar at the University of Dakar Senegal 1961*, edited by J. Vansina, R. Mauny, and L. V. Thomas, 375–89. Oxford: Oxford University Press for the International African Institute, 1964.

Vincent, Joan. *Teso in Transformation: The Political Economy of Peasant and Class in Eastern Africa*. Berkeley: University of California Press, 1982.

Walser, Ferdinand. *Luganda Proverbs*. Berlin: Reimer Verlag, 1982.

Webster, J. B. "Usuku: The Homeland of the Iteso." In *The Iteso During the Asonya*, edited by J. B. Webster, C. P. Emudong, D. H. Okalany, and N. Egimu-Okuda, xv–80. Nairobi: East African Publishing House, 1973.

Were, Gideon S. *A History of the Abaluyia of Western Kenya*. Nairobi: East African Publishing House, 1967.

White, Luise. *Speaking with Vampires: Rumor and History in Colonial Africa*. Berkeley: University of California Press, 2000.

Wrigley, Christopher. "Bananas in Buganda." *Azania* 24 (1989): 64–70.

    "The Kinglists of Buganda." *History in Africa* 1 (1974): 129–39.

    Kingship and State: The Buganda Dynasty. Cambridge: Cambridge University Press, 1996.

Index

Numbers in *italics* refer to illustrations.

BOOKS IN THIS SERIES

For EU product safety concerns, contact us at Calle de José Abascal, 56–1°,
28003 Madrid, Spain or eugpsr@cambridge.org.